GrassRoutes

Seattle

Seattle

An Urban Eco Guide

Serena Bartlett

with Daniel Laing

SASQUATCH BOOKS
SEATTLE

To Lady and Doodle (and Sky Boat)

*Certainly, travel is more than the seeing of sights; it is a change
that goes on, deep and permanent, in the ideas of living.*
—Miriam Beard

Printed in the United States of America
Published by Sasquatch Books
Distributed by PGW/Perseus
15 14 13 12 11 10   9 8 7 6 5 4 3 2 1

Cover design: Rosebud Eustace
Cover and interior illustrations: Daniel Laing
Interior design and composition: Rosebud Eustace
Interior maps: Lisa Brower/GreenEye Design

Library of Congress Cataloging-in-Publication Data

Bartlett, Serena.
  Grassroutes Seattle : an urban eco guide / Serena Bartlett.
    p. cm.
  Includes index.
  ISBN-13: 978-1-57061-609-9
  ISBN-10: 1-57061-609-4
  1. Seattle (Wash.)--Guidebooks. 2. City and town life--Washington--Seattle. 3. Ecotourism
--Washington--Seattle. I. Title. II. Title: Grass routes Seattle.
  F899.S43B37 2010
  979.7'772--dc22

                              2010003606

Sasquatch Books
119 South Main Street, Suite 400
Seattle, WA 98104
(206) 467-4300
www.sasquatchbooks.com
custserv@sasquatchbooks.com

CONTENTS

Acknowledgments

I am unendingly grateful to all the people who have helped me with this book, to Seattle itself for inspiring me, and for all the wonderful people I met on the path. I'd especially like to thank Daniel Laing for his love and support throughout this process, the contributors, and the small-business owners, urban farmers, and conscientious locals for making Seattle such a rich and delicious collage of sustainability.

The GrassRoutes Story

Like cracking open a dusty geode, travel has revealed to me the many facets of the world, allowing me to compare my known surroundings with the previously unexplored. No other activity has had quite the same impact, offering a unique experience of both commonalities and differences in the quilt of humanity.

After each journey my reality was challenged with new ways of thinking and acting, and I found I had new interests and an altogether different perspective. The most important souvenir I brought home wasn't tangible—it was a more open mind.

I became a detective of sorts, unearthing cultures and becoming familiar with local customs by seeking out nontraditional attractions and cities off the beaten path. Wherever I was, the locals gave me the chance to have unique experiences rather than manufactured ones. When I returned home I kept up the habit, discovering a wealth of intrigue in my own country. Whether trekking across another continent or walking a few blocks to a nearby neighborhood, no matter what my pocketbook dictated, I always managed to find new cultural gems.

GrassRoutes was born out of my growing collection of ideas and inspirations drawn from my journeys. I made up my mind to promote world citizenship, but search as I might, I found no vehicle that expressed my ideas about travel, so I decided to create one.

The concept evolved from a bundle of notes collected on the road. Since I have always viewed cities as whole entities, I didn't want my guides to be divided into chapters covering specific neighborhoods. Also, chowing down on some messy barbecue doesn't equate with dining on braised rabbit, so I chose not to organize the guides simply by activity. GrassRoutes guides had to be designed around the mood of the traveler and the timing.

But organization wasn't the only thing I wanted to do differently. GrassRoutes, true to its name, champions local businesses and their corresponding contributions to the greater good of the community. Restaurants that serve sustainably grown produce share these pages with shops that showcase works by local artists. Wildlife preserves are in the mix with amusements that use energy-saving techniques. Volunteer listings give visitors the opportunity to interact with residents while giving back. Being conscientious about society and environment is a recipe for peace: this is one message I hope to convey.

Another is that travel can fit a limited budget. GrassRoutes is more than a guide to a city's attractions—it is a reaffirmation that authentic cultural experiences are not out of reach for anyone.

As you enjoy your travels, you can be satisfied knowing that you are a conscientious consumer. With such a bounty of local businesses dedicated to the spirit of positive change, it is becoming easier to support such a philosophy. Each listing in every GrassRoutes guide meets this standard in one aspect or another. So while you are venturing out into the world and meeting real people in new places, your dollars are staying in the community.

In this spirit, I bring you GrassRoutes guides, created to benefit readers and communities. I hope you will try something new, even if you thought it was not possible. All you need to have a genuine cultural escapade is an inquiring mind, a detective's spirit, and the desire to get acquainted with the world around you.

Read more about the GrassRoutes philosophy: *www.grassroutestravel. com/story*.

Urban Eco-Travel Tips

To help you prepare for your adventure, here are some tips that I have compiled over my years of world travel.

Trip Planning
Don't overplan. Pick dates that make sense, and make the fewest reservations you can get away with to take into consideration factors of time, exhaustion, and exploration.

Before embarking on a trip, tell as many people as will listen where you are going, and get their feedback and tips. Have the same talkative approach when you get to your destination so you can meet locals and learn their favorite spots.

Look at books and magazines featuring the culture and history of the area before embarking on your trip, and keep a well-organized travel guide and a clear map with you while you are exploring.

Time Allotment

When picking dates, consider what kind of trip you want to have. One game plan is to spread out your time between different sights as a good introduction to an area. Another is spending prolonged time in one or two cities to truly get to know them. Either way, in my experience it is good to slow down the tempo of travel enough to smell the proverbial roses.

Reservations

Be sure to reserve a hotel for at least the first night so you have somewhere to go when you get off the plane. Even if you prefer to travel on a whim, I recommend starting on day two—after you get your bearings.

Before you book a room, try to get an idea of your destination first, so you can place yourself in the area that most interests you. If your entire vacation will be spent in the same area, I suggest staying in the same centrally located hotel the whole time so you avoid having to carry your stuff around. After all, you probably didn't travel to see different hotels, but to see the city itself!

Whenever you do book a hotel, make sure you know its cancellation policy.

In general, don't reserve many transit engagements. That way, if you want to extend your stay in a given spot, you can do that without too many trials and tribulations. Local transit arrangements are usually easy to book without much advance notice.

Restaurants tend to have widely varying policies on reservations, so check ahead to see whether your dream meal requires one. Or forgo the reservations: when you get to your destination, look around and act on a whim, or best of all, get the locals' advice. It is hard to get a good sense of a restaurant from its web site.

Be sure to reserve tickets for any special events you'd like to attend.

Packing

Pack light, but anticipate a variety of activities. I like to have a good pair of pants that can match with different shirts. I also bring one dressier outfit and a bathing suit.

To pack dressy or delicate clothes without a garment bag, I fold delicates around pajama bottoms or sweats and roll them, then use either disposable shower caps or reusable plastic bags to protect them. I also stow some plastic wrap in case shoes, shampoo bottles, or odds and ends need covering. There are some recycled versions of plastic wrap, look for them at natural food stores or independent grocery shops. I used to bring one felt-coated non-slip hanger from home, but a friend gave me the great idea to head to the nearest dry cleaner and ask for extras from them if you're staying somewhere where there aren't accessible hangers.

Bring more than enough underwear, but wear clothes that can keep their shape for two or three days of use, especially pants or skirts. You'll be meeting and interacting with new people every day, so no one will know you wore the same outfit two days in a row.

Buy sundry items like sunscreen after you arrive. Remember, you will have to carry what you bring, so don't weigh yourself down.

Check the climate and current weather conditions of your planned locations and pack accordingly.

Try taking your luggage for a stroll in your own neighborhood before hitting the road. Then you'll know right away if you've overpacked, with enough time to do something about it.

Read GrassRoutes' latest packing tips and gadgets: *www.grassroutestravel.com/packing_tips*.

Toiletries

It is amazing the time, energy, and stress saved by bringing along a few extra items in your toiletry kit. These things boost my self-sufficiency when I am on the road, and I always like that. I'm not talking about remembering to bring your toothbrush and toothpaste—I'm talking about finessing your toiletry kit, because let's face it, what you put in there is personal. The following is a list of some handy items for both sexes, followed by a list of girls-only things.

General

Aspirin/ibuprofen/acetaminophen—Whatever your choice for general pain relief, these products can be surprisingly hard to come by at times, and sold by the pair they are way overpriced.

Gauze and tape—I find this combo to be more flexible than adhesive bandages for various cuts and helpful for off-the-cuff art projects, too. For an instant spa treatment, use the gauze as cheesecloth, wrap an extra tea bag from the hostel/hotel inside, wet the package with warm water, and place it over your eyes after you get back from a long day.

Clove oil—This fast-acting tooth pain remedy numbs lightly. You won't catch me traveling without it.

Hand sanitizer and tissues—Because you never know.

Arnica and calendula creams (avoid the gel versions if possible)—Arnica goes on bruises and sore muscles; calendula goes on open wounds and scrapes. If you want simple and effective natural remedies for such ouchies, I recommend packing tubes of these two creams.

Leatherman multitool—Even for city travel, I don't think I've gone on a trip and *not* used mine, if only to get the wine bottle open.

Tabacum and a handkerchief—If you have a tendency for motion sickness, there's no better trick than the one a fellow travel writer taught me: tie a handkerchief around your eyes (not too tight!) and take the recommended dose of this natural remedy. Try to get near a vent or moving air, face forward, and you'll be much more likely to turn around that sick feeling.

First aid antibiotic ointment—From paper cuts to all-out scrapes, healing ointment protects against infection on the road. And it doubles beautifully for shaving cream, never leaving red bumps, in case the airport security folks made you dump your canister.

For Girls Only

Mannose—If you have a tendency for compromised urinary tract health on the road, I recommend this age-old remedy for eliminating the issue. Mannose-D is in cranberries, and taking one teaspoon of mannose is like drinking five bottles of undiluted, unsweetened cranberry juice. This remedy is available at health food stores and natural medicine outlets.

Lavender oil—This essential oil emits a calming scent and masks body odors. I mix mine with a little lotion to avoid putting the oil directly on my skin, which can be too concentrated, especially for sensitive skin.

GladRags pads—Try these reusable pads and Keepers Cups if you are willing—they save tons of trash and have traveling bags to make their use doable on the road. Admittedly, these products are not for everyone.

Instant ice pack and instant heat pad—I don't know about you, but cold cures my headache pretty fast, and heat calms my sore back or upset tummy quickly. Learning about cold and heat's ability to relieve pain and relax tenseness in my body has changed my travels for the better. Just make sure you don't buy Icy Hot pads—those are completely different than plain heat pads. For "that time of the month," it's great having these temperature options on hand.

Ummelina's eye creams—These bio-rich organic creams come in many varieties, so there's bound to be at least one you'll fall in love with. While traveling, it is easy to see puffiness and stress showing in the delicate skin around the eyes, and I've found no better way to deal with it to date. *www. ummelina.com/global-remedies.cfm?categoryID=61.*

Safety
All major cities around the world have some amount of crime. Please use your wits and stay safe. Try to avoid traveling alone to new places at night.

En Route
Travel with equipment that helps make the journey to your destination peaceful. When I travel, I bring earplugs, headphones, and a sleep mask so my voyage will be blissfully quiet. I find this is easier than asking others to tone it down.

Get enough sleep before you fly. I recommend drinking lots of water the day before traveling and the day of—more if you tend to get dehydrated easily or are prone to headaches from dry plane air. Boosting your dose of vitamin C won't hurt either. To prevent your ears from popping on takeoff and landing, purchase a natural gum, like rain forest–friendly, chicle-based chewing gum.

When You Get There
Don't plan two activity-heavy days back to back. In general, it is good to have a combination of restful, educational, and physical experiences. Balance your time rather than trying to jam in too much activity. Ask yourself what you really want to see, and cut out the rest. Keep in mind that you can always come back, and be realistic about what you and your friends and family have the energy for.

Consider breaking into smaller groups when people in your party have different ideas of what they want to see and do.

Carbon Offsets

Despite the debate about the effectiveness of carbon offsets, they represent an important stopgap measure that can really do a lot of good. Carbon offset providers use a calculator programmed to estimate what a given trip will rack up in carbon dioxide emission. This mechanism considers factors like trip distance and the number of passengers in the vehicle so you'll only be responsible for your share. To offset the estimated carbon dioxide emission, you then pay one of these providers to plant trees or otherwise reduce carbon elsewhere.

You aren't throwing your money away if you know where to get certified offsets. For instance, some of the best carbon offset products are certified by Green-e, a consumer protection program run by Center for Resource Solutions. Other carbon offset providers doing a stellar job, and thus endorsed by Environmental Defense Fund (*www.fightglobalwarming.com*), are Carbon fund.org and AtmosClear (*www.atmosclear.org*).

Major travel web sites are helping out by making carbon offsetting a click option when you purchase your ticket.

Green Travel

Air travel is not great in terms of being carbon neutral, but many airlines are starting to invest in energy efficiency to make up for their jet fuel emissions. When you book a flight, pressure them to do so, or buy your own credits when you fly from one of the certified carbon offset providers. Travel often necessitates flying, so when you can, try to use airlines that are more conscientious, and you are sure to make a more positive contribution to the greater good. Weigh your options and do the best you can.

Public transit and biking are the greenest solutions around, but other great ways exist to get around, like using vehicles that run on compressed natural gas, electricity, fuel cells, or biofuels. In these pages, I point you to the latest and greatest green transit solutions in the area you'll be visiting.

Read more about green travel: *www.grassroutestravel.com/green_travel.*

Eating

These days eating green is a tricky undertaking. Here are some tips to stay conscientious and also get your grub on whether you're away or at home.

- Lots of smaller farms operate organically but just don't have the bucks to maintain an organic certification stamp. Search these out on your next farmers market excursion.

- Organic produce that's out of season and shipped from far away can be more taxing on the environment than buying conventional, local produce in season.

- Biodynamic farming is a wonderful philosophy of growing that takes into consideration many factors beneficial to the earth. It isn't always easy finding biodynamic produce; try farmers markets or search online for a biodynamic farm. Some are a part of CSA (community-supported agriculture) programs. Otherwise, buy local, in season, and organic.

- For more affordable and accessible organics, buy from a local farm, join a CSA, or subscribe to an organic food box service.

- Find out which conventional produce you should avoid because it's grown unsustainably or requires soil sterility and high levels of chemicals that stay on board when you take a bite. Stone fruit and leafy veggies are two examples of things to buy organic, always.

- Conventional produce that doesn't require a large amount of pesticides or to which pesticides aren't as apt to stick, such as fruits and vegetables with thick peels, are safe to eat.

- When you are ordering at one of the restaurants in this book, you may find some ingredients that aren't sustainable on the menu. Just go for the dishes that you know have ingredients that can be sustained.

- Kosher, halal, and organic, hormone-free meats are always better choices in terms of taste, quality, humaneness, and sustainability.

- Be especially careful when it comes to seafood. Shrimp, tuna, big-fin fish—all no-nos. Squid, catfish, tilapia, anchovies, and mackerel, on the other hand, are all totally tasty and easy to sustain. The Monterey Bay Aquarium has an up-to-date explanation of the best seafood choices: *www.montereybayaquarium.org/cr/seafoodwatch.aspx.*

Read more about eco-friendly dining: *www.grassroutestravel.com/eating.*

Banking

Did you know that the most important factor in true sustainability is economic? Think local jobs, banks that give loans to new small businesses, and more. Business owners who live where they work care more about the longevity of their community and local environment, and when you spend your money at locally owned businesses, you support that sincere effort.

Most of the businesses in these pages have direct links to the local economy, injecting most of their revenue right back into the community. Don't consider the sustainability movement without looking into the economics of it—indeed the solution to many challenges in society today lies in the communion between green industry and economics. For more info, check out Van Jones's Green For All (*www.greenforall.org*) or the Business Alliance for Local Living Economies (*www.livingeconomies.org*).

For specific establishments and more about keeping money circulating locally, see Community-Supporting Banks on page 230, and refer to *www.grassroutestravel.com/buy_local*.

Using GrassRoutes Guides

Organization by type of venue runs the risk of muddling, say, an upscale restaurant with a drive-thru, just because both are technically restaurants. Instead, shouldn't guides be organized by what kind of experience you are looking for?

GrassRoutes guides employ a new system of organization that makes searching for activities, restaurants, and venues easy. This guide is organized by situation, with chapters such as "Up Early," "Do Lunch," and "Hang Out" that pay attention to your state of being.

All phone numbers are in the 206 area code unless otherwise stated.

As authors, we want to tell our experiences from our own perspectives. The initials after each review denote the author:

SB: Serena Bartlett
DL: Daniel Laing
IM: Issac Marion

As well as a few contributing guests:

IB: Ilsa Bartlett
AK: Andrew Keuftiel
JW: Julia Wingert

Our Criteria

Urban eco-travel is defined by businesses and activities that give back to their local communities through environmental, social, or economic means. To appear in a GrassRoutes guide, a business or activity *must* have a local presence or be locally owned. In addition, if we can answer yes to at least one of the following questions, the destination passes our test:

- Does it bank locally?

- Does it hire locals?

- Does it use energy-efficient appliances?

- Does it sell fair-trade merchandise?

- Does it have a positive community benefit (for example, bringing people together or providing community outreach)?

- Does it use fair-trade, organic, or locally grown products?

- Is its location environmentally sound (for example, the building is not on a landfill, or the building is made with green materials)?

- Does it participate in reuse/garbage reduction?

- Does it care about the environment, community, and economy around it?

- And last, but certainly not least, do we love the place? Does something make it special? Does it blow our minds?

With these considerations in mind, we've created a series of icons to accompany our reviews. These icons (see key on opposite page) indicate which of the criteria above are particularly noteworthy at a particular business or organization.

✑	art/cultural/historic preservation	Ⓢ	free
			green cleaning
	banks locally		green energy use
	bikeable		hires locals
CO	cash only		inspirational
	community pillar		local organic produce/ ingredients
	composts		
$	cost: cheap		locally owned
$$	cost: moderate		on public transit route
$$$	cost: pricey		recycled material use
	dog friendly		recycles
	educational	R	reservations recommended
	electric vehicle use		romantic
	employee health care	V	vegetarian
	employees reentering workforce	((ᵠ))	WiFi available
	fair trade		

The GrassRoutes Team

Serena Bartlett

Author Serena Bartlett revels in discovering new and fun ways to tread more lightly on the planet. She has lived and traveled in more than 25 countries as an active spokesperson for eco travel. Serena is a regular contributor to a number of national and Bay Area publications, writing stories on everything from making shampoo with garden ingredients to green business tips to an interview with one of her role models, Riane Eisler.

Serena has appeared on KRON4's *Bay Area Backroads*, ABC7's *View from the Bay*, and other programs as a green travel expert; she has also been a featured guest on several radio stations. Serena is a sponge for creative solutions for becoming more self-reliant, like sewing her own sheets and quilts, designing jewelry, wild forays in the kitchen, and growing her own edible garden. She is a ski bum at heart and a swimming junkie, equally comfortable on a pack trip with her poodle or as a city slicker.

Find out more about her travel guides at *www.grassroutestravel.com* and more of her writing, recipes, and art at *www.serenabartlett.com*.

Daniel Laing

Born and raised in Oakland, Daniel's style of freehand line drawing continues to evolve with each new GrassRoutes guide. His art has been shown at several galleries, design studios, and cafes. Daniel studied anthropology at UC Berkeley, where he learned to see beyond the superficial by putting aside preconceived notions. He can be found zipping around the streets of Oakland and San Francisco on his speedy bike, scaling the bouldering walls at the local climbing gym, in the front row of a Sonic Youth concert, or buried in a book. See more of Daniel's designs and artwork at *www.grassroutestravel.com/illustrations*.

Issac Marion

Isaac Marion is a native of Seattle and Mt. Vernon who is skilled at seeking out the unusual and describing it with precision. His witty contributions to this guide are just one of his myriad writing styles. He's the author of *Warm Bodies* and a growing collection of short stories. Find out more about his writing, videos, music, and paintings at *www.burningbuilding.com*, *www.myspace. com/isaacmarionmusic*, and *www.youtube.com/user/isaacinspace*.

Ilsa Bartlett

A Bay Area writer and blogger focusing on meditation and science.

Jamie Freedman

A musicologist with a popular blog and a wonderful music column who always knows the local tunes (for more, see page 159).

Andrew Keuftiel

A well-traveled foodie who always finds the best spots to hang and meet new friends.

Julia Wingert

A local educator and facilitator who knows all the ins and outs of Seattle's public transit.

Dutsi Bap

Our cheerleader, research assistant, and referee, Dutsi boosts morale and provides support crucial to the GrassRoutes team. He completed therapy dog certification and believes that the meaning of life is to eat roast chicken, run in the park, and take long naps at the feet of our writers.

Puget Sound Overview

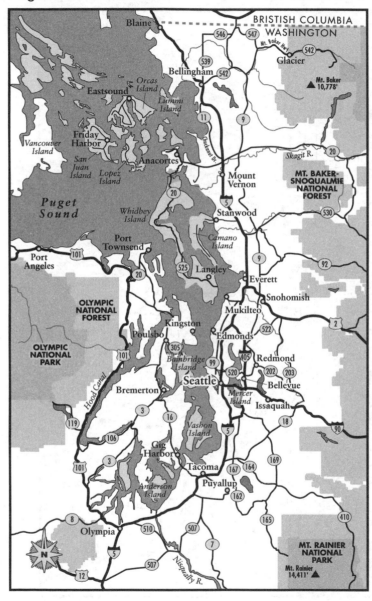

Greater Seattle Area

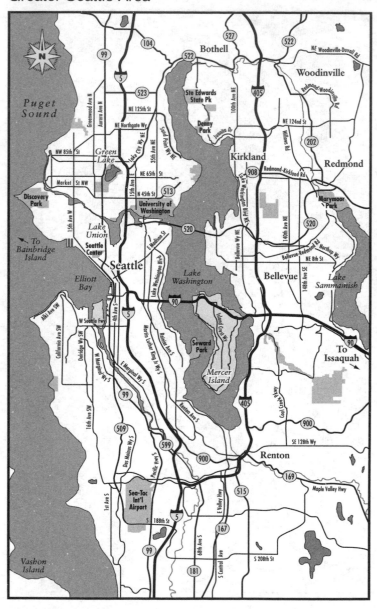

Downtown/Belltown

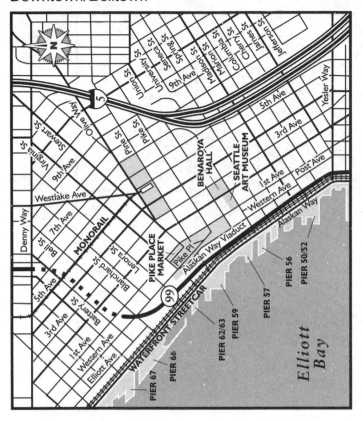

Pioneer Square

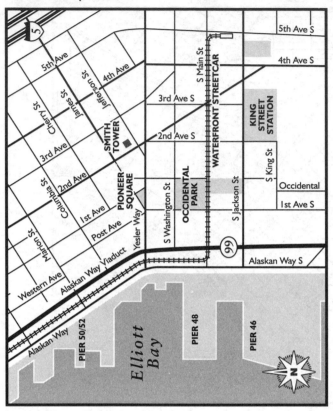

Fremont/Wallingford

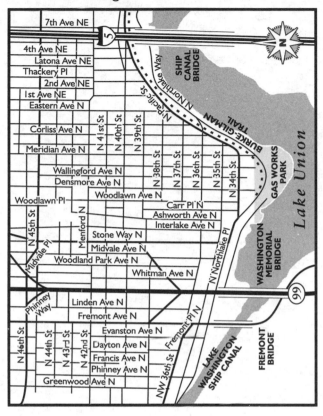

SEATTLE
About Seattle

If history has taught us one thing about Seattle, it is the city's resilience in the face of economic turmoil. Indeed, Seattle has had its share of booms and busts, but it seems that anything that has failed to destroy this city has only made it stronger. And when destruction has been an unfortunate reality (as in the case of the Great Seattle Fire of 1889), Seattle bounced back with unrelenting vigor. Perhaps the Seattle mentality knows no despair, or maybe Seattleites just have a lot of energy from all that coffee. Whatever the case may be, Seattle has suffered many a debilitating crash, only to raise its collective mug triumphantly for another refill, so to speak.

In under a century and a half, Seattle has blossomed from a small outpost with a population of 3,500 to the major metropolis we have come to take for granted in our daily lives. But the story of Seattle begins long before Euro-American settlement with the Coast Salish people, notably the Duwamish tribe. Over a thousand years before Seattle's iconic Space Needle was erected, the Duwamish brought architectural design to the Puget Sound in the form of large wood plank houses, which they built on the coast or along waterways. Here they developed a complex culture based on fishing, hunting, and gathering. The eventual displacement of the Coast Salish by white settlers combined with the ravages of a damp climate sealed the fate of Seattle's earliest known architecture.

By the late eighteenth century, various European powers were embarking on voyages to the Pacific Northwest. From one of these came Captain George Vancouver, who would give the Puget Sound its name after his lieutenant, Peter Puget. Although Lewis and Clark's 1805 expedition had established the basis for American claims to the Oregon Territory (which included what was to become Washington State), settlement of the Puget Sound basin was hindered for nearly half a century until the resolution of the U.S.-Canada border dispute in 1846. The ready availability of timber gave rise to a network of small towns north of the Columbia River and into the Puget Sound area.

In the fall of 1851, somewhere near the Burnt River in eastern Oregon, a man named Brock stopped to chat with a group of settlers bound for the Willamette Valley. The group, led by Arthur Denny, took the man's advice to inspect an unblemished land of forests, lakes, and mountains north of the Columbia. The Denny Party, as the group is referred to today, initially settled at Alki (now West Seattle), but the absence of a protected deepwater anchorage ultimately drove the settlers to relocate across Elliott Bay. Brock led Denny to make Seattle history—affecting the lay of the city today—and a main thoroughfare named for Denny is a nod to this auspicious meeting.

The village of Duwamps was founded on the location of present-day Pioneer Square; obviously this name did not stick. Instead, David Swinson "Doc" Maynard, who had settled the land south of the Denny Party's, proposed the name "Seattle" after the leader of the Suquamish and Duwamish tribes. Chief Seattle, seeking to accommodate the white settlers, formed a friendly relationship with Maynard, who in turn negotiated support for the native people in a more honorable way than other white leaders.

Henry Yesler, another man whose name appears around town to this day, was an entrepreneur and Seattle's first millionaire. He arrived in the town in 1852 and built a steam-powered sawmill on the waterfront where Maynard's and Denny's plats met, thus sealing Seattle's dominance of the lumber industry. Although the Denny Party had consisted of Methodists, Seattle soon developed a reputation as a wide-open town, similar to San Francisco's Barbary Coast, where prostitution and gambling ran amok.

As the nineteenth century drew to a close, the focus on where the newly constructed Northern Pacific Railway's trans-continental railroad would end became the center of attention. Nearby Tacoma offered cheaper land prices to the bottomline-driven railroad barons, and a practical industrial setting. This caused an uproar in the more established port town of Seattle, and what ensued was 11 frantic years of freight debate. In the end Tacoma was the chosen terminus, but Seattle attracted the Great Northern Railway in 1884 (nearly the same route the Amtrak train takes today).

The era encompassing the mid-1800s through to the early twentieth century was marked by plundering and general lawlessness. Schools barely functioned, indoor plumbing was rare, and sewage plagued the tides. The town had the bizarre distinction of having such bad potholes that at least one drowning occurred. Women played a significant role in civilizing the town, thanks to a brief allowance of women's suffrage (Seattle being one of the first areas in the United States to do so in any capacity).

Seattle's first big economic boom was fueled by the lumber industry, shipping logs to San Francisco and earning it the nickname "Timber Town." A forest of 300-foot, 1,000- to 2,000-year-old trees once blanketed Seattle. As the lumber industry eventually went into decline, the city began its practice of using recession times to rebuild infrastructure. This method proved to be quite successful, especially in the wake of the Great Seattle Fire of 1889. Although the blaze had ravaged most of the central business district, an entirely redesigned plan was promptly executed that addressed many of the shortcomings that had contributed to the fire's spread. Buildings were constructed of brick rather than wood, fire hydrants were located more frequently, and the city retired its volunteer firefighter program (which was competent but inadequately equipped) in favor of a professional force. The high demand for labor nearly doubled Seattle's population from 25,000 to 40,000 in the year after the fire. New businesses and big-name financial institutions (like what used to be America's biggest bank, Washington Mutual) rose from the ashes.

Four years following the fire, the threat of a national depression loomed over the heads of Americans as the Panic of 1893 set in. Although the city was hit hard, Seattle's second and most dramatic boom to date came as a direct result of the Klondike gold rush, which erased the town's debt literally overnight. During this era, Seattle became a major transportation center and spawned new businesses such as the American Messenger Company (UPS), Nordstrom, and Eddie Bauer. Massive immigration ensued and many of the neighborhoods that make up modern-day Seattle first came into being. City engineer R. H. Thompson led a massive effort to level the hills south and north of the newly bustling city. Known as the Denny Regrade, the project's displaced earth was used to build the industrial Harbor Island and the waterfront. The dramatic expansion of the city prompted planners to begin beautification, providing parks and boulevards under a plan designed by the Olmsted Brothers firm. Lack of zoning during Seattle's expansion led to an intermingling of different land uses and economic classes. The 12-year-long gold rush era culminated in the 1909 Alaska-Yukon-Pacific Exposition, showcasing the development of the Pacific Northwest.

War swept the globe in 1914, causing a massive swell in shipbuilding for Seattle. A decade later, the city experienced severe labor strife—perhaps the harshest of the Great Depression. But with the outbreak of World War II, the U.S. government was suddenly in need of tens of thousands of planes a year, and the Boeing airplane company filled the orders and grew to be the largest employer in Seattle. At the end of the war, however, Boeing had to shut down factories as production decreased dramatically.

Despite its various economic booms and busts, Seattle began to establish itself as an arts center. Skid Road produced a thriving jazz scene with such luminaries as Quincy Jones and Ray Charles. The thriving music scene evolved with the decades, epitomized by whatever counterculture movement was going on (from beats to hippies to "batcavers"—the first goths), which was a natural progression to the '90s when Seattle was made famous for its unique grunge sound.

In an attempt to counteract the decline of the downtown area, Seattle became the host of the Century 21 Exposition—the 1962 World's Fair. In its wake, the fair left behind Seattle Center and the now-iconic Space Needle, though at the time it was painted a shade of orange called "Galaxy Gold." A monorail line was also built in conjunction with the fair, although today it serves as little more than a tourist attraction, running on too limited a schedule and route for any sort of practical use. It is great for people watching as long as you aren't concerned with getting to and from on a reliable schedule (it erratically breaks down).

The 1970s ushered in yet another bust following the cancellation of Boeing's supersonic transport program. Over 40,000 jobs were lost between 1970 and 1971, and a famous billboard sarcastically suggested, "Will the Last Person Leaving SEATTLE—Turn Out the Lights." Seattle was soon joined in recession by the rest of the country in the oil crisis of 1973. The sustained economic boom that had characterized the 1950s and '60s came to an end, yet Seattle escaped a fate similar to that of Detroit by being a port city that did have a substantial population of educated and skilled workers.

Seattle's recovery from the Boeing recession is perhaps best demonstrated with the stories of Pike Place Market and Pioneer Square. On one hand, the city shot itself in the foot with the socially and morally irresponsible internment of the Japanese during World War II, since 80 percent of the vendors at Pike Place were ethnically Japanese. In a rebound to keep the famous market alive, an initiative was passed in 1971, despite intense opposition by the Seattle Establishment. Today, Pike Place Market is without a doubt Seattle's most important tourist attraction, pulling in 9 million visitors each year. Similarly, historic Pioneer Square faced impending doom, only to be saved by a reenergized downtown. As businesses began to occupy the cheaply acquired buildings, the restaurants, galleries, boutiques, and other services soon followed.

In 1979 Seattle received a big break when Microsoft founders Bill Gates and Paul Allen moved their startup company from New Mexico to their native home. By 1995 Microsoft had grown into one of the most profitable corporations in the world, making Gates and Allen billionaires and thousands of their employees—past and present—millionaires. Some of those millionaire employees then moved on to start their own companies. Paul Allen became a major investor in new companies after departing Microsoft and remains a major force in local politics. He currently owns three Pacific Northwest professional sports teams: the Seattle Seahawks of the NFL, the Portland Trailblazers of the NBA, and Major League Soccer's Seattle Sounders F.C. Microsoft has served as a catalyst for many technological innovations, in addition to dedicating itself to philanthropic causes, donating software and funds to many schools and libraries.

Seattle is still converging and deciding where it wants to be in the scheme of things. It is a city caught between politeness and intensity, creativity and capitalism, solitude and nature. Any trip to the Emerald City—a nickname arising from its beautiful water geography—will be a mere thread in the ever-changing fabric of this Puget Sound city. DL

General Visitor Information

It is hard to go anywhere in central Seattle without finding free maps, and guide pamphlets with loads of local info (albeit ad-driven). The Seattle Convention and Visitors Bureau is a great place to start, especially if English is your second or third language. Practical info on whatever your interests are here, with people to help explain if you need it. Get directed! (*www.visit seattle.org*, Spanish: *www.visitseattle.org/visitors/espanol*, 1 Convention Place, 701 Pike St, Ste 800, Seattle, WA, 98101, 206.461.5840, e-mail to request a free Visitor's Packet: *visinfo@visitseattle.org*)

For International Visitors

Welcome—we hope you love it here as much as we do!

Required Documents

Before you plan to travel here, contact your country's nearest U.S. embassy or consulate to determine the necessary documents required for travel to the United States. You are required to obtain a visa or passport, and may need to pass certain health guidelines, so allow enough time before your desired departure date to figure all this out. The info changes frequently, so check online for updated specifics: *www.usa.gov/visitors/visit.shtml first.*

Customs

You must complete customs and immigrations formalities at your first point of entry into the United State, whether or not it is your final destination. At that point you will speak with a customs officer and present your forms and documentation. If you are flying or taking a train these forms will be handed out prior to entry into the country. Just keep in mind the officers are the equivalent of police, so they aren't always talkative or very friendly, but that doesn't mean everyone in the city is like that! You'll be welcomed by kind bus drivers, airport personnel, and others whose job isn't to protect the country.

Travel Insurance

The United States has no compulsory government travel insurance plan. It is advisable to purchase private travel and health insurance, especially since there aren't many options for low-cost health care in the United States.

Electricity

The standard electrical current in the United States is 110 volts. Most outlets accept two- or three-pronged plugs (much closer together than the British kind, and not round like those used in most of Europe and Asia, which are also different voltages). Laptops and other electronic devices should be equipped with a power converter—if not, get one before you plug in!

Currency

There are a number of large banks that will let you exchange foreign currency for U.S. dollars, but it is advisable to change money *before* coming to the United States (often at better rates), or at least at the airport, even if there are some fees. It can often be difficult or inconvenient to find good money-changing spots in the United States, unlike in Asia and Europe.

Emergencies

It is always a good idea to acquaint yourself with the emergency resources of an area while you are visiting. Here is some important info in the case of an emergency:

9-1-1

Dial 9-1-1 on your phone only to stop a crime in progress, report a fire, or call for an ambulance due to a medical emergency. In most cities there are a limited number of emergencies that the 9-1-1 lines can attend to at a given time, so determine how urgent your situation is before making the call.

9-1-1 from Cell Phones

If you are dialing 9-1-1 from your cell phone, you will be connected to highway patrol and need to provide the dispatcher with details about the location of the emergency, your cell phone number, and, as always, the nature of the emergency. The location of cell phone calls cannot be necessarily determined like landline calls can, and sometimes calls can be cut off. If this is the case, call back. If you are in a moving vehicle, stop driving so as not to distance yourself from the location of the emergency. Check with your provider if there is a different emergency number you must dial from your phone.

Know Your Non-Emergency Number

Often incidents to not require the immediacy of a 9-1-1 call. For Seattle, the non-emergency numbers are the following:

625.5011 Non-Emergency Police

386.1400 Non-Emergency Fire

Emergency Updates

The Seattle Office of Emergency Management answers all sorts of questions and provides resources for visitors and locals on subjects ranging from winter weather preparedness to city pandemic flu plans, earthquakes, landslides, and other hazards. A breeze through this info will get you in the know about how to prepare and how to act, whether you are a first-timer visitor or a long-time resident. For the latest updates and information during an emergency, go to: *www.seattle.gov/emergency* or call 233.5076.

Hospitals and Clinics

Bastyr Center for Natural Health (Homeopathic Medicine)
3670 Stone Wy N, Seattle
834.4100
http://bastyrcenter.org

Harborview Medical Center
325 9th Ave, Seattle
731.3000
www.uwmedicine.org/Facilities/Harborview

Seattle Children's Hospital
4800 Sand Point Wy NE, Seattle
987.2000
www.seattlechildrens.org

Northwest Hospital and Medical Center
1550 N 115th St, Seattle
364.0500, 877.NWH-HOSP
www.nwhospital.org

Swedish Medical Center (multiple locations)
First Hill: 747 Broadway, Seattle
386.6000
Ballard: 5300 Tallman Ave NW, Seattle
782.2700
www.swedish.org

Climate

Let's not beat around the bush: Seattle is not known for fabulous weather. But after spending so much time there, I think maybe it should be—it is just a different kind of fabulous. There's rain nearly every other day in fall, winter, and spring, but there are just as many rainbows—and once you get into the wet weather, you learn to see the beauty in its many forms. There are deep, dark raindrops; a light and sprinkling kind; and all shades in-between. What this means for the plant life is bursts of vibrant green that reflect off the many bodies of water surrounding the city. On dreary days there are a plethora of fanciful indoor activities, and on sunny days everyone and their mother congregates outside for colorful street festivals, park lounging, water activities, and outdoor movies. The weather fuels this city, rather than hindering it. Just don't expect a tan. The average yearly temperature hovers around 59 degrees, so at least you know you won't freeze, and if it does get too brisk, head to Hothouse Spa and Sauna (see page 183) and you'll be good as new. Here are a few web resources for the dreary details: *www.seattleweather.com* and *www. seattle.gov/html/visitor/weather.htm*. On paper it might not look so good, but Seattle is another story in real life, trust me.

Neighborhoods and Surrounding Areas of Interest

The lowdown on some of Seattle's most fascinating micro-communities.

Ravenna

Serving as a residence for many grad students and professors, Ravenna is a popular place to take your bike, whether you aim to cruise down Ravenna Boulevard (a.k.a. Professors' Row) or take the route connecting Green Lake to the Burke-Gilman Trail. Ravenna was once covered with old-growth timber rising nearly 400 feet—that is, until the logging boom laid waste to the entire forest, save for those trees in the Cowen Park ravine. These surviving trees had been ignored for decades until their gradual disappearance under suspicious circumstances in the 1920s. At the very least, this legacy has helped galvanize community efforts to restore the ravine and its riparian habitat. What remains is a charming 'hood many are proud to call home. Avoid Park Road during the holidays, unless sitting in bumper-to-bumper traffic to see an elaborate Christmas display is your idea of tradition. DL

Eastlake

This largely residential neighborhood can be reached by a number of bus routes from the University of Washington, which is especially convenient if you've decided to volunteer or take a class there. Most of the small businesses that populate Eastlake can be found on Eastlake Avenue, sure enough. The park at the west end of E Louisa Street serves as the Independent Petanque Club of Eastlake's "home field," which was constructed from granite curbs recycled from Pioneer Square and pitching mound material courtesy of Safeco Field. DL

Georgetown

This one is a top pick. *Seattle Weekly* fittingly described this neighborhood as "industrial bohemian chic." You'll find coffeehouses, bars, a record store, a scooter shop, and many more small businesses making creative use of old brick buildings deserted by industry, transforming the cold, sterile interiors into warm, inviting spaces. SB

West Seattle

It's strange to think that the original settlement founded and later abandoned by the Denny Party would eventually return as part of the city. Here you can find many sites with historical information, including the Museum of History and Industry and the Log House Museum at Alki Point. "The Junction" at the intersection of California Avenue SW and SW Alaska Street is a bustling business district representing the heart of West Seattle. The highest point in Seattle can be found at the intersection of 35th Avenue SW and SW Myrtle

Street, where you can behold spectacular views of the Olympic Mountains to the west and the Cascade Range to the east. *DL*

SoDo

Originally referring to a location south of the Kingdome, SoDo is now taken to mean "south of downtown." The conversion of vacated factories and warehouses into lofts and studios emulates SoHo in New York City during the 1970s. SoDo differs from the template laid out by the Manhattan neighborhood, though, having not experienced so much gentrification as some of the industrial buildings continue to serve their original purpose. *DL*

Pioneer Square

Pioneer Square is at the very core of Seattle and is home to one of my favorite bookstores, Wessel and Lieberman Booksellers (see the Bookish chapter, page 45), and many others; a bunch of corporate art galleries and several great local ones; plus tourists, locals, hacky sack players, bums, outdoor art, old red bricks, and many a good story. It's a pretty area with some of Seattle's oldest structures, but it's small—wedged between the waterfront, downtown, the International District, and SoDo—and perfectly easy to navigate to and from if you have lunch plans at Salumi (see page 68) or Szechuan Noodle Bowl (see page 70), or you're just in the mood for a sit in the square. *SB*

University District

Dubbed the "U District," the University of Washington campus is home to a diverse community and once served as the site of the Alaska-Yukon-Pacific Exposition, Seattle's first world's fair. University Way NE, or simply "the Ave," serves as the main thoroughfare in this youth-dominated area. Here you'll find some distinctly local spots among the prominent chain-store population, including Flowers Bar and Restaurant (see page 69); Big Time Brewery and Alehouse (see page 152) and its house-made beers; Cafe Allegro (see page 39), with its counterculture ambiance; Bulldog News, which offers hundreds of periodicals for your browsing pleasure; the University Book Store (see page 50) for the very bookish; and Red Light (see page 132), the Ave's top vintage clothing shop. For a change of scene, stroll through the campus to Drumheller Fountain, where beautiful rose gardens abound, and with any luck you'll have a clear view of Mount Rainier. *DL*

Central District

Seattle's historically African American neighborhood is rich with cultural institutions, city landmarks, and comforting soul food restaurants. Founded by some of the city's original settlers, the Central District later became a source of civil rights activism. Countless historic houses have been designated city landmarks, and the Douglass-Truth Public Library holds the largest African American literary collection in the Seattle Public Library system. When I'm feeling homesick for my native Oakland, I come here for scores of authentic soul food restaurants, such as Nellie's Place Cafe and Ezell's Famous Chicken (see page 139). The Langston Hughes Performing Arts Center has something to offer on any given day, such as a performance by a local boys' choir or a production of a play written by the legendary Harlem Renaissance playwright himself. DL

Ballard

Full disclosure: I live in Ballard. I've lived here for a little over a year, and during that time I've gone from liking it, to hating it, to loving it. When I first arrived it seemed like a nice area—not too scary, not too trafficky, but not too remote from the city either. Then I started to feel ashamed of where I lived, because everyone I met raised their eyebrows and said, "Ballard? I thought only 70-year-old Vikings lived in Ballard." True, Ballard has a long history involving a lot of Nordic fishermen, and yes, Scandinavian kitsch can still be found at a few restaurants and souvenir shops, but the area is evolving. I eventually discovered downtown Ballard, the area surrounding NW Market Street, and realized that there is a thriving culture here full of young and exciting people and plenty of things to do. The residential areas are very suburban and teeming with families and squealing children, but Market Street and Ballard Avenue offer nightlife options such as the über-popular King's Hardware (see page 148) and the quirky, classy hidden gem Hazelwood. The Ballard vibe is much more relaxed than Capitol Hill or the U District, although some may complain about the weaker diversity rating and the creeping menace of condo developments. It's less interesting than those eastern neighborhoods perhaps, but it's also less intense. I personally enjoy the balance of calm and crazy. IM

Columbia City

Columbia City is a bit of an anomaly. A tiny enclave of culture dropped from the sky into the wildlands of the largely rundown Rainier Valley. There are bookstores, art galleries, and nice restaurants aplenty here, but within walking distance you may also encounter smashed windows, barred storefronts, and blocks of smoke shops and liquor stores. The area is a combination of lower-income families from diverse cultures and the younger hipsters that bring with them neighborhood gentrification. Come for the cute shops and tasty restaurants; stay for the fascinating social dynamic. *IM*

Belltown

Once home to Seattle's burgeoning film exchange, Belltown has evolved into a vibrant arts and music district full of trendy restaurants where you can find just about any kind of cuisine. This enclave is known for its clubs, such the famed Crocodile Café and sister clubs Tini Bigs (see page 148) and Watertown in the Denny Triangle (bounded by Denny Way, Olive Way, and 5th Avenue). *DL*

Downtown

Downtown Seattle as we know it would not have been possible had it not been for the Great Seattle Fire of 1889. Today, upscale restaurants and shops thrive where strip clubs and pawnshops once stood. The architecture is something to behold: Rainier Tower seems to defy the laws of physics with its 11-story concrete base that tapers toward ground level; influences of the Empire State Building can be seen in the stair-stepping profile of the 1201 3rd Avenue Tower; the 27-story Seattle Tower showcases a 1920s art deco style; and Columbia Center, although not quite as attractive, plays host to the largest firefighter competition in the world. Where ashes once blanketed the city blocks, Seattle's bustling shops and diverse architecture now stand. Downtown is also home to the Washington State Convention and Trade Center, which stretches across 12 lanes of I-5 to reconnect First Hill with the downtown area. *DL*

Capitol Hill

Seattle's version of San Francisco's famous Castro district can be found at the heart of Capitol Hill, and it's called Broadway. The strip is defined by its movie houses such as Harvard Exit Theatre (see page 144), clubs such as Gravity Bar, and countless vintage clothing and bookstores. The Pike-Pine corridor just east of Broadway has been developing a reputation for its small trendy shops and clubs, such as Century Ballroom. More retail spots and restaurants line the less ostentatious 15th Avenue E. DL

Fremont

"The People's Republic of Fremont," as it is sometimes called, was once a center of the counterculture movement, but it has experienced some gentrification. There is much to this quirky neighborhood that conjures images of Berkeley, including the infamous statue of Lenin salvaged from Slovakia and the Volkswagen Beetle (which had a California license plate) immortalized as part of the Fremont Troll sculpture beneath the Aurora Bridge. You can also find an old rocket fuselage that I imagine would have those geeks at Lawrence Berkeley National Laboratory pretty excited. Fremont hosts the Summer Solstice Parade and Pageant, known for its nude Solstice Cyclists. Drawing yet another parallel with the San Francisco Bay Area is Fremont's Silicon Canal, as opposed to Silicon Valley, where a growing number of tech companies have a presence, including Adobe Systems and Google. Fremont residents are a particularly proud lot, and have proclaimed their neighborhood "The Center of the Universe." DL

Wallingford

Every neighborhood should have its own neon sign. At the heart of this neighborhood named for a major landowner of the late nineteenth century is the QFC supermarket, atop of which stands the large illuminated FOOD GIANT sign—wait, that's what it used to say. It has since been altered and now proudly announces that you are indeed in Wallingford. Thanks, giant neon sign! Wallingford's business district is populated by many small shops, some restaurants and watering holes, two Guild 45th movie theaters, and Dick's Drive In restaurant. At the northern edge of the district, a clashing of streets following the contours of Green Lake and those abiding to the city grid plan go by the name Tangletown for the retail pocket there. To the south are Lake Union and a jutting peninsula where the former Seattle Gas Light plant rests, surrounded by Gas Works Park. Tying Wallingford to nearby Fremont, Gas Works Park serves as the traditional endpoint of the nude Solstice

Cyclists and it is also the starting point of the World Naked Bike Ride. Even living a city that averages fewer than 60 clear days a year, Seattleites sure do like to "freewheel." DL

International District

The threat of intense racial discrimination and the ravages of the Great Seattle Fire of 1889 failed to deter the few Chinese Americans who stayed in Seattle, and through their strong will and sacrifice of security, the International District (a.k.a. the ID) exists. The new Chinatown established after the fire was destined to become the hub of a neighborhood that is more representative of the eastern Asian continent. The Chinese American population was soon joined by Japanese and Filipino immigrants, and, following the Vietnam War, by a wave of Southeast Asians. The neighborhood eventually gained federal status as the Seattle Chinatown Historic District, thanks to organizations dedicated to its preservation. Hing Hay Park, the Wing Luke Asian Museum (see page 109), the Uwajimaya supermarket (see page 118), and the community-maintained Danny Woo International District Garden are a just a handful of the many notable establishments in this part of town. DL

Queen Anne

Named for the style of architecture that dominated the hill in the late 1900s, Upper Queen Anne has long been a popular spot for the city's economic and cultural elite, especially for its magnificent views. From Betty Bowen Viewpoint you can see everything from the Puget Sound to West Seattle and the islands, and Kerry Park offers a perspective of downtown, Elliott Bay, and the Space Needle. Queen Anne Avenue N is dominated by restaurants, like 5 Spot (see page 31), and some portions of the main thoroughfares reveal the Olmsted Brothers' comprehensive boulevard design, a project that was never fully executed. Upper Queen Anne is connected to Lower Queen Anne via "the Counterbalance," which is named for the weight and pulley system that once hauled streetcars up its steep incline. Lower Queen Anne is known for Seattle Center (see page 143). DL

That's Not All, Folks!

Believe it or not, this list doesn't cover all the Seattle neighborhoods, but it does present the liveliest ones. On a trip to the Emerald City you may well hear about some of these other areas: Beacon Hill, Bitter Lake, Blue Ridge, Broadmoor, Broadview, Bryant, Cascade, Cherry Hill, Crown Hill, Denny Regrade, Denny-Blaine, First Hill, Greenwood, Harbor Island, Industrial District, Interbay, Judkins, Lake City (Cedar Park, Matthews Beach, Meadowbrook, Olympic Hills, Victory Heights), Laurelhurst, Madison Park, Madison Valley, Madrona, Magnolia, Maple Leaf, Montlake, Mount Baker, Northgate (Haller Lake, Licton Springs, Pinehurst), Phinney Ridge, Rainier Beach, Rainier Valley (Brighton, Dunlap), Rainier View, Roosevelt, Sand Point, Seward Park, South Lake Union, South Park, Squire Park, University Village, Upper Fremont, View Ridge, Washington Park, Wedgwood, Westlake, and Windermere.

Surrounding Areas of Interest

Edmonds

www.ci.edmonds.wa.us
www.walnutstreetcoffee.com
www.ricksteves.com/about/travelcenter.htm

Edmonds is a quaint and quiet waterside town, best known in my circles as the home of intrepid European traveler Rick Steves. But there's more than his incredible travel book library and headquarters in this town, just about 25 minutes to the north of Seattle. Look for live music and neighborhood coffee shops, indie shopping, and great views of the water.

Bainbridge Island

www.ci.bainbridge-isl.wa.us
www.bgiedu.org
www.yesmagazine.org

Just across the Sound from Seattle lies green-coated Bainbridge Island. It is easy and fun to take a ferry there, and there's more to see than the rich houses for which the island is famous. Its also the home of *Yes Magazine*, a number of sustainable education centers, small farms, a winery or two, some great bookshops, beaches, and excellent Thai food.

Bellevue

www.ci.bellevue.wa.us
www.bellevuesquare.com

Seattle's sister city to the east (across Lake Washington), Bellevue, isn't at all a biological twin—rather a more shopaholic incarnation. There are many fine restaurants and great authentic dives, and it has an equally strong neighborhood feel as some of the Seattle locales. Culture is prevalent, but mixed in there is one of America's best malls, so—as I said before—the propensity for shopping is high. A number of large companies are based here, and more and more of them are taking the green movement seriously and putting new protocols into action.

San Juan Islands

www.visitsanjuans.com
http://orcasislandchamber.com

A gorgeous string of islands that are practically touching Canada, the San Juans are simply beautiful. Orcas, the most famous isle, is a wonderful vacation spot, home to a free-spirited and imaginative community and some of the most epic kayaking experiences. Wind between the small islands to catch a glimpse of the wild Pacific Northwest, then climb to the top of Mount Constitution to get a view of them all—plus Vancouver, BC, on the horizon line.

Tacoma

www.cityoftacoma.org
www.museumofglass.org
www.tacomaartmuseum.org
www.kingsbookstore.com

Home to King's (a favorite bookstore) and a terrific art museum, glass artist Dale Chihuly's hometown is all that. Complete with a free cellphone tour of Chihuly's installations around the city, Tacoma is a great escape and easy to walk. Tacoma is about 30 minutes due south of Seattle, and taking a bus there is a breeze. I would recommend traveling with a partner if it is your first time in Tacoma.

Woodinville

www.ci.woodinville.wa.us
www.woodinvillewinecountry.com

A nearby mecca of mostly locally owned, small-scale farms and wineries, Woodinville is not far from Seattle, but it's a world away, so to speak. Heading north and east for just over 30 minutes brings you into town.

Getting Here

Tips to get from A to B

Here are some options for travel that include everything from flying to walking. Even a conscientious traveler of the globe must at times make use of transportation options beyond walking! Weigh time, cost, and energy usage to determine which transport choice best suits your needs and the needs of the planet. Though it can be more time-consuming, transit provides a smoother transition to the next spot. Choose efficient routes to avoid wasting unnecessary fuel.

The Puget Sound is an international travel destination, with one major, and several smaller airports, plus a slew of train options and rideshare offerings. Here's the vital info to get you to Seattle.

By Plane

Seattle-Tacoma International Airport (Sea-Tac)

Main Terminal: 17801 International Blvd

433.5388, 800.544.1965

www.portseattle.org/seatac

This modern airport is a hub of international travel, with many direct flights to and from most Asian countries, South and Central America, Canada, and many others. An underground tram comes every two minutes, easily connecting the terminals. Chain restaurant options abound in each terminal, but as prices are higher than usual, I recommend bringing a bagged lunch or waiting until you are released from the security line to get some real grub. Although you cannot bring more than 3 ounces of liquid with you, and you may even have to relinquish gels like lip balm to airport security officers, you can still bring an empty water bottle to fill at a water fountain once inside the terminal and avoid spending extreme amounts of cash on bottled water. Security regulations change with great frequency; check with the Federal Aviation Administration (*www.faa.gov*) to see what the current restrictions are. At the end of the baggage claim area is a pleasant fountain with huge local rocks and a sculpture garden with historic planes flying from the glassy ceiling. It is a courteous airport (if there is such a thing), and there are plenty of ways to easily get downtown. United, Southwest, and Alaska Airlines and its subsidiary Frontier Airlines have main hubs at Sea-Tac, but most major airlines fly to and from this airport. SB

Seattle Seaplanes

329.9638
www.seattleseaplanes.com
Call to schedule charter flights and 20-minute scenic flights
If you want to arrive in Seattle in extravagant style, hire Seattle Seaplanes to fly you from spots around the Puget Sound and back over and into Seattle, pointing out the sights on the way. For a romantic start to a vacation with your sweetie, try these fun vehicles that fly in the air and on the water. SB

By Train

Amtrak

King Street Station, 303 S Jackson St
www.amtrak.com
Traveling by train isn't the most convenient way to get to and from Seattle, but it is the most romantic, the most scenic, and, unless you have a CNG or fuel cell vehicle, the greenest. Find your way to the south end of downtown, and King Street Station (see map, page xxvi) will sweep you through its marble walkways and off into a train car zooming toward your future destination—or vice versa.

If you're visiting the capitol city on your way out of town, alight on the platform at Centennial Amtrak Station just 8 miles outside of Olympia on the Yelm Highway and catch one of the hourly buses Intercity Transit operates into town until 8:20pm Monday through Saturday and 7:55pm on Sunday. The tracks north and south of Olympia run through lovely wilderness and backcountry areas, with occasional views of the Olympic Mountains and Mount Rainier. SB

By Boat

Washington State Ferries

801 Alaskan Wy, Pier 52
464.6400, 888.808.7977
www.wsdot.wa.gov/ferries

Washington State Ferries operates the country's largest ferry fleet. Commercial users, tourists, and daily commuters (most of whom are traveling to and from Bainbridge Island) are carried up and down the Puget Sound to 20 different ports. Among the destinations is Orcas Island, where on a clear day you can see Vancouver, BC, on the horizon from the island's summit. Fares vary, so call or check the web site for more information. *DL*

By Bus

Greyhound Bus Lines
811 Stewart St
628.5526
www.greyhound.com
Daily 6a–11:30p

Taking the bus doesn't get nearly enough props. No confusing driving directions, no road ragers, no gas pumps or searching for change at a toll, and all the time in the world to zone out to the views whizzing by, great tunes, and a new book. All this and you're actually getting somewhere. Greyhound has a relatively nice bus station in Seattle that connects to the complete network of bus routes crisscrossing North America. *SB*

By Car

- From Vancouver, BC, take Interstate 5 south.

- From Idaho or states to the east, take Interstate 90.

- From Utah and southern Idaho, take Interstate 84 and connect to I-90 via Interstate 82.

- From points east of Utah, connect to I-84 by way of Interstate 80.

- From California and Oregon, head north on I-5.

- From the Pacific Northwest coast, take Highway 101 and make your way west to I-5.

Getting Around
Movin' and groovin' in town

As soon as you set foot in this city, you'll want to start exploring. The public transportation system is excellent and covers a lot of ground; there are very few places you can't go with a Metro pass (see below) in hand. Metro maps are essential tools for no-stress searching, even if your aim is to get lost. After a day of following your nose, you'll know which cable car, bus, or streetcar to take home.

By Public Transit

Seattle Metro
King Street Center, 201 S Jackson St
553.3000
http://transit.metrokc.gov, http://tripplanner.metrokc.gov

As a devout bus rider in the city of Seattle, I must say that riding Metro is an experience of love. There's the love of your neighbors, who quite often entertain en route, the love of adventure, and, of course, the love of the environment.

Hordes of Seattleites mitigate their oil addictions by utilizing mass transit, which runs from the heart to the limbs of this green city. It is one of the unique spaces where all expressions of human existence cooperate. Hipsters, young children, people in suits, and the occasional man in leather and a feather boa all need to get somewhere, and they choose to do it en masse. The bus itself isn't the only mode of transportation, though—the Metro web site offers a host of options. Carpools, vanpools, ride matches, and shuttles between transit posts all exist to serve travelers and commuters riding to make a difference. Overwhelmed? That's love, baby.

Catching the most expedient bus using route maps can, at times, be a bit of a circus. Fortunately, Metro has bestowed upon us the Trip Planner (known affectionately as TP), an online tool that generally gives solid, simple instructions to get where you're going. From time to time, though, it advises an unnecessarily circuitous route, which you, as a sentient being, can circumvent. Dare to experiment with TP by changing walking distances, transfers, and travel times to find a more direct path. Know that TP's maps are abysmal, so it's helpful to have another online mapping program open to verify your course or to seek other possible travel routes. Also, if you visit a place ahead of time, make a mental note of the route numbers serving that area; it helps to eliminate extra steps later. When all else fails, Metro has some really friendly drivers, who are always willing to help. In a few rounds, you will be another savvy bus rider, saving the planet one trip at a time! *JW*

Seattle Center Monorail

www.seattlemonorail.com
Sun–Thurs 9a–9p, Fri–Sat 9a–11p
Fares: $1.50 youth 5–12; $2 seniors, disabled, and Medicare cardholders; $4 adults

It's a little surreal to find yourself in a major U.S. city and look up to see a pretty little monorail buzzing around downtown. Seattle's monorail looks deceptively like the kind you'd find at a big zoo, to ride around the park and see all the animals from above. This monorail gives you the same kind of viewing advantage, minus the lions and tigers but plus a fun little whirl through the far side of Experience Music Project (see page 85) at the end of the line. It does feel somewhat out of place, however. Seattleites themselves have a slew of jokes about the monorail, and the saga of votes and re-votes for initial construction and various expansions have provided many columnists with an opportunity to show their wit and sarcasm. I ride it with glee anyway. It's convenient for downtown back-and-forths, and it's far better than trying to drive the mess of one-way streets alongside classically cautious Washington drivers and dealing with gigantic parking fees. *SB*

South Lake Union Streetcar

www.seattlestreetcar.org

One of my very favorite places to stroll in this wonderful city is South Lake Union, with its combination of new energy, lake views, parks, and big buildings with unexpected purposes. Getting there is easy with the new South Lake Union Streetcar (originally the South Lake Union Trolley, or SLUT, an unfortunate acronym that seems to have stuck, despite the official name change), a trolley car with a north- and southbound loop stopping at Fairview Avenue and Ward Street; Lake Union Park, Westlake Avenue, and Mercer Street; Terry Avenue and Mercer Street; Westlake Avenue and Thomas

Street; Terry Avenue and Thomas Street; Westlake and 9th avenues; Westlake Avenue and Denny Way; and Westlake and 7th avenues. In December 2008 a new measure passed to expand SLUT with more lines and greater ease of use. Admittedly it's another pro–tech biz project—Paul Allen, who's behind Experience Music Project and other big projects around the city, got SLUT constructed with the help of Mayor Nickels to make it easier for employees to get to his private asset management company, Vulcan. Even so, I'm intrigued by the spirit of business in this city—it's interesting to watch the ebbs and flows of various corporations and their influence both on the psyche of the city and the physical landscape. Riding this wide-windowed streetcar gives me the chance to ponder these ideas en route. *SB*

Sound Transit's Link Light Rail
Various stops from Downtown Seattle to Sea-Tac Airport, plus a planned network of future routes
888.889.6368
www.soundtransit.org
Finally there's an easy light rail train to and from the downtown corridor and the airport, and by 2016 a full network of these electric trains will be speedily whirring around the sound. As this new and exciting public transit system gets up and running, it'll be even easier to skip a car while touring Seattle! Check for updates online to get new fares, routes, and maps.

By Solo Transit

Segway of Seattle
93 Denny Wy
284.7634
www.segwayofseattle.com
Mon–Sat 10a–6p, Sun 11a–5p
Inside Seattle's downtown Vespa dealer is the best selection of Segways for rent or purchase. Pick the whizzy I2 for paved commutes or the rugged X2 with hefty treads on the tires for trail riding. The gyroscopes inside these funny two-wheeled personal transit contraptions make it hard to fall off them—just make sure you don't bump into anything. Take some tips from the guys at this shop so you learn how to use your own body weight to get

the thing going forward (and backward). Segways are fun, environmentally friendly, and offer an easy way to get around the city, and riding one has the potential to make you feel like a kid again. SB

Scooters

As long as you have a good waterproof jacket and don't mind the occasional helmet head, renting a scooter is an ideal way to get around Seattle. Electric scooters are readily available and are easy to plug in at gas stations and hotels around the city. They can be a blast as long as you take the necessary precautions. Since Seattle is too spread out for many to walk, but it's not so expansive or wild to warrant four wheels, scooters make perfect solo transit devices for an adventure from locale to locale. Here are some ideal spots to rent these gasless mobiles:

Scoot About
535 Westlake Ave N
407.3362
www.scootabout.biz

Big People Scooters
5951 Airport Wy S
763.0160
www.bigpeoplescooters.com

Scooter Gallery Seattle
1001 NE Boat St
547.7400
www.scootergalleryseattle.com

Taxis
Yellow Cab, 522.8800
Seattle for Hire Cars, 709.2003, www.seattleforhirecars.com

Taxis aren't a huge part of Seattle's transit network, but in the downtown corridor they are easy to hail and great for late-night escapades. You can even find taxis in Seattle's sprawling network of neighborhoods, but unless you are right near a main intersection, transit point, or downtown city block, I'd call to request a cab. Most of the companies listed above have alternative fuel vehicles for at least a portion of their fleet. SB

Casual Carpool

www.craigslist.com

Finding a ride with a fellow road tripper can be done through the crisscrossing interchanges of Craigslist's vast network. I'd ask detailed questions and try to arrange a meeting before accepting a ride from anyone, but I have to say I've met some great friends and had fantastic experiences getting from point A to point B via Internet-induced cotransit. *DL*

Zipcar

Locations throughout the city
866.494.7227
www.zipcar.com

For the savvy ecotourist, the Zipcar car-sharing service offers an array of fuel-efficient vehicles available at hourly and daily rates. Zipcar is the largest car-sharing network in the world, and you can join the service online, make reservations, and pick up your car at a designated spot. Drop the car back off whenever you're done, 24 hours a day, 7 days a week. Gas, insurance, and designated Zipcar parking spaces are all included in the rental price. Best of all, this service is becoming more widespread, so you can use it in other cities where you travel. The company offers discounted plans for businesses, groups, and drivers who need to use the service more frequently. *DL*

Top Picks

If you only had one crazy, cramped day in this city

I've chosen 11 of my top Seattle spots, in part because 11 is my favorite number and also as a nod to Spinal Tap fans who admire guitar amps that go the extra digit for maximum sound projection. Here are the 11 places that typify the dynamic, sustainable city of Seattle.

Richard Hugo House (see pages 53 and 97)

My favorite literary resource by far is the Richard Hugo House. There are always four writers, poets, or performers in residence, with community hours to share their skills and inspiration with anyone who e-mails for an appointment. The Hugo Zine Archive and Publishing Project has more than 20,000 zines organized by music or religion or race. Cabaret performances on the house stage are almost always free of charge, and theater productions and regular events fill gaps in the calendar between classes and workshops. If you like words, you'll get this place. And love it.

Canlis (see page 173)

With its old-world sophistication and air of romance, Canlis is one of the finest restaurants in America. Loving preparations of the restaurant garden's own produce show up on beautiful plates every season of the year. Follow the dress code, make a reservation for a window seat, and get ready for one of the most memorable meals of your life.

Vida Spa (see page 181)

This regional spa sensation offers the most nourishing, deeply satisfying relaxation experience I've had in a long time. Beyond the bells and whistles of the showier pampering spots, Vida Spa stays holistic and simple at the same time, offering Ayurvedic teas for different body types in a calm atmosphere that's free of kitsch. Get yourself massaged, steamed, and dusted, and you'll have lasting radiance.

Belle Epicurean (see page 36)

Never have I felt so pretty as when seated at the front window inside Belle Epicure, legs crossed, sipping a morning cappuccino with a croissant to dip. Belle Epicurean is the fancy side of Seattle. In a city where there is a strong urge toward beauty, this is a place with sheen. Delicate French pastries and sandwiches, served in a marble cafe atmosphere like that found in Paris, make me remember that this is a big city.

Theo Chocolate (see page 194)

From start to finish, cocoa pod to pure chocolate bar, Theo Chocolate products are fair trade, shade grown, and always organic. The Fremont factory and retail shop is a city treasure—a place where anyone who's interested can discover the process chocolate goes through to become a confection.

Kobo (see page 119)

Fusing local craft and foreign design, the Kobo showroom has an unbelievable collection to behold. See what talented artists and furniture makers have thought up—a wonky side table in tiger maple, a set of cups printed with Northwestern fern leaves. Even if you are here just for the eye candy, Kobo is an authentic representation of Seattle style.

Neumos (see page 158)

This mid-sized concert hall, restaurant, bar, and lounge gives back by regularly hosting nonprofit events and community fundraisers, and donating to Amnesty International and the Vera Project (see page 158). Seeing Living Legends, The Shins, or Vampire Weekend with a die-hard Seattle music crowd is a necessary leisure.

Fremont Abbey Arts Center (see pages 104 and 205)

One of the most solid stages for Seattle's underground sounds and art is consistently Fremont Abbey Arts Center. Whether featuring a highly regarded play fresh from the Edinburgh Fringe Fest or one of owner Nathan Marion's own multimedia performance showcases (called The Round), Fremont Abbey is where it's at when it comes to community-supported art in the Emerald City.

Georgetown (see page 10)

Georgetown is perhaps Seattle's most chameleonlike neighborhood. My first experience here was drinking a cup of coffee and taking in a unique scene as an old factory tumbled with the help of two ginormous cranes. Fantagraphics Books, a slew of art and performance spaces, a coffee shop, and an old-fashioned pharmacy just around the corner—no matter how I swing it, I still can't get enough of this neighborhood. I think Georgetown totally typifies the mood of this newish city, complete with creative strokes of genius and confused growth. It's a must-see for anyone checking out Seattle for the first time—or for any time in my mind. Chances are, no two visits will be the same.

Kippered Herring at Pike Place Market (see page 125)

It's true that Pike Place Market is one of Seattle's most prized gems, but I am always a little sad when I consider how different the market is today from its beginning. The original stall owners were largely Asian Americans, many of whom lost all that they owned when America unconstitutionally imprisoned them during World War II. Now the market has lost some of its soul, but the kippered herring at one of the fish stands gives me a reason to continue coming to Pike Place. Not all locals visit the market regularly, but those who do know about this sustainable smoky treat with gobs of omega-3 fatty acids and heart-healthy protein. In fact, the market used to be the world's foremost supplier of kippered herring, and I hope more people rediscover its tastiness. Delish!

Washington Park Arboretum (see page 83)

With its glens, hills, and dales, Washington Park Arboretum can hold my fascination easily for an entire afternoon. The endless array of trees, many of which bloom in early spring or flame golden and red in the fall months, are crisscrossed with walking (or jogging) paths. This beautiful park is what any visitor to Seattle should take home in his or her memory—the clear, gently rippling water, snow-dusted mountain peaks, and shrouds of blossoming maples and camellias in the fresh, moist air.

Up Early

All things early bird, plus morning treats

Sometimes I simply wake up early with extra gusto. I remember vacations in my adolescence when I rose before anyone else and snuck out for a private walk, a personal view of the place where I found myself. A morning walk such as this, or a nice long breakfast, can help you start your day off on the right foot. Take the time to enjoy the simple things as the world is just waking; follow your nose on a whim. I like taking it easy, stepping back for a moment from all the electronic systems, and just letting my feet go for a stroll. Here are some of my favorite ways to spend the first hours of the day in Seattle. Some are great solo, but you can always bring a friend.

 Mae's Phinney Ridge Cafe

66412 Phinney Ave N

782.1222

www.maescafe.com

Daily 7a–3p

The cow-centric kitsch that overtakes Mae's Phinney Ridge Cafe is oddly balanced by the slew of regulars who come to stew over morning papers, fair-trade coffee, and green eggs and ham just like Dr. Seuss wrote about. Trout and salmon are smoked by a talented line chef, so any dish with these fabulous fish comes highly recommended. Biscuits and gravy are made for both meat eaters and vegetarians, and the tofu breakfast is tastefully healthy. If you look closely around town, you might see Mae's delish handmade ice cream pints or cinnamon buns at nearby grocery stores. *SB*

The Essential Bakery Café

2719 E Madison St

568.7718

www.essentialbaking.com

Mon–Thurs, Sat 6a–6p; Fri 6a–9p; Sun 7a–6p

Any time a baker has been picked to be on the Bread Bakers Guild team to compete in France, his or her bakery gets flooded with fresh and enthusiastic faces waiting their turn to taste. So you can imagine what the excitement is like surrounding the team captain's bakery, the Essential Bakery. The bakery makes lines out the door look easy. The loaves—whether seeded or smooth, round or rectangular—define bread. Leave with a baguette in your bicycle basket and I'm willing to bet you'll soon find yourself with a wheat addiction, especially when you stop to spread some goat cheese on top. Pastries and morning rolls are fresh from the oven in the early hours. Look around town to find Essential Baking Company's loaves, they're delivered fresh to many shops and cafes. *SB*

Gas Works Park

2101 N Northlake Wy
684.4075
www.seattle.gov/parks/park_detail.asp?id=293
Daily 4a–11:30p

What do you do when you've got the deed to an obsolete crude oil plant on a prime piece of property? There are lots of answers, but for the city of Seattle it was a clear opportunity for a new and cool park. Safely restored and repurposed as a picnic area and unique, colorful playground, Gas Works Park is a beautiful treasure. It is a symbol of re-envisioning the way we treat the planet, and it is placed at the edge of Seattle's deep-teal ocean bay, in view of mountains and the downtown skyline. If romance is in the air, take out your camera and get some schmaltzy-cute photos of you and your sweetie. If you have young ones, you'll relish their smiles as they discover the fun structures and maze of machinery. *SB*

Green Lake Park

7201 E Green Lake Dr N
684.4075
www.seattle.gov/parks/park_detail.asp?ID=307
Daily dawn–dusk

Come here for the best morning swim. I have tried to convince people that swimming in a lake is so much more fun than in the chlorinated pools I spent the better part of my youth flailing around in. Even in Seattle, where I get "Would you like some cheese with that whine?" in response to my incessant complaining about the weather, I'll swim in a lake. And this is no ordinary lake. Green Lake is the multipurpose park-lake-trail-theater-sport-picnic place. My top five fave activities here are swimming in the lake,

Gas Works Park

playing lakeside Frisbee, taking art classes at Alki Bathhouse, walking my poodle Dutsi around the lake, and reading on a park bench. On brisk mornings, I jump in at the clearing near the Stone Avenue N side where the lake bottom is smoother, and then I walk back toward my friend Nathan's house, picking up two cups of joe at Zoka Coffee Roaster and Tea Company (see page 43) on the way. SB

$ 5 Spot

1502 Queen Anne Ave. N
285.7768
www.chowfoods.com/five
Mon–Fri 8:30a–12:00a, Sat–Sun 8:30a–3p

It's a little hard to review the 5 Spot, because it's basically a brand-new restaurant every three months, when a new "theme" is adopted that completely revamps the decor, music, and a large chunk of the menu. This month was Key West mode, so the walls were covered with tropical paintings, pirate flags, and a giant, fanciful blue ship hanging from the ceiling. Sounds kitschy, and it is, but in a fun way. And the food—cafe standards with some spicy gourmet flair—speaks for itself. *IM*

$$ Bay Café at Fisherman's Terminal

Ⅴ *1900 W Nickerson St*

🏠 *282.3435*

☕ *Mon–Fri 6:30a–2:30p, Sat–Sun 7a–2:30p*

Perched in the last corner pocket of Ballard, near the locks at Fisherman's Terminal, Bay Café is where I come to sit by the water, watch the raindrops dance on the bay, and sip a malted milkshake straight from heaven. Greasy cheddar omelets and gravy and biscuits fill my belly, especially on days when I dream of being a fisherman and want something to stick to my chilled bones. Breakfast is served all day, so you can either skip out on the family for a solo early morning coffee on the water or sleep in with them and truck over together for all the classic morning fare, complete with Norman Rockwell prints and pretty teal and purple wooden trim. *SB*

Ⅴ Silence-Heart-Nest

((ᵩ)) *3508 Fremont Pl N*

📠 *633.5169*

www.silenceheartnest.com

✚ *Mon, Wed–Fri 8a–2:30p; Sat–Sun 8a–3p*

Growing up in a family culture that sometimes tended toward the new age, I've long had suspicions about anything with such a frilly name as this Fremont vegetarian restaurant. Phrases containing words like "chakra" or an echo of "purple crystal energy" make my skin crawl, so when I initially passed by this bright, white-curtained eatery at the "Center of the Universe" (i.e., Fremont), I was none too impressed. Where did they come up with a name like that? Then I thought a little about each of the words separately. Silence is something rare and sacred, and I can't recall the last time I really had any. Heart, well, besides the fact that I love to draw them, a mighty enough image is conjured. Nest, yes, I do have a power animal and it is a grizzly bear, so a hibernating nest, or den, is an appealing concept. I made up my mind to enter, and after being seated by an elegant white-haired woman in a glittering sari, I was cheered by the real cream in my coffee and the sweeping bird-pattern brushstrokes on the wall. Then the food came. Julia had vegan cashew gravy dousing her homemade biscuits and a hearty slice of Neat Loaf, something I myself would never have gravitated toward, but I enjoyed every mouthful she allowed me. I had the huevos rancheros, made with free-range eggs and fresh *queso* and *pico de gallo*. The tortillas were even crisped just as they should be! Plus a number of weekday breakfast items are just $6, and include bottomless coffee, if you get there before 11am. We each picked an affirmation card from the table. Mine gave me a lot to think about: "Do not be afraid of tasting the bitterness of failure. Be brave! The sweetness of success will before long befriend you." *SB*

🄪 Myrtle Edwards Park

🏕 *3130 Alaskan Wy W*

🏌 *684.4075*

🚌 *www.seattle.gov/parks/park_detail.asp?id=311*
Daily dawn–dusk

What used to be named Elliott Bay Park is one of the most ideally situated parks in Seattle, a city where I've found patches of green around every corner. During late spring and summer, the fishing pier gets packed with sun seekers and real live fishermen reeling in all sorts of Puget Sound fish (with uncertain lead levels . . .). There's a bayside concrete trail with a gravel path alongside it for weak-kneed runners. In the early morning if you're patient, you can go before other joggers rise and watch the athletic morning crowd wash on in and then out again and off to their suits and briefcases. Dulsi and I stick around for the whole show, retracing our steps a second time on the 1.3-mile lap. For those nonmorning moments, return to Myrtle Edwards Park on the Fourth of July for a seafood buffet and fireworks. *SB*

🄪 Meridian Playground

🏕 *N 50th St and Meridian Ave N*

🏌 *684.4075*

🚌 *www.seattle.gov/Parks/park_detail.asp?id=1104*
Daily 4a–11:30p

Duck under the high stone archway on the corner of 50th Street and Wallingford and you'll be enveloped in a dewy park, speckled with fun play structures and hushed with the exception of the street beyond. I arrive before the kids when I'm staying in Wallingford; it's a short uphill walk from

Tangletown's center and a perfect respite from other, more jostling morning excursions. It's also home to one of Seattle's most cherished P-Patches, community gardens originally named after the Picardo Family Farm, who began this local tradition. Some 55 P-Patches are dotted around the city, but this one is notable, as some of the plots are run by toddlers at the nearby preschool! *SB*

Glo's

1621 E Olive Wy

324.2577

Mon–Fri 7a–3p

If I had to divide breakfast into two main categories, one would be simple and the other would be messy. Sometimes my stomach is a bit queasy and I just want my same old, same old: oatmeal with soymilk and a little maple syrup. But on days when I know I'm gonna see some action, I can think of nothing better than eggs draped over tortillas with beans, avocado, cheese, and tomatoes . . . a messy breakfast. Enter Glo's, Capitol Hill's busy, messy breakfast spot. Though there's nothing especially inspiring about this place, some mix of the crowd, prices, plates, and personalities makes it a smash hit with everyone I direct here. Eggs Blackstone, sausage and gravy, huevos rancheros—I have several items on my top picks list. Come early so you can eat sooner. *SB*

The Breakfast Club

12306 Lake City Wy NE

361.2583

www.361club.com

Mon–Fri 6a–2p, Sat–Sun 7a–2p

For a short while I lived in small-town New Jersey, and though it was a great many years ago, the corn cob–loving, Danish-eating, true-American-diner-needing me is still alive and well. This small-town breakfast gem is as authentic as the dust on the wares in antique stores in other pockets of northern Seattle. There are more ticky-tacky, kitschy items here than anybody would wish to have in their own abode, but I love spending my $7–10 in this palace of pancakes, waffles, and oversugared power breakfasts. Come on weekdays with a good friend or a young cousin and talk about your most deviant opinions under your breath while you wait for your cheery waitress to bring the goods. And the small-town thing goes deeper than just the look of the place: service is slow and gourmet cuisine has yet to be discovered, but isn't that what we like about this sort of place to begin with? *SB*

Sazerac

1101 4th Ave

624.7755

www.sazeracrestaurant.com

Mon–Fri 7a–9p, Sat–Sun 8a–2:30p, 5–10p

Asparagus soup, steel-cut oats with huge local raisins, simple scrambled egg whites, pulled pork—all are at your beck and call downtown in the morning hours at the base of the Hotel Monaco. Nothing too jazzed up, but never as mundane as the other downtown breakfast places, Sazerac is also one of the few that makes a concerted effort to keep prices reasonable while utilizing local, organic ingredients. The breakfast menu here is influenced by Cajun and Creole roots, and if you're a real protein hog, you can even start with oysters instead of half a grapefruit. *SB*

Coffee Time

Sipping a morning cup in many ways

Speaking as a true coffee lover, but only a part-time coffee drinker, I can say that when I choose to have a cup, I like a good one. Seattle is populated with roasters more obsessed than I am with quality java—they are perfectionists. All locally owned and very much entrenched in the community, these stops are frequented by a cross-section of people who are in the know about the importance of fair-trade and organic brews. Find coffee, tea, and snacks at these admirable cafes, and avoid the chains at all costs, even in Seattle where the coffee chain was practically invented. A regular cup at a locally owned coffee shop has a much more positive effect on the community in the long run than an organic cup at a chain. Each of these spots has its own vibe, an indicator of what the spirit of the surrounding neighborhood is really like. Whether you're on a strict diet of only two cups a day or you like to come and go with morning bevvies like I do, there's something for everyone at Seattle's coffee meccas.

Caffe Ladro

 7011 California Ave SW (and other nearby locations)
938.8021
www.caffeladro.com
Daily 5:30a–10p

Project: Take an early dinner and a long bath. Go to bed before the double digits. Wake up at 6am and walk or take public transit over to Caffe Ladro. Order a large coffee made from fair-trade Mexican beans and pull out the Jack Kerouac paperback curled in your bootleg. Sit on the sidewalk watching West Seattle wake up—dog walkers and spandex-clad joggers, children with scarves and backpacks, and women with heavy-looking bags in both hands. Rest your neck on the broad boards of the sidewalk benches, and close your eyes for a moment to remember the art you saw on the walls when you were waiting for your hot coffee. Rinse. Repeat. SB

Belle Epicurean

 1206 4th Ave
262.9404
www.belleepicurean.com
Mon–Fri 6a–6p, Sat–Sun 9a–2p

It may be passed over as just another shiny downtown coffee counter, but Belle Epicurean is anything but run-of-the-mill. I find this oasis in the midst of the area with Seattle's most big-city feel—checkered with high-end fashion houses, fine hotels, glitzy restaurants, and the whir of people jetting to and fro. Stop in and waltz over the veined marble floors toward the sandwiches and sweets, to the sound of an espresso orchestra punctuated with multilingual conversations and the sweet hush of newspaper pages turning. Everything here is infused with beautiful details, each tasty offering is made with well-thought-out attention, giving it a certain *je ne sais quois*. However silly it may sound, don't leave without trying one of Belle's Buns (pastry chef Carolyn Ferguson's name for them). There is potato-rosemary brioche, and a lovely pear and almond version in addition to classic pecan, also made with two-day brioche dough. Plain butter croissants are perfectly formed. For breakfast you can order an egg with some Gruyere stuffed inside. A rainbow of sandwiches are made for lunchtime including local smoked salmon with herbed chevre, turkey with housemade cranberry relish, roast beef with swiss cheese and horseradish aioli, and a spicy deviled egg salad baguette that goes wonderfully with candied nut–dappled spinach salad. As many ingredients as possible are sourced from local organic farms, and there is plenty of room on the menu for seasonal or daily inspirations based on what is freshest and readily available at the nearby Pike Place Market. Two windowside tables have the best views of the 4th Avenue buzz if you can snag them. I can easily take up one of these spots for hours, lingering over coffee and treating myself to a Black Forest slice with cherry curd and hazelnuts when I've finished the article I've come to work on. SB

Java Bean Coffee

2920 Avalon Wy SW, 938.5665
6521 5th Ave NE, 522.0860
5819 24th Ave NW, 788.9677
www.javabeancoffee.com
Mon–Fri 6a–7p, Sat–Sun 7a–7p

For some reason I hadn't heard of Seattle's Java Bean Coffee until I really started exploring the city—only the names Seattle's Best, Starbucks, and Caffé Vita had managed to trickle down to California. But Java Bean should be what people think of when they imagine this city's famous beverage. All the blends are carefully built from organic, fair-trade, and shade-grown coffees. While one of the coffee-fanatic baristas is doing latte art on your morning cup, she'll be explaining the health benefits of coffee or updating you on the local salmon populations. Java Bean has several locations around the city, and each sells all the blends as beans or brewed to perfection. If you give a nice tip, you can ask for a pretty pattern on your foam to ensure that sparkle glints in your eye. SB

Green Bean Coffeehouse

Green Bean Coffeehouse

 312 N 85th St, #101

706.4587

www.greenbeancoffee.org

Mon–Tues, Thurs 8a–6p; Wed, Fri 8a–10p; Sat 9a–6p

Greenwood is a great hideaway neighborhood just north of Wallingford that is home to the community-based, nonprofit Green Bean Coffeehouse. It goes without saying that the house-roasted coffee comes from beans grown in the shade of native South American trees rather than on clear-cut acres, and the house-made granola alone is worth the trip. Each month a new activist or issue theme is featured, and community events hovering over related subjects scatter the calendar. Bring your children so they can play with the handmade children's toys at the back of the seating area while you catch up with a long-lost friend or sit around the communal table making some new ones. *SB*

Cafe Allegro

4214 University Wy NE
633.3030
www.cafeallegromusic.com
Mon–Fri 6:30a–10:30p, Sat–Sun 8a–10:30p

Cafe Allegro is music to my ears. A full calendar of live music, performed in the wood-clad upstairs area of the cafe, provides melodies from many musical traditions. It is a classic Seattle experience to duck into an unexpected show here, order an apricot croissant from the Essential Baking Company (see page 29), and rub shoulders with aspiring poets as you listen to the sounds of someone strumming a guitar. The owner began working here as a barista back in the 1970s and has evolved the cafe with tender care. Organic, fair-trade coffee from Brown and Co. satisfies those grabbing a cup to go or laboring over a novel or newspaper for hours. *SB*

Zeitgeist Coffee

171 S Jackson St
583.0497
www.zeitgeistcoffee.com
Mon–Fri 6a–7p, Sat–Sun 8a–7p

Sometimes I get a strong feeling of desire to look a certain way, be in a certain place, or acquire a certain object. If I pursue my desire until I get it, there sometimes occurs an unnerving aftereffect: finding out that what I wanted isn't all it's cracked up to be. That's a little how I view Zeitgeist Coffee. This coffee shop is very cool—the art hanging on the walls, the funky outfits of regulars, the beats and strums from local musicians and DJs over loudspeakers, and the hard-core coffee make it one of the most sought-after places to drink a cup of joe. But the atmosphere is made for this passing feeling of desire, not for dwelling. The noise level is always up over my reading limit, and there's too much going on for a moment of clearheaded thought. But that's why I like it and why I want to go, perhaps too often. Even if I change my mind after I order, I am still set with one of the best cups of coffee in this caffeine-crazed city. *SB*

🍸 Cafe Solstice

4116 University Wy NE
675.0850
Mon–Thurs 6:30a–11p, Fri 6:30a–9:00p, Sat 7a–9p, Sun 7a–11p

The consummate student coffeehouse, this large cafe has blankets of students spread across it at any given time. Be one with the University District scene at Cafe Solstice—a cup of tea and a crumbly cookie go together terribly well with an outpouring of studious conversation and furrowed brows. *SB*

Bauhaus Books and Coffee

301 E Pine St
625.1600
www.bauhauscoffee.net
Mon–Fri 7a–1a, Sat 8a–1a, Sun 8a–1a

Even if Bauhaus Books and Coffee wins the popularity contest, beating out multilocation Seattle java houses, I don't begrudge its fame. After all, Bauhaus is a taste of the real Seattle, and like it or not, it is a major attraction if you want to be front and center on Seattle's hipster scene. This über-cool coffee joint is ideal for soaking in the atmosphere, sipping a primo mug of coffee, and entering into Cap Hill as a local, whether it's the truth or not. Instant residency can be confirmed if you score one of the few prime downstairs spots next to a plug for your laptop, tighten your Converse laces, unzip your hoodie, and munch down on an apricot pastry. Amazing book collections are waiting to be taken off the shelves as a low-tech alternative for entertainment and further Seattle insights. *SB*

🖊 Cherry Street Coffee House

2121 1st Ave, 441.7176
103 Cherry St, 621.9372 (and three other downtown locations)
www.cherryst.com
Daily 6:30a–5p

Seattle isn't a city where the only downtown coffee options are Starbucks. Its blocks are crowded with all manner of coffee shops, none better than the community-oriented Cherry Street Coffee House. Five downtown locations make it easy to get your caffeine fix from an inspiring, local business with a philosopher at the helm. Owner Ali Ghambari is known around town as a do-gooder entrepreneur, bringing together local art (the newest location at

1st Avenue and Lenora Street is covered in art by local muralist Sam "Sneke" Swanson), peaceful messages (greeting cards with Ali's own musings on them, such as "It doesn't matter how dark it gets out there when you are the light"), good role models (big pictures of MLK and Gandhi on the walls), and delicious coffees and snacks. I come for lunch most often—the soup and sandwich deal for around $7 is filling and healthy, especially when Egyptian Lentil is in the kettle. SB

Herkimer Coffee

7320 Greenwood Ave N, 784.0202
5611 University Wy NE, #100C, 525.5070
www.herkimercoffee.com
Mon–Fri 6a–6p, Sat–Sun 7a–6p

"Graphite with a hint of black cherry." "Chewy, with overtones of pencil shavings." If you think some of the adjectives used at wine tastings are weird, then welcome to the wild world of Herkimer Coffee. Regular cuppings at both cozy locations propel these oddities further by describing the body, texture, aroma, and flavor of each carefully blended cup as if discerning the subtitles would reveal some sought-after truth. I am not sure I am as serious as these folks about coffee, but I sure am glad they do things the way they do. The studious and open feeling of the Greenwood Avenue coffeehouse itself elevates this java higher. The roasting beans, grown on small farms with no pesticides or clear-cutting, are always wafting sweet smells, and the marbleized latte pours are always thoughtfully and artistically enhanced. Get some beans to go, and learn the Herkimer methodology for home preparation and brewing from its illustrious blog at Barista Exchange; *www.baristaexchange.com/profiles/blog/list?user=2kc574vaffzui.* SB

Fuel Coffee

610 19th Ave E, 329.4700
1705 N 45th St, 634.2700
2300 24th Ave E, 328.0700
www.fuelcoffeeseattle.com
Daily 6a–10p

On the Seattle coffee scene, you have to really know your stuff in order to set your shop apart. Fuel Coffee does, and in order to prove its might, Fuel has cornered the city with three homey little coffee hideouts. Gorgeous lattes are the main draw for me, never lonely with a devilish vegan brownie baked right next to the beans. Dutsi is happy to laze outside during the summer— the organic dog treats made at Fuel erase my poodle's impatient tendencies. Locals flow in and out of the doors, some grabbing coffee to go in their own mug, while writers, techies, and day traders stay inside, letting the coffee flow and the colorful atmosphere inspire. *SB*

 C&P Coffee Company

5612 California Ave SW
933.3125
www.candpcoffee.com
Mon–Fri 6:30a–8p, Sat–Sun 7a–8p

Serving the highly regarded roasts from nearby Lighthouse Coffee Roasters, C&P Coffee Company feels a little like the clubhouse or student hangout of a prestigious university. When I first walked up the welcoming brick stairs and found an oasis with perfect WiFi connectivity, I did a double take, thinking I was back in boarding school about to bump into my sophomore crush. There's a studious vibe here that aids in opening your mind to more motivated thoughts, and the din never rises above a humming radio. Enjoy the study snacks from the Essential Baking Company (see page 29) and the local art gallery, too—you may be the only out-of-towner privy to these local collections. Regular community events like wine tastings, knitting groups, and live music fill the calendar, and if you're smart, you'll go online to print the monthly coupon before heading over. *SB*

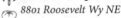 Cloud City Coffee

 8801 Roosevelt Wy NE
527.5552
www.cloudcitycoffee.com
 Daily 6a–7p

My mother and I are obsessed with finding the perfect cafe in which to write in each city where we've lived or traveled. There has to be good coffee (that's a no-brainer) as well as WiFi, comfortable seating, a slightly upscale atmosphere, and good eats so you can work for hours on end without missing a meal. Cloud City Coffee is as close as I have come so far on my Seattle escapades to finding a place that meets all these requirements, and as soon as my mother gets to go and approve it, I think it has a good chance of becoming our pick. It has abundant seating, unlike some of the more crowded cafes, and the space is welcoming to people who aren't interested in going somewhere anytime soon. Just walking through the doors gets me ready to wax creative. Every day there's a special scone flavor fresh from the on-site oven: raspberry on Sundays and caramel apple on Thursdays are my favorites. True North Coffee and a full menu of sandwiches, salads, and soups, as well as breakfast fare, uplift the taste buds without making you feel like you're copping out by eating at a coffeehouse. *SB*

Zoka Coffee Roaster and Tea Company

2200 N 56th St
545.4277
www.zokacoffee.com
Daily 6a–10p

Nothing can compare to my first experience at Zoka Coffee Roaster and Tea Company, in the northern Seattle neighborhood of Green Lake. I walked up the steep hill, the morning traffic whizzing behind me, badly in need of a strong dose of caffeine. After a splurge at Mighty O Donuts (see page 190), I turned back to face Zoka, and to my surprise there was a long line of runners sporting their finest short shorts and zippy sneaks filing out the corner door, some chatting with their fellow exercisers and others continuing to jog in place. I found myself in the line and eventually got my coffee and a prized window seat with computer plug. Never a better writing session! This top-notch coffee joint has a good mix of vibrancy and functionality, together with fabulous coffee and reliable WiFi. This is my numero uno coffee location when I've got my laptop in tow. *SB*

Victrola Coffee and Art

411 15th Ave E
325.6520
www.victrolacoffee.com
Daily 5:30a–11p

Probably the best espresso in Seattle can be found at Victrola Coffee and Art. Streamline Espresso tastes just like its name: a closely woven blend of raw cocoa and blackberry flavors under a sultry crema. Ask for whatever your coffee preference and the Victrola baristas will oblige—service and quality are king at this especially casual coffeehouse. Enjoy live performances and colorful walls always hung with local art. Pick up beans to go—organic, fair-trade coffee is readily available. *SB*

Espresso Vivace

 532 Broadway Ave E
 860.2722
www.espressovivace.com
Daily 6a–11p

Espresso Vivace is a bit of a local legend. Coffee guru David Schomer is responsible for several innovations in both the equipment and methods of brewing, and he has received national press for his slightly quixotic quest to create the perfect espresso. Coffee aficionados will appreciate the amount of craft that goes into the drinks here—the level of training required of the baristas is far beyond that of your typical coffee slingers, and it shows in the rich crema and perfect rosettas on every cup. As you might have guessed already, this is another of those magical little holes-in-the-wall where the lines extend out into the street and people wait in the rain with a smile.

Vivace has three locations located on or near Capitol Hill, and the clientele is largely in-the-know cool kids, but of the more relaxed, worldly variety. In keeping with the hard-core coffee-cult aesthetic, the walls are decorated with photos of various masterful rosettas, snapped by the employees who poured them. If you like your coffee like you like your religious deities—serious, powerful, and worthy of worship—Vivace could be your new Sunday morning ritual. *IM*

$ Caffé Vita Coffee Roasting Company

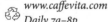 *124 4th Ave E, 360.754.8187 (Olympia location)*
1005 E Pike St, 709.4440 (and other Seattle locations)
www.caffevita.com
Daily 7a–8p

Caffé Vita was started in Seattle, and in this locally owned chain the Olympia store is the most vibrant of all. The Seattle locations serve the same tasty roasts as many other coffee shops licensed to brew Vita, and hipsters and office workers huddle around their über-specific hot drinks and focus in on their laptops, rarely talking to one another. Sourcing coffee from the Americas, Indonesia, and Africa, Caffé Vita brews up cups that are dark and earthy, acidic and fruity. Head to Olympia for the most authentic Vita experience, or run in for a quick bagel and cup of joe if you are lost in Capitol Hill. I like to come here when I'm on deadline—the focused atmosphere can really light that fire of motivation, or maybe I'm just soaking it up from all the serious cats around me. *SB*

Bookish

Reading retreats in every flavor

Technologies come and go, but as far as I'm concerned, the beauty of a bound book will never fade. Not only a comical, moving, challenging, or inspiring experience, the role of a volume of words impacts every aspect of life, from early learning to individual solace. I think about where I've been with a good book: in a new city, at a favorite cafe, sitting in my grandfather's rocking chair, on top of Mount Whistler giving my legs a little break from the steep slopes. Search for a book and watch as it in turn takes you on a journey. Make your own book, share the experience of reading, and take your books on your world travels. Find a special spot for yourself after gleaning a new title from one of these Seattle bookstores.

Seattle Center for Book Arts

Events at various locations
937.9756
www.seattlebookarts.org
Schedules vary, call ahead

The Seattle Center for Book Arts (SCBA), is the strong, reinforced spine holding together the pages of Seattle's booming literary community. It offers children's workshops, annual book parties, lit fests, and a year-round calendar of classes. If you're in town during Easter and join in an egg hunt, don't be surprised if you find a mini-journal inside your colored plastic treasure—each year SCBA donates book-related goodies to many local hunts. My most memorable moment in Seattle was peeping in on a letterpress workshop hosted by SCBA at Cornish College for the Arts. They let me join right in, and my lesson on historic fonts still inspires me. I daydream of taking SBCA's popular bookbinding course, covering accordion, scrolling, case bound, and basic techniques. Take your notes and scribbles from your Seattle travels with you and bind your own personal guide to the town! *SB*

⑨ Seattle Public Library

1000 4th Ave (and other Seattle locations)
386.4636
www.spl.org
Hours vary by location

The written word is a powerful medium in cranial Seattle, where thinkers tend to congregate to push out their ideas onto paper. It is important to take in ideas and stories while you are creating your own, and sneaking into one of Seattle's many public library branches is the quickest way to disappear into that world. Choose the Fremont branch (731 N 35th Street, 684.4084), just steps from the famous Fremont Troll (see page 79), for a wide selection of videos to rent or for a novel to sit and read while looking out over the canal. The brand-new Central branch (1000 4th Street, 386.4636) is a gigantic glass structure that looks a bit toppled, but inside organization reigns supreme. The Ballard branch (5614 22nd Avenue NW, 684.4089) has a "free" box just outside the entrance, a full section dedicated to boat books, lots of available computers with free Internet access, and a denser selection of sought-after titles than some of the smaller libraries.

Seattle is serious about books, and its vast network of neighborhood libraries is evidence of this, plus author talks, free workshops for kids and adults, and art shows and lectures are scheduled all the time. Seattle's libraries are more worth visiting than those in other West Coast cities not only because they are such a key ingredient in what composes the local culture, but also because the sheer number of free educational and community-supported events can fill up your calendar fast, without your having to spend a dime. Get involved! *SB*

⑨ Subtext Reading Series

Various locations and times
www.speakeasy.org/subtext

The ideal situation would be to take the train into town, hop around the food carts for a bite, and find your way to a Subtext reading, rife with local underground literary talent. Check out the schedule beforehand to make sure you get in with the gritty syllables thrown together by these talented wordsmiths. *SB*

East West Bookshop of Seattle

 6500 Roosevelt Wy NE
800.587.6002
www.eastwestbookshop.com
Mon–Thurs 10a–9p, Fri 10a–10p, Sat 10a–9p, Sun 12–6:30p

To a black-clad, slick New Yorker, this shop may seem, well, "woo-woo." But its mantra, "Know Thyself," gives the shop a clear mission that is well addressed. Find books in all traditions of spiritual and scientific advice, from the mind to the heart. Come for a poetry reading or to flip the pages of the latest meditation manual. *SB*

Elliott Bay Book Company

 1521 10th Ave
624.6600
www.elliottbaybook.com
Mon–Sat 9:30a–10p, Sun 11a–7p

Seattle is known for independent bookstores in large part because of Elliott Bay Book Company, the backbone of this city's literary crowd. Come for readings or to browse the vast collection of DIY and green how-to books, travel guides, poetry, or fiction, and then head to the cafe. It is easy to spend an entire day at Elliott Bay Book Company—a great day. At press time the store was moving from its incredible Pioneer Square location to Capitol Hill where it will hopefully thrive for many decades to come. *SB*

Fantagraphics Books

1201 S Vale St
658.0110
www.fantagraphics.com
Mon–Sat 11:30a–8p, Sun 11:30a–5p

Georgetown is an important neighborhood for Seattle's unique culture, not only because of the music, art, and tile works on these few blocks, but also because of the epic history of comics and graphic arts at Fantagraphics Books. It is most famous, perhaps, for being one of the first galleries to show Matt Groening's works, but plenty of other big names in the comic book

Fantagraphics Books

world have called this place home for their artwork at one time or another. Look around at the menagerie of graphic art books and comics, see what is on the walls, and check out the music collections while you are at it. Whatever treasure you find here, you'll be taking part in a necessary vehicle of Seattle culture. *SB*

🎁 Friends of the Seattle Public Library Book Sale

www.friendsofspl.org/booksale.aspx

I'll start with the negatives . . . well, the one drawback. Books, plural, weigh a ton. I can never get all the ones I want to fit in my suitcase. They're horrible traveling companions if you have an indecisive tendency or a voracity for reading that can't be quelled; they'll give you whiplash at an airport as surely as a fender bender. So that's the sad part: when we travel, we can't "beam up" books to our own private libraries back home, but the good old post office does give book-rate discounts to save your sore muscles. So I say no excuses—just empty out your suitcase, head to this epic sale, and get a buddy to drive you to the post office. That's how I managed my bookish fervor after a rather explosive visit to this biannual (spring and fall) sale. Friday night is the member preview sale, when local writers speak and members may purchase up to 25 items. Saturday is chaos—the whole city seemingly descends on the endless tables of $1 books. Sunday the books are half price, so most cost just two quarters, doubling the incidence of suitcases and other large carry aways. And though the selection dwindles, there are always enough cult fiction books, random hardbacks, and collage-ready picture books for my pile of art supplies. Yes, I am sad books are so heavy, but I've had so much experience lugging my must-have collection around the globe that one more box of words taken to the post office won't hurt. That is, until I find I have no more shelf space. . . . *SB*

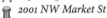

Epilogue Books

2001 NW Market St
297.2665
www.epiloguebooks.com
Mon–Sat 10a–7p, Sun 11a–6p

Once you're done with that pile you scored from your last trip to the Friends of the Seattle Public Library Book Sale, bring them to Epilogue Books for cash or trade. You'll either set yourself up with some lunch money or find yourself situated behind some new pages. Optimal selection, a full calendar of special events, and cheap DVDs for movie night all make this place worthy of being repeatedly named favorite independent bookseller by *NWsource Magazine*. *SB*

Abraxus Books

5711 24th Ave NW
297.6777
www.abraxusbooks.com
Daily 10a–8p

They don't call Seattle one of the most literate cities for nothing, and Abraxus Books just adds to the sprawling network of bookishness pervading the town. Dive into Abraxus as an unabashed detective not quite sure what quest you are on—the stacks of used titles are more of an adventure than an errand to pick up a specific book. History, culture, and environment are big here—the theme I picked up my first visit was "East meets West" because of the large number of how-to Zen books and memoirs from western Buddhists. A trip here is a guaranteed good time. *SB*

University Book Store

4326 University Wy NE

634.3400

www.bookstore.washington.edu

Mon–Fri 9a–8p, Sat 10a–7p, Sun 12–5p

This large beige building houses one of Seattle's favorite reading resources—University Book Store. More than just a convenient spot to stockpile Huskies gear or groovy school supplies, there are new and used books on all matter of subjects, and one of the easiest-to-navigate floor plans, with intuitive organization and helpful folks manning the information booth. The children's books are another draw, as is the local-friendly bookstore cafe. Read up! SB

Left Bank Books Collective

 92 Pike St, #B

 622.0195

www.leftbankbooks.com

Hours vary, call ahead

Counterculture isn't so counter in Seattle. Sure, the condos and fresh injection of chic chain shops give the city a fancy globalized makeover, but the bread and butter of local thought certainly tends toward the contrarian. Freedom of thought takes the main stage at Pike Place Market's Left Bank Books, a collectively owned anarchist book and bumper sticker shop that's been around more than 30 years. Find stickers for every mental state or political perspective, as well as archived zines from all over the world. Some of Left Bank's "titles of all time" give a clearer picture of what you'll find: Alexander Berkman's *ABC of Anarchism*, Howard Zinn's *A People's History of the United States*, and so on. Members of the collective can offer suggestions if you're new to the scene or help you find a specific title. I dropped by with a bushel of fresh epazote from the market, and Alana, a member of the collective, hooked me up with *Open Veins of Latin America* by Eduardo Galeano to read while I stirred my pot of flavorful beans. SB

📖 Secret Garden Bookshop

2214 NW Market St

789.5006

www.secretgardenbooks.com

Mon–Fri 10a–8p, Sat 10a–6p, Sun 12–5p

A glorious hamlet for readers and writers, the Secret Garden Bookshop greets everyone who enters its doors with a breath of fresh air. It's a community center for most residents of Ballard—the bookshop they pass by when walking along the neighborhood's main drag and the place they call to reserve new titles after hearing an inspiring author interviewed on the radio. It's a pretty place: well lit, well organized, and well staffed. I can't help wanting to do a signing here—the warm glow emanating from this store on a windy night in May as an author event took place suckered me in for the better. Ask any of the staff and they'll point you to books written by community members like Theo Pauline Nestor's *How to Sleep Alone in a King-Size Bed* or *The Art of Racing in the Rain* by Garth Stein. SB

📖 Wessel and Lieberman Booksellers

208 1st Ave S

682.3545

www.wlbooks.com

Mon–Sat 11a–6p

I covet beauty. Fleeting beauty and ancient beauty. Material beauty and immaterial beauty. Perhaps it's due to my Taurus rising. Just off the red bricks at Pioneer Square, Wessel and Lieberman Booksellers is a beauty to behold. The refurbished old building that holds a number of locally owned shops is itself worth the visit. I like to circumnavigate the block before entering, so I can see the hacky sack games by the sculptures on the square and gawk at the entrance of Wessel and Lieberman to relish the excitement. Huge art books cover tilted wooden panels, set just at waist height so you can easily flip through each superior manual. Rare texts, oversized volumes, antique art books filled with prints, portfolios, and illustrations are the specialty here. Since Pioneer Square is one of my favorite places to wander—because of the huge number of book stores, art galleries, tourists to watch, and changes underway—I am glad such beauty exists there. Even if you're not as cuckoo for books as I am, one lingering moment at Wessel and Lieberman will at the very least spark your curiosity. And those tourists I spoke of rarely find their way inside this shop, so the atmosphere is most often airy and personal. *SB*

Open Books: A Poem Emporium

2414 N 45th St
633.0811
www.openbookspoetry.com
Tues–Sat 11a–6p, first Sun of the month 12–4p

Devoted to all types of poetry, Open Books: A Poem Emporium has thousands of poetry books, CDs, tapes, videos, rare books, first editions, and out-of-print editions. Thousands. Aside from my squeeze through the poetry section at the Central branch of the Seattle Public Library (see page 46), I don't think I've ever witnessed such a menagerie of congealed syllables. I find the array of tapes and CDs especially valuable—savoring a poem by hearing it read aloud can have an entirely unique impact. That said, Open Books invites poets to come read in the cozy space, and there's nothing quite like hearing poems read by the poet and then meeting him or her in person. My two favorite finds here are *Legitimate Dangers: American Poets of the New Century*, a compilation written by 85 poets born after 1959, and the complete Kay Ryan collection. *SB*

Seattle Arts and Lectures

Various locations and times
621.2230
www.lectures.org

Each year, Seattle Arts and Lectures hosts an array of prolific presenters. Here you can listen to short stories, poetry, and literary criticism from the nation's most sought-after writers and thinkers. Forget your nightmares of university lecture halls—you'll be hanging on these speakers' every word. During a recent season of speakers, Jane Hirshfield and Gary Snyder offered poetry, Michael Pollan talked about food, and John Updike spoke before we sadly lost him. Censorship and women's rights activist Shirin Ebadi and prolific portrait photographer Annie Leibovitz are just two inspiring characters who have lectured for special events. These are the cool kids that you always wanted to meet, and here in Seattle you can. *SB*

Richard Hugo House Zine Archive and Publishing Project

1634 11th Ave
322.7030
www.hugohouse.org/house/zapp
Hours vary, call ahead

It's a little intimidating to behold the huge archive of zines at Richard Hugo House, one of my first loves of Seattle that still makes my heart skip a beat. Divided into clearly organized sections like gender and sex, humor, and politics, the store offers zines and mini-zines from all around the world, newly preserved in the library on the House's second floor. Peruse the collection of more than 20,000 zines and stay late for a free cabaret performance—there's always a lot going on here (see page 97). SB

Get Active

Hikes, runs, rides, bikes, boats—anything and everything to get you moving

Whether you are simply getting from point A to point B or you are seeking some good sweaty fun, getting active always has a refreshing result. I started on the swim team at a young age and have been known to go through various ski-bum phases now and again. I've also been challenged by Pilates and yoga, and bouldering rocks, indoors and out. Whatever thrill level you're seeking, from kayaking the ocean to jogging in Discovery Park, Seattle is a beautiful place to get active outdoors, and when it's raining there are myriad ways to get moving indoors.

REI—Seattle Flagship

222 Yale Ave N
223.1944
www.rei.com
Mon–Sat 9a–9p, Sun 10a–7p

Curious about wilderness first aid? Interested in taking a bike trip across Turkey using tips from an Emerald City native? Nearly every day, Seattle's REI flagship store hosts some edgy, wild, or superhuman event—famous adventurers come to talk about and show pictures of their last epic climb, the

The Running Trail at Alki Beach Park

benefits of kelp and eelgrass are discussed in a workshop, and a three-part avalanche awareness class fills up quickly with backcountry skiers. Although you'll find REIs all over this country and beyond, this store is true to its Pacific Northwest roots, preaching environmental preservation as a position of responsibility that we each possess as human beings. The flagship location is certainly part of the local scene as much as it is popular with tourists, but I find these informational and often free extras are the best route to enjoying the great outdoors, Seattle style. *SB*

⑨ Alki Beach Park

1702 Alki Ave SW
684.4075
www.seattle.gov/parks/park_detail.asp?ID=445
Daily dawn–dusk

Alki Avenue is lined by a beach—2-plus miles of it—so you can imagine how perfect it is for strolling at a relaxed pace with a poodle or whatever prized pooch you're hanging with. This pretty corridor has eateries and outdoor sculptures punctuating the smooth-paved path at the side of the four-lane street. On those rare perfect summer days, all of the city comes to Alki Beach Park with sunscreen and umbrellas; it's unusual to find a place that takes such complete advantage of good-weather days. Come back at night, crowd around one of the safely built fire pits, and warm yourself with new friends (specific info on Alki Beach Park fire pits and fire safety can be found here: *www.seattle.gov/parks/parkspaces/AlkiBeachPark/fire.htm*). *SB*

Lincoln Park

8011 Fauntleroy Wy SW
684.4075
www.seattle.gov/parks/park_detail.asp?id=460
Daily 4a–11:30p

This family park's original name was Fauntleroy Park, after the fiancée of past resident and U.S. Lieutenant George Davidson. It is a great place for families, with its ribbons of beach strewn with driftwood, walking trails of the paved and unpaved variety, excellent boating launch points, centuries-old shade trees, and a saltwater pool dating back to the 1940s. Whatever your purpose, Lincoln Park is an enjoyable open space and a prime location for getting active while soaking in Seattle's natural beauty. *SB*

Schmitz Preserve Park

5551 SW Admiral Wy
684.4075
www.seattle.gov/parks/park_detail.asp?id=465
Daily 4a–11:30p

Dive into the depths of an old-growth forest within Seattle's city limits at Schmitz Preserve Park. This prized nature preserve has become not only a great place to hike through woods and past creeks, but also a chance for hands-on environmental education. It is named for German immigrant land donor Ferdinand Schmitz, who was as serious about entrepreneurial prospects as he was natural preservation. Trails are all wide enough to keep hikers from easily getting lost and for bringing lots of doggies along for the walk. *SB*

Lake Washington Rowing Club

910 N Northlake Wy
547.1583
http://lakewashingtonrowing.com

Just as learning to fly a plane may give someone the sensation of being a bird, so sculling simulates the glide of a gilled fish through the water. Learn the basics in group or private rowing lessons, then as your skills progress, you can take part in competitive training and quads. Even if you are in town for only a short visit, you can take part in activities by contacting the Lake Washington Rowing Club in advance. If you live in town, meet up with one of the members and have him or her show you around to get a good idea of the spot as you consider membership. *SB*

Swimming Pools in Seattle

General info: 684.4075
Wading pool hotline: 684.7796
www.seattle.gov/parks/pools.asp

Of all of the cities I have explored and discovered, Seattle has by far the most complete and well-organized resource for finding a swimming pool: the Pools page of the Seattle Parks and Recreation site. The folks at this government department even go so far as to divide the pools into four categories: indoor pools, outdoor pools, wading pools, and beaches. Click the icons that dot an interactive map of Seattle to find Pritchard Island Beach (8400 55th Avenue S) for great summer rafting on Lake Washington; East Queen Anne Playground Wading Pool (1912 Warren Avenue N), which is especially fun for children; or the Ballard Pool (1471 NW 67th Street), which features a modern 25-yard pool, a 99°F hot tub, and a rope swing over the deep end. *SB*

Amy Yee Tennis Center

2000 Martin Luther King Jr. Wy S
684.4764
www.cityofseattle.net/parks/athletics/tennisct.htm
 Mon–Fri 6a–10:30p, Sat–Sun 7a–9:30p

I'm still not completely sure what it is about the sport of tennis that makes it so well loved all over the Pacific Northwest, but whatever it is, I have found no shortage of great tennis courts in many cities and towns all over BC, Oregon, and Washington. Seattle's Amy Yee Tennis Center certainly ranks among my favorites. The 10 indoor courts and 4 outdoor courts, plus the wide array of group and private classes and amateur leagues, make it a lively hub of activity even in blustery rainstorms. Tennis lovers can find new playmates here, and couples wishing to take up a sport together will find tennis a perfect way to share time and get a workout in. Call ahead to reserve a court for a nominal fee, or to sign up for a lesson check the full updated class schedule online. *SB*

Sound Mind and Body
437 N 34th St
547.2706
www.smbgym.com
Mon–Thurs 5:30a–10p, Fri 5:30a–10p, Sat 7a–7p, Sun 8a–7p

One of the most spacious and airy workout options in Seattle, Fremont's Sound Mind and Body gets you spinning within sight of Chihuly glass and floor-to-ceiling window views of the bustling neighborhood. Try some afternoon meditative yoga, but keep an eye out for the gym's popular Latin dance classes and sign up early. There are special training sessions for skiers—getting those thigh muscles ready for bumpy runs is much easier with the help of the stretches and exercises taught at Sound Mind. Hop next door to PCC Natural Market (see page 73) for an after-workout snack—the free weights are plentiful, but they do have the tendency to make me hungry! *SB*

Rain Fitness
159 Western Ave W, #355
283.7246
www.rainfitness.com
Mon–Fri 5:30a–10:30p, Sat–Sun 8a–7p

One of the best views of the Puget Sound is from the vantage point of the treadmills at Rain Fitness, the largest nonchain gym in Seattle. It's not where you'd expect to do some sightseeing, but with the huge panes of glass and the laid-back, non–meat market atmosphere, you might even forget you're at the gym. Everything is reliably clean, and travelers can have access to all the free classes and equipment for a single-day use fee. If you're staying longer, one-, three-, and six-month memberships are available—just ask at the front desk. *SB*

⑨ Green Lake Park

7201 E Green Lake Dr N
684.4075
www.seattle.gov/Parks/park_detail.asp?id=307
Daily dawn–dusk

Running in Seattle just doesn't get better than this. If you're like me and you're happy to avoid hills or half-day jogs that leave you stranded in a neighborhood far afield, Green Lake Park has a meandering, evenly paved 2.98-mile loop ideal for us relaxed types, but serious enough for the ever-increasing number of spandex-clad Seattleites training for some marathon. On weekends, the ring around this dab of blue is colored with a rainbow of neon polka dots. As I come closer to the lake, I see that they are just the short shorts of the run-a-holics, bouncing on nimble calves before congregating in lines out of the nearby coffeehouses. Swimming, outdoor yoga, and a community center with regular activities are all active options for this swath of open space (see the Up Early chapter, page 29), but it's a great, nonintimidating place to jog for a beginner like me. SB

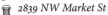 Stone Gardens Gym

2839 NW Market St
781.9828
www.stonegardens.com
Fri–Mon 10a–10p, Tues–Thurs 6a–11p

Seattle is ideally situated near some pretty spectacular outdoor climbing spots, and it's also home to mossbacks (i.e., tried-and-true Northwesterners), outdoorsy types, and REI. Needless to say, climbing is quite popular in these parts, and Stone Gardens keeps us all satisfied when we're not on our way to climbing in nearby BC or ascending from a West Coast forest. Take a private two-hour class for $50 and you get not only a 15 percent discount on all the gear in the shop, but also a two-week pass to the gym and indoor climbing facilities—a steal, if you ask me. If you want to skip the basic belay lesson and go straight to the 5.10 and ups, take a two-and-a-half-hour rappelling and gym-lead climbing class with a pro instructor. On any given weekend, you may find a speed climbing competition, a kids' climbing league championship, a bouldering lesson in progress, or a new, fun workout technique under your own belt. SB

Movement Classes

The sheer number of muscles in our bodies means we really need a full range of motion in order to exercise them all. In my mind, yoga, Pilates, and stretching techniques are at the very core of a holistic activity schedule. Being gentle on your body can be just as much of a workout as going all out physically at some of these spots. Here are my favorite places to get moving in a class setting around the city:

Studio Evolve

3333 *Wallingford Ave N, Ste B*
547.9616
www.studio-evolve.com
Mon–Fri 7a–9p, Sat 8a–6p, Sun 8a–8p

With the philosophy that there's a deeply important connection between body and mind, Studio Evolve promotes health and happiness before the more superficial goals of some gyms or yoga studios. In addition to offering Pilates, SPRe bodywork, and Yamuna body rolling, this light-filled place hosts some of Seattle's top massage therapists for an après-class massage. SB

8 Limbs

500 E Pike St, 325.1511
4546½ California Ave SW, 933.9642
7345 35th Ave NE, 523.9722
www.8limbsyoga.com
Mon–Fri 9a–1:30p & 3:30p–7p, Sat–Sun 9a–1:30p

The complete yoga mind is fostered at Seattle's local 8 Limbs chain. Seasonal classes fill a weeklong schedule with intensives mixed in, like prenatal yoga, Valentine's Day partner yoga, and yoga sutras. While you are waiting for your session to begin, you can shop in the boutique to deck out your workout wardrobe or find a new meditation tape for your car. This studio wasn't voted the best yoga place in town by three different city papers for nothing—some of the most practiced teachers offer classes here. SB

Seattle Yoga Arts

109 15th Ave E

440.3191

www.seattleyogaarts.com

Mon–Thurs 8a–8:45p, Sat 9a–12:15p, Sun 9a–7:30p

The team of women yoga instructors at Seattle Yoga Arts represents years of delving into profound questions and studying healing movement techniques. Hone your body for life with the skills taught here. I recommend founder Denise's Tuesday morning class or her gentle Thursday evening session that's easy on tired bodies. *SB*

Bodycenter Studios

4250 8th Ave NW, Ste 100

633.4800

www.bodycenterstudios.com

Hours vary, call ahead

This holistic Pilates studio hosts a range of classes for all body types and skill levels. Pilates is an amazing exercise that has a toning, centering effect on anyone who gives it a whirl. After I tried it, a few moves stayed with me that I can perform anywhere—even on an airplane if I have to! If you overdo it on your first attempt, massage appointments are available as well as physical therapy for further healing. *SB*

Maya Whole Health Studio

701 N 36th St

632.4900

www.mayawholehealth.com

Hours vary, call ahead

Totally opposite to the sweat-'til-you-drop workout spaces you may find, Maya Whole Health Studio is a calm, rosy space—quiet and open, ready for the next movement class to begin. Many chic gals get their groove on here—the Pilates Essentials course and the popular seasonal detox work-shops are some of Maya's highlights. The studio welcomes out-of-town visitors for single class prices, so just check ahead to ensure the classes are at your appropriate level. *SB*

Weight Lifting in Seattle

Shun your image of Seattle as filled only with hipsters, grunge guitar-ists, and tech geniuses—after all, Mark Twain did have a point when he said, "All generalizations are false, including this one." Regularly ranked one of the top national teams, Seattle's Calpians weight lifting team calls Seattle home. Buffing up the metallic way is lots of fun—a mix of endurance and that quick pop that thrusts the barbell over your head. It's satisfying, to say the least. There's a great com-munity around fitness in Seattle and around weight lifting, too. I've got my hand-me-down weight bench set up at home, and thanks to my weighty findings in Seattle, I got reinspired to use it for more than a clothing rack. Here are some fun spots to get your muscles moving in and around Seattle:

🏋 Thrush Sports Performance

1627 45th St E (Sumner)
253.826.9887
www.thrushsportsperformance.com
Hours vary, call ahead

No bells and whistles here. Thrush Sports Performance is the most serious weight gym in or around Seattle. It is where the Washington weight lifting team, the Calpians, trains, but it isn't an exclusive place. If you are inter-ested in this sport and want to try it out, this gym is a great resource. Careful instruction, including safe practices, is the keystone here. If you aren't plan-ning on benching, you can watch a league match or find out where one's tak-ing place. It's nothing like a baseball game, trust me. *SB*

Seattle Muscle

235 Summit Ave E
228.6610
www.seattlemuscle.com
Mon–Thurs 5a–11p, Fri 5a–9p, Sat 9a–5p

Seattle Muscle isn't for the faint of heart—it's more for the pointed of determi-nation. Serious workouts are prepared by one of Seattle's premier fitness gurus and a master of physical transformation, Ron McQueen. Skip the chain work-out experience and opt instead to get the one-on-one training you'll need to

Salumi

buff up or shed pounds. The draw for me is the tailored program and personal touch, neither unrealistic nor pushy. This is anything but generic. *SB*

Do Lunch

Outstanding midday eating of every sort

Lunch is my favorite meal of the day. When I lived in Switzerland, it was an event, with several courses and mandatory attendance by the entire family. In fact, some parts of the world consider lunch the largest meal of the day, followed by a siesta. There are many types of lunches to be had in Seattle: savory vegetarian delights from Flowers Bar and Restaurant, authentic borscht at Piroshki on 3rd, or healthy Cuban fare at Paseo. I had to dedicate a spot for lunch. From business power lunches to lazy afternoon munching, it's a state of mind. Let's do lunch!

FareStart

700 Virginia St
433.1233
www.farestart.org
Hours vary, call ahead

If I could have 12 top picks, this would be the one I'd add to my current list. FareStart is a great dining program featuring some of Seattle's best chefs, who come to run the kitchen for one night each month. Check the web site ahead of time to figure out who will be at the stoves, and get ready for a menu inspired by what was freshest at the market and out of the sea that very morning. Lunchtime offerings from FareStart's skilled students, low-income workers learning culinary professions at this philanthropic eatery, give you more chances to sample the fine organic cuisine at this do-gooder restaurant. *SB*

Nijo Sushi Bar & Grill

83 Spring St
340.8880
www.nijosushi.com
Mon–Wed 11a–11p, Thurs–Fri 11a–12a, Sat 4p–12a, Sun 4p–10p

"I crave sushi," are invariably the first words uttered by my cousin when she comes to visit from her new home in Austin, Texas. You see, she was born and raised in the Pacific Northwest, and she isn't used to the lack of reliable fresh fish in her current community. Nijo Sushi is where we go where she gets into town. It's quick and easy, affordable and fresh, inventive and delicious. What more could we ask for? Perhaps that nothing on the menu be more than $12, and Nijo obeys our wishes once more; the only exception is the superfluous sashimi salad at $15, with generous slices of a rainbow of sashimi, decorated with lumps of fish roe and slivered *tamago*, or egg. A few indulgent rolls with mayonnaise sauces are worth mentioning if you feel like getting a little Americanized with your lunch: the Lion Roll with seared salmon; the Hawaiian Roll with tempura scallions; and the soft-shell crab Spider Roll, my perennial favorite, rolled up with cucumber, avocado, *tobiko* fish roe, and spiced sushi sauce are always winners. More traditional eel rolls, fried oyster and *agedashi* tofu bento boxes, and *sunomono* marinated seaweed salads cater to those seeking an authentic Japanese lunch. Everything is fresh, and you can even sneak a peek into the back where the fish comes in right from the seafood market in the center of Seattle's International District. The daily meat, fish, and produce markets are crucial to the culinary culture of this entire town! SB

Seven Stars Pepper Szechuan Restaurant
 1207 S Jackson St
568.6446
Mon–Thurs 10:30a–10p, Fri–Sat 10:30a–2a

This neighborhood lunch joint is best for four things: hot pot, green onion pancakes, hand-shaved noodles, and sweet duck. The rest of the menu is, in my opinion, not worth returning for, but since these three crown jewels are prepared so adeptly and consistently well, I can justify my adoration of Seven Stars Pepper Szechuan Restaurant. Plus the price is always right. SB

Pho Bac
 415 7th Ave S
 621.0532
Daily 8a–9p

Clear, sweet, mild, and filling. Hearty, tender, bright, and healing. Pho Bac's mixed beef pho (or chicken pho for those who aren't excited to eat tripe) recalls a dictionary of adjectives, all of which add up to one satisfying lunch.

It's impossible to overspend at this kitschy soup stop, which is ideal for mid-museum visits or for filling a hungry belly after hours walking up and down downtown Seattle and the International District's gridded streets. File past the yellow awning and the neon cow sign for this meaty stock or for any number of noodle soups. Spring rolls are a regular addition to the top of my big open bowl. SB

Thai Tom

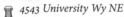 4543 University Wy NE

548.9548

Mon–Sat 11:30a–9p, Sun 1–8p

In the middle of big, expansive cities, there are always a couple of spots that can be aptly described as the cool kids in town. Lines of regulars, most of whom are avid readers of that town's free weekly paper, openly proclaim their addiction for whatever grub the cool kids dish out. Thai Tom is one of this small group on Seattle turf, together with Musashi's (see page 140) and perhaps a few others, that serves cheap and authentic meals, none for more than $7. The trick here is to come for lunch or takeout to avoid the chaos of this tiny kitchen, unless you're there for the free light show of flaming woks that can be viewed from the narrow marble counter. Try anything with yellow curry—just expect to get an overdose of rice with pretty much any order (more to soak up the sauce with, I say). Tofu and chicken dishes are supplied with genuine sear marks and oodles of flavor. It's clear that Thai Tom is all about good food, but I can't help thinking patrons wouldn't be as satisfied if there wasn't the allure of the squeeze once inside. SB

Snoose Junction Pizzeria

 2305 NW Market St

 789.2305

www.snoosejunctionpizzeria.com

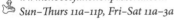 Sun–Thurs 11a–11p, Fri–Sat 11a–3a

Wait! Don't sit down just yet. Hold that pizza over your head and take a look at those 100-year-old bolts ensuring earthquake safety or the tables made from old bowling lanes. Owners Emily and Mark are inextricable from the conscientious business movement and the Ballard scene—in fact, the very name Snoose Junction recalls the era when Ballard was a stop-off for incoming

Scandinavian ships. Each item on the menu is carefully created from the finest local and organic ingredients. Even the Hawaiian pizza features hormone-free Black Forest ham and fresh pineapple as opposed to the canned stuff. Add roasted eggplant, Mama Lil's sweet peppers, or Cascioppo Brothers' hot Italian sausage for just two extra bucks, or go with one of the specials: the T.S.P. (That Seattle Pizza) has gobs of artichoke hearts, plus roasted garlic and red onions. Even though they've taken it off the official menu, order a Baked Potato Pie covered with slabs of Yukon gold potatoes, smoked bacon, and gooey cheddar with a dab of sour cream for good measure. Stay for a dessert of over-the-top *sfogliatelle*, an orange-infused ricotta cheese blend wrapped in pastry sheets, or dress up your low-key lunch with a swill of Chianti or an espresso stout, always on tap. *SB*

India Bistro
2301 NW Market St, 783.5080
6417 Roosevelt Wy NE, Ste 105/106, 517.4444
www.seattleindiabistro.com
Sun–Thurs 11:30a–9p, Fri–Sat 11:30a–9:30p, Sat 9a–5p

India Bistro may not be the most authentic of Seattle's Indian kitchens (a few of those are mentioned in the Sweet Tooth chapter, page 188), but it is home to one filling lunch buffet. For under $7 you get an order of naan and an all-access pass to mildly prepared, mostly vegetable curries, rice dishes, grilled items, and a few dessert choices. A casual comfort reverberates between these sunny walls, like taking a brief getaway to a foreign land without having to conform totally to the other nation's culture. *SB*

Starlife on the Oasis Cafe
1405 NE 50th St
729.3542
Daily 8:30a–12a

Just when you thought you had seen all of the tried-and-true Seattle coffeehouses, along comes Starlife on the Oasis, a cafe that exemplifies this city's vibe. It's hidden away in the University District, so finding this cozy spot is a lucky thing for anyone wishing for a moment of solace. I came upon this homey spot in a late-morning daze and in need of some time to gather my notes. After getting a tip about Starlife from a student, I decided to visit and had the most satisfying cup of coffee imaginable. The vibrant and healthy lunch menu is a highlight, no matter what you order. To top it off, I tried one of Starlife's famous vegan cookies—the chocolate chip version—and it was everything I could have wanted. That's coming from someone who normally turns up her nose at cookies of the vegan variety. *SB*

 Cedars Restaurant
4759 Brooklyn Ave NE
527.4000
www.cedarsseattle.com
Mon–Sat 1:30p–10p, Sun 12p–9p

Although I have honestly been happy with every dish I've ordered at Cedars Restaurant, I could dine solely on the appetizers. Bright and fluffy tabbouleh, fried chickpea-flour pakoras, hummus and tahini, oven-fresh pita bread, and smoky eggplant baba ghanoush are a Mediterranean dream come true. At the end of a long morning walk, I found Cedars. The discovery coincided with the very first time I recognized a new friend in public in Seattle—it was a good sign. This neighborhood joint is right up my alley. From the tandoori to the mango lassi, Cedars is a breath of fresh air, with a pleasant whiff of Indian spice. *SB*

Nordisk Filmklubb
Nordic Heritage Museum
3014 NW 67th St
789.5707
www.nordicmuseum.org, www.slseattle.com/home/announcements

The consummate film lover will relish the chance to discover this Scandinavian matinee held several times a month during weekday lunch hours. Hosted at the Nordic Heritage Museum in Ballard (many residents of this neighborhood are of Nordic descent), you can join neighbors and fellow film buffs for a noontime bagged lunch and watch films like Godt Hjerte's *Winter Quarter. SB*

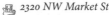 La Isla Seattle
2320 NW Market St
789.0516
www.laislaseattle.com
Mon–Sat 11:30a–12a, Sun 11:30a–10p

As far as I can tell, La Isla Seattle's claim to be the only Puerto Rican restaurant in the state of Washington holds true—but regardless, it is certainly a surprisingly authentic celebration of that rich culinary tradition. Imagine you are no longer suffering from Seattle rain fatigue and have been beamed over to San Juan, a pile of green banana *alcapurrias* or freshly baked pulled chicken empanadas giving your taste buds a trip. Salted cod fritters called *bacalaitos* are battered with island herbs—they are my favorite item on the lunch specials menu. This place wouldn't be complete without the bar, whose piña coladas, mojitos, and other rummy drinks are known to be strong and delicious. *SB*

$ Paseo

CO *4225 Fremont Ave N*
V *545.7440*
www.paseoseattle.com
Tues–Sat 11a–9p

We know you've seen the lines wrapping around that block of Fremont Avenue, and you've either marveled at the wonder of it or found out it is a cash-only lunch spot getting more buzz than ever. But Paseo for a late lunch is still an undiscovered place: a few stay-at-home dads feed heaping bites of slow-cooked beans and rice to their kiddlywinks, and late risers shuffle in for a Caribbean bowl rather than simple cereal for breakfast. Alex, my Vancouver writing buddy, and I took turns stuffing our faces with balanced blue corn chips dipped in simmered chicken thigh, black beans, saffron rice, fresh salsa, and cheese. Our classic Caribbean Bowl—which with a tip came to a mere $10—fed us both heartily, so we took a breather down to the Fremont neighborhood to check in on Lenin and friends. *SB*

Salumi

309 3rd Ave S
621.8772
$$ *www.salumicuredmeats.com*
Tues–Fri 11a–4p

There's a smug feeling derived from finding the salumi sandwich and lining up outside the tiny mustard-colored storefront with Seattle's serious lunch eaters. Feast your eyes on authentically prepared Italian cured meats, all organic and grass fed: lardo, coppa, oregano salami, and lamb prosciutto dangle along the wall. Choose the soup of the day plus a meaty sandwich and devour them on a central seat in Pioneer Square. This shop is Mario Batali's father's place—so you can see what an inspiring tradition this perfect salumi can be. *SB*

⩔ Flowers Bar and Restaurant

4247 University Wy NE
633.1903
Daily 11a–2a
$

Vegetarians in a rush who want choices will adore Flowers Bar and Restaurant's veggie buffet, just $8. A luscious spread of vegetarian dishes from various ethnic persuasions is laid out each afternoon for early diners, ensuring a tasty bargain for smart Seattleites. You can be in and out quickly unless you happen upon one of the slow waitstaff, but considering the price it is no big deal. This place is cool, calm, and collected, just like the trip-hop that is perpetually playing. *SB*

$ Piroshki on 3rd

710 3rd Ave
322.2820
www.piroshkirestaurant.com
Mon–Fri 7a–6p, Sat 8a–2p

A few pieces of my heritage show up in my eating preferences—I love borscht (well, really anything with beets), I adore herring, and pickling is a regular word in my vocabulary. This family restaurant is home to some of these favorites of mine. Piroshki on 3rd's classic borscht, floated with a cloud of sour cream, is a must-order. Piroshkis come in several variations, with some of the pastries stuffed with garlicky vegetables, some with spiced meats, and others with aged cheeses. None is more than $4, and they are made with egg whites and low-calorie soybean oil, so even careful eaters can indulge. If, however, you want more than just a piroshki snack, order beef stroganoff, pelmeni dumplings, or pierogis stuffed with potatoes. No inner chill can survive a satisfying meal at Piroshki on 3rd. *SB*

$ Szechuan Noodle Bowl

420 8th Ave S
623.4198
Tues–Sun 11:30a–9p

At any given time there is some combination of wise-looking grandmas delicately forming fresh Szechuan-style dumplings in the window of this hole-in-the-wall of holes-in-the-wall. Back before World War II and the tragic Japanese internment, this place was a Japanese-owned business, and the landowners were among the lucky few who had their land returned to them after the war. Now these skillful ladies have been here for some time, keeping vegans, meat eaters, and every ethnicity to pass through Seattle happy and stuffed on their always fresh dumplings. These moist pockets of steamed veggies and meat come in any number your stomach can manage and in more flavors than you thought possible; I always try to gather together a posse before heading over so we can try them all. In between the Uwajimaya supermarket (see page 118) and Pioneer Square bookstores, this spot is perfect for a solo bite—just have your cash handy. *SB*

$ Fu Man Dumpling House

14314 Greenwood Ave N
364.0681
Tues–Sun 11a–3p, 4:30–9p

Throw out the table manners, the etiquette, the pomp and circumstance, and let's get to eating. Fu Man Dumpling House is at the cusp of being discovered, but this hole-in-the-wall dumpling factory serves only the tastiest garlic-packed steamed delights, which you can eat there or take home to your freezer. You'll be hard-pressed to spend more than $10—that's because you'll skip everything else (except maybe the hot and sour soup if you are getting a sore throat) and get the crispy fried balls of delight. Just be sure to bring a date who is accustomed to less than perfectly fresh breath: these dumpling makers love their onions and garlic. *SB*

Agua Verde Cafe and Paddle Club

1303 NE Boat St

545.8570

www.aguaverde.com

V

Mon–Sat 11a–9p, Sun 12–6p

Even when it is raining out, the obliging staff at the University District's Agua Verde Cafe and Paddle Club will let you rent a rowboat or canoe so you can paddle post-meal with your dining buddies—the best way to digest in my opinion. Try Agua Verde's iced margaritas, which bring sunshine to my day even when it is far from sunny. Pick and choose from the extensive taco list; my favorite is the yam and catfish taco, made with a fish that is sustainably caught and also sustains my taste buds. Maybe the reason this fresh-Mex spot is so popular is because it seems sunshiny here all year long, and for Seattle that is a rare treasure. *SB*

Farm to Table

Edible bounties direct to your tavola

Connecting with the source of the food we eat is a wonderful step toward sustainable living. How can you look at produce or a list of ingredients the same way after having the experience of talking with the local berry farmer or seeing an egg hatched before your eyes? Somehow we got sidetracked and chemicals slipped into the food stream, but we can think a little bit before chomping down and make sure what we are eating is as natural as we are. Escape to the countryside without leaving Seattle's bustling blocks and you'll find pocket farms and markets full of local bounty. After all, we are what we eat!

Ballard Farmers Market

Ballard Ave NW between 20th and 22nd aves NW

www.fremontmarket.com/ballard

Year-round, Sun 10a–3p

Ballard's quaint little farmers market could be a tourist's perfect afternoon out or a distracting enough second-date place for locals. Although plenty of talented home chefs are crawling around the picturesque Ballard bungalows,

Interbay P-Patch Community Garden

I get the impression that the farmers market isn't their sole supplier. Families and slow-paced couples out along the historic waterfront stumble through the market, ecstatic to find the handmade cheeses and local smoked fish but not intending to be regulars—though I'm sure the story of the fresh salmon jerky will make it back home. Bring a basket to sling in the crook of your elbow and buy up not only picnic makings, but also gifts for all your friends and family made by the people selling them. *SB*

Magnolia Farmers Market

Next to Magnolia Community Center, 2550 34th Ave W
www.seattlefarmersmarkets.org/markets/magnolia
End of May through mid-Oct, Sat 10a–2p

Seriously focused on local, organic produce, the Magnolia Farmers Market is the supplier of not only most of the decked-out kitchens in this ideal neighborhood, but also many of the great restaurants. Cafe Flora bases its menu on what the farmers at the market bring, and making connections with these wise foragers brightens the restaurant's fantastic mushroom menu in the early fall. You can find these treasures and more, plus olallieberries, blackberries, mulberries, and marionberries for canning projects. *SB*

PCC Natural Markets

600 N 34th St (and nine other Seattle locations)
632.6811
www.pccnaturalmarkets.com
Hours vary by location

PCC is the big small market in Seattle. I can hear George Carlin echoing his wordplay jokes in my head, "jumbo shrimp . . ." But these markets are smaller in scope than the national natural food markets, and bigger than your local food co-op (although it started as one). There's a special experience of food featured at PCC—a respect for taste and for the season, for the growing process and the eating ceremony. It is handy to find them scattered around town, always there with a delicious prepared snack or the ingredients for a future picnic or backyard supper club. The staff members are more friendly than your average bunch of locals, and they tend to know a lot more about the food than meets the eye, so although you may have experienced the "Seattle stare," don't be afraid to talk to strangers at the PCC Natural Markets. Anyway, who doesn't have a few minutes to talk about something tasty? *SB*

University District Farmers Market

In the University Heights lot at NE 50th St and University Wy NE
www.seattlefarmersmarkets.org/markets/u_district
Year-round, Sat 9a–2p

I don't know whether it was a neighborhood vote or just a few vocal farmers market planners, but the farmers-only attitude at the University District Farmers Market keeps it pure in a refreshing way. Here you'll find heaping boxes and baskets of whatever came from the ground the previous week. If you are a haggler, talk to the farmers and get bulk discounts on items for big canning projects like pickled Romanesco broccoli, onion and cranberry relish, or oil-cured seafood (refrigerate the fish after packing it in a sealed jar with oil and seasoning). You'll find it hard to avoid the kitchen after an inspiring trip to this local food congregation. *SB*

⌀ Broadway Farmers Market

Behind the Bank of America at 10th Ave E and E Thomas
www.seattlefarmersmarkets.org/markets/broadway
Mid-May through early Dec, Sun 11a–3p

Without fail, Capitol Hill is pulsing with ogling shoppers and live music every seasonal Sunday, rain or shine. Although this market is ideally placed amid one of Seattle's most vibrant areas, it also serves as a regular pasture for lazy locals, whiling their weekend away with the help of an armful of braising greens, a sculpturesque winter squash, and a jar of local sage blossom honey. *SB*

ⓒⓞ West Seattle Farmers Market

In the Junction, California Ave SW and SW Alaska Ave
www.seattlefarmersmarkets.org/markets/west_seattle
Year-round, Sun 10a–2p

Skagit and King, Jefferson and Douglas, Thurston and Grant, Lincoln and Snohomish—a trip to the West Seattle Farmers Market could easily turn into a lesson in Western Washington geography. King County, where Seattle is located, offers Trevani Truffles; luxurious beef and lamb soup stocks from Sea Breeze Farms; and organic vegetables from Whistling Train Farms. My irresistible meal consisted of dreamy bacon from Wooly Pigs, cheese from Samish Bay, and summer tomatoes and basil from Stokesberry Sustainable Farm in Thurston County to the south. Falling in love with your senses is a fantastic entrance into Seattle society—one bite out of this market and you'll be set on eating your way through the rest of the town. *SB*

⌀ Lake City Farmers Market

Next to the library at NE 125th St and 28th Ave NE
www.seattlefarmersmarkets.org/markets/lake_city
June–Oct, Thurs 3–7p

This farmers market typifies the Seattle vibe: families spotting their children on the jungle gym next to brainy know-it-alls (who grow wiser with each rainy day) and an overall spirit of inventive genius—both in the kitchen and in the worlds of technology and business. Lake City has its own convergence of these city forces, but they are represented by a colorful if somewhat modest market (compared to the more abundant markets elsewhere in the city) with a very regular crowd. I would venture to guess many local families have the market sketched in red pencil on their calendars as a ritual outing and a chance to get a bouquet of flowers and some curly kale. Come with a raincoat, a book under your arm, a couple of empty canvas bags, and a sense of adventure, Seattle style. *SB*

Uprising Seeds
2208 Iron St (Bellingham)
360.201.0468
www.uprisingorganics.com
Hours vary, call ahead

Ensuring that native, non–genetically modified seeds survive in this ever-changing pool of genetic science, Bellingham's Uprising Seeds regenerates local seeds. Rare plants and those adapted for growing in the Pacific Northwest are among some of the specimens here, and everything is certified non-GMO and organic. You can find Uprising Seeds' seed packets and seedlings at locally owned garden stores around Seattle, at the Bellingham Farmers Market, and at the Uprising Organics Farm itself. You can also order any of the 75 varieties of heirloom edible plant seeds over the phone to be shipped directly to you. *SB*

Seattle Tilth
Main offices and garden: Good Shepherd Center, 4649 Sunnyside Ave N, Rm 120
Demonstration garden: Bradner Gardens Parks, 1733 Bradner Pl S, Mount Baker neighborhood
633.1451
www.seattletilth.org

The award-winning nonprofit group behind P-Patches and other gardens across the city, Seattle Tilth, is a crucial resource for residents interested in directing their lives toward sustainability. Purchase a handful of red worms and a garden worm bin to break down your waste, or take a class about composting, conserving resources, and gardening in the local climate. Volunteers are welcome to help keep the community gardening ethic alive and well. Even if you are a beginner, it will do you good to learn a bit about the soil and get some under your nails! *SB*

Major Annual Events at Seattle Tilth

A bunch of events and classes throughout the year are put on at various locations by Seattle Tilth. Here are some annual favorites:

January: Annual Member Meeting (everyone invited)

March: Annual Tilth Celebration

May: Seattle Edible Plant Sale, Issaquah Edible Plant Sale

July: City Chickens Coop Tour, Monster Milk and Cookie Bake

September: Harvest Moon Square Dance

October: Tilth's Sustainable Soiree

December: Tractor Pull Square Dance

Columbia City Farmers Market

Columbia Plaza, 4801 Rainier Ave S
www.seattlefarmersmarkets.org/markets/columbia_city/
Mid-Apr–Oct, Wed 3–7p

This market is one of the best for prepared foods like sauces, bread and pastries, cheeses, and jam and honey, but I make sure to have cash on hand each visit for the eggs and poultry from some of the most idyllic and sustainable farms in the country. Although the plaza where the Columbia City Farmers Market takes place was recently purchased, the group that attends and organizes the market is dedicated to keeping it going, even if that means the market moves to a new location within the next couple of years. *SB*

P-Patch Community Gardens

www.seattle.gov/neighborhoods/ppatch

Seattle is no Fresno, and it doesn't pretend to be the largest grower of produce, but there is a huge network of both small- and large-scale farmers across the state of Washington. Apples and Walla Walla onions are two famous Washington State exports, but the gardening culture trickles down and spreads to far more varieties of fruits and veggies. Seattle's P-Patch gardens are keystones of Seattle communities, bringing together volunteer efforts to share in the bounty of the soil. Although gardening in Seattle has many upsides, a primary perk is that you sure don't have to worry about watering too often! Visit various P-Patches across the city, or volunteer for a day to help turn the beds with the neighbors. There are some 55 P-Patch gardens, so keep an eye out and you'll be sure to come upon one. Some of my faves are Delridge (5078 25th Avenue SW), Ravenna (5200 Ravenna Avenue NE), Linden Orchard (Linden Avenue N and 67th N), and Queen Pea (5th Avenue N and Howe Street). *SB*

Hang Out

All the best chill-out spots, from cozy reading nooks to relaxed microbrews with your buddies

Sometimes the best way to get the sense of a place is to slow down and stop attempting to see everything and do everything. Try a pub game, attend a laid-back concert, or pop into a teahouse and give new meaning to loitering. Seattle is fast and slow, caught between Washington's relaxed vibe and the busyness of being a flourishing city, and it is easy to find a great chill-out spot to take in all sides of this city. Bring friends or venture out alone for a moment on the treadmill of usual livelihood.

Roanoke Park

 950 E Roanoke St
684.4075
www.seattle.gov/parks/park_detail.asp?id=379
Daily 4a–11:30p

Roanoke Park may not be the city's largest open space, but the 2-plus acres of natural green kept in pristine condition on the street with the same name are a perfect place to hang out in Seattle finery. The bursts of color from the leaves and flowers and the pure quality of the light (sometimes rays stream through openings in the cloud cover) make this *the* park to ponder nature. There are fruit trees ripe for foraging September through early December, weather depending, and a play area for children to climb on while you and your friends chat on the lawn. *SB*

Lake Washington Ship Canal and Wetlands

3015 NW 54th St

783.7059

www.ci.seattle.wa.us/tour/locks.htm

Daily 7a–9p

The terminus of the winding Lake Washington ship canal at Hiram M. Chittenden Locks is the perfect place for lazing on a sunny summer day. Watch the fish frolic up the fish ladders, and then march through the botanical gardens and wetlands, stopping to smell an especially fragrant blossom or sketch one of the alienlike succulent plants. Ships pass along the view from patches of green space ideal for picnicking or restrictive Frisbee tosses. Bring your sunglasses and sunscreen and a ukulele for an afternoon full of laid-back, Seattle-style memories. *SB*

Cavalry Cemetery

541 35th Ave NE

522.0996

www.acc-seattle.com

Always open

I apologize in advance if you think it morbid, but I have a fancy for taking time out in cemeteries when I travel. Cavalry is a primarily Catholic cemetery in Ravenna, with soldiers and priests buried side by side on 40 acres. Gravestones date back to the early days of Seattle in the late 1800s. Sit on the southwest-facing hill and look out at the view. On a sunny day, I bring a book, a jar of kombucha, and a bun from the Essential Bakery Café (see page 29), and sit under one of the shade trees at the height of the cemetery plaza. *SB*

Olympic Sculpture Park

2901 Western Ave

654.3100

www.seattleartmuseum.org/visit/osp

Daily, 30 minutes before sunrise until 30 minutes after sunset

After experiencing a scary helicopter accident, two members of the Seattle Art Museum's board of directors made plans to open this park and succeeded in doing so in 1997. Bordering the land's edge with some 50,000 tons of riprap, the sculpture park and nearby Myrtle Edwards Park (see page 33) were shored up and planted with native trees and hedges. The sculpture garden

Fremont Troll

is also speckled with permanent and traveling outdoor art shows like the famous *Eagle*, a sweeping metal gestural burst by Alexander Calder. Even in the rain, this park is a sight to behold, but the best way to experience what this place has to offer is to take an hour-long tour, focusing on either the ecology and environment or the Duwamish and Unocal site heritage and current art installments. *SB*

⑤ Fremont Troll
N 36th St and Troll Ave N
Always open

I had an interesting experience with Seattle's famous Fremont Troll. I was lurching past the Fremont branch of the Seattle Public Library, dismayed that it was temporarily closed, and I wound another block toward the bridge overpass where the Troll—a massive concrete sculpture—has been keeping watch since 1990. I had a small but oddly heavy backpack with me, so I stopped to rest at the paved bench below his grand grimace. At the base of his neck I found an open volume. It was a book of poetry—an *End of the World Graffiti* chapbook by Seattle poet Raegan Butcher. I sat and read, and the time flew by without my knowledge until dark crept upon my squinting eyes and I could no longer clearly make out the words on the page. I bid the Troll farewell and found my way to a nearby cafe to finish my reading endeavor, made possible by my gift from the Fremont Troll. SB

Skillet

Various locations, check web site
694.7836
www.skilletstreetfood.com
Mon–Thurs 9a–2p

Street food takes on new meaning at Seattle's Skillet, a silver bullet–like moveable kitchen that roams the town, spreading good eats to all who find its ordering window. Start with a refreshing sip of rhubarb-lemongrass lemonade while you await your pan-seared Idaho trout with tomato-braised cranberry beans and red onion and watercress salad to be prepared. That's what I did, and I was not disappointed. My honey ordered the burger, as I knew he would, and he was smitten with the slathering of melted Cambozola cheese and crispy bacon inside the brioche bun. Put simply, chasing down Skillet is worth the racing heart, the ripped seams, the beads of sweat, and the panting. Once you track down the restaurant, make your selection and hang around with friends or a book or a hacky sack, and then grub with other satisfied diners. The weekly menus, created from organic, seasonal farm produce and sustainably acquired seafood, never fail to make my mouth water. I wish more Airstreams hid kitchens like this. SB

Boom Noodle

1121 E Pike St
701.9130
www.boomnoodle.com
Sun 12p–10p, Mon–Thurs 11:30a–10p, Fri–Sat 12p–12a

This is shiny Japanese food, uppity in all the right ways to fit in with the finest Pike and Pine eateries. I go to Boom Noodle for its gracious happy hour, 4 to 6pm Monday through Thursday and 10pm to close Friday through Saturday, and order chilled sesame tofu layered with shiitake mushrooms and bamboo shoots, and house-made edamame purée with sweet potato crisps and Japanese cucumber and eggplant.

Regular menu items are affordable and go along well with these early bird bargains: cold *somen* noodles with chilled tempura broth, green beans with crispy pork and Japanese pickles, fresh handmade cream puffs for dessert, and delectable drink concoctions are all good reasons to be a regular here if you come to this neighborhood often. It is a great atmosphere to lounge in, chatting with friends, catching up on your solo time, or embarking on a new romance. Boom Noodle allows you to enjoy the food and drinks in a stunning array of futuristic design and cool people. I spend more time here than I probably should, but then again, it does get rainy in Seattle, and being indoors seems so nice during those times. . . . SB

Discovery Park

3801 W Government Wy
386.4236
www.cityofseattle.net/parks/environment/discovparkindex.htm
Daily 6a–11p

When I first began learning about seafood sustainability, I quickly discovered that although some 75 percent of species had been fished over capacity, there were some species that it was important to keep eating correctly. That is to say, eating salmon from a conscientious line fisher ensures that entire expanses of fishing waters are reserved for sustainable population cultivation and healthy, balanced fishing methods that fit in with the natural ecosystem or food chain. I thought about this a lot at Discovery Park as I took the self-guided tour through the park's Salmon Bay Wildlife Corridor. Then I walked up to Magnolia Bluff, which overlooks the sweeping viewpoint of the Puget Sound, and crept back through wildlife sanctuaries and protected tidal beaches, where I removed my shoes and let my toes wriggle in the sand. The park is a monument to America's astounding beauty, and it is so accessible from a perch in Seattle that I am easily able to spend hours on end there without missing the concrete jungle nearby. SB

Explore

Places where the wide world is explained, nature abounds, and adventure is waiting

Curiosity can lead down many a path; we've all seen our friend Curious George get in over his head. But fostering a healthy curiosity about the world is as important as taking our very first steps. If we fill our imagination with programmed images and digital friends, we miss out on all there is to explore for ourselves in the big wide world. History and science, nature and adventure are waiting around the bend to expand your knowledge of the world around you. Seek out the big questions, ask your own, and most of all, enjoy the ride!

Burke Museum of Natural History and Culture

NE 45th St and 17th Ave NE
543.5590
http://burkemuseum.org
Daily 10a–5p

The Burke Museum of Natural History and Culture, squeezed into the University of Washington campus, is larger than life. Housing one of the most epic totem pole collections around, the Burke Museum is one of the best places to get in the know about the native peoples of Washington and the Northwest. After just a few hours between these walls I came out with a pretty good picture of the forces that shaped the region—from the perspective of the stones, plants, animals, and humans. Curiosity comes alive in the faces of visitors perusing the exhibits and getting under the skin of this century-old museum. *SB*

Seattle Clock Walk

www.zombiezodiac.com/rob/ped/clock/map.htm

This free online map, complete with photographs, directs you on a walking tour around central Seattle in search of the city's most interesting timepieces. Start with the sullen black hands of the Union Station clock, set in the grayish-pink granite veneer of the transit building, before heading to another train depot, King Street Station, and another Roman-numeral face, this time centered on a bronze-encircled cross. Follow the directions on the web site for the complete tour, and have yourself an unexpected exploration of Seattle's take on the passing of the hours. *SB*

Washington Park Arboretum

2300 Arboretum Dr E

543.8800

http://depts.washington.edu, www.arboretumfoundation.org

Daily 7a–dusk

Aside from the internationally recognized collections of prized camellias and hollies, this 230-acre arboretum is a real treasure because it looks like Puget Sound did before it was settled: rolling hills covered with weeping hawthorns and mountain ashes. On a clear spring day it looks a little like these winding paths were made for a romantic comedy movie set. I wear my green sneakers and a cozy zippered hoodie for long walks through the extensive gardens—some are planted in a structured organization, while others look like frames from the animated film *Bambi* come to life. It's easy to loll around here or to get heady about the flora and learn about horticulture from serious plant geeks. I love it! *SB*

Northwest African American Museum (NAAM)

2300 S Massachusetts St

518.6000

www.naamnw.org

Wed 11a–4:30p, Thurs 11a–7p, Fri–Sun 11a–4p

The three primary sections that make up this cultural resource tell about the past and present of the African American experience in the Pacific Northwest. As I strolled through the Journey Gallery, I imagined that I myself was making the long, perilous journey first to North America, and then across plains and mountain ranges of the continent to the West Coast. Hearing about the travels and trials of these unsung heroes gave me a chance to be introspective not only about my own human determination, but also about race and leadership. The museum has an open space for traveling exhibits to fill—one month there will be a showcase of local black artists, another month an exhibition on Ethiopia. *SB*

Woodland Park Zoo

5500 Phinney Ave N
548.2500
www.zoo.org
Daily 9:30a–5p
Admission: $8–16.50

Father's Day is one of those holidays about which I feel little pressure. The old standards are just as good each year, and unlike birthdays, I don't feel I'm expected to come up with some extraordinary theme or gift. Father's Day is my favorite holiday to celebrate at the zoo, but any time an old-school adventure is desired it's a place that's easy to enjoy. Marvel at the new flock of flamingos and the other well-cared-for creatures. Bring Dad or wander solo amidst the finery of feathers and fur, and chances are you'll end up like I do: fully entertained and stuffed on hot dogs. *SB*

Seattle Aquarium

1483 Alaskan Wy
386.4320
www.seattleaquarium.org
Daily 9:30a–5p
Admission: $10.50–16, free for children age 3 and under

Where am I at 1:30pm on an adventure day out in Seattle? If I can make it in time, I'm in the Seattle Aquarium's underwater dome with a 360° view of the fish feeding. Follow your nose through one of the two water-enclosed tunnels leading to this large fish-viewing cave, and you'll have a hard time discerning what to breathe, water or air? Farther along the winding hallways of marine life is a large window on a 120,000-gallon tank modeled after nearby Neah Bay that allows a unique peek at the richly decorated native underwater scene. Aside from scuba diving, I can't think of a better way to get up close and personal with the watery kingdoms of the Puget Sound and at the same time come away with an idea of how to help protect this environment. *SB*

ᗕ Space Needle

ᗷ *400 Broad St*

ᗘ *905.2100*

www.spaceneedle.com

ᗕ *Daily 9a–12a*

Admission: $8–16, free for children age 3 and under

The Space Needle began life as the symbol of the 1962 Seattle World's Fair and has since become one of the most recognizable structures in the world, and even in a city of many wonders it remains atop the must-see list of many tourists. If you give in to your friends' or family's whims, or to your own desire to squeeze in the elevator and gradually ascend the Needle, be sure to first set aside any claustrophobic tendency. This is one place to brag about visiting, especially if you go all out with a reservation at Sky City, where you can enjoy a seafood meal while rotating at 500 feet. If you're visiting in the winter, make the date December 31 for the West Coast's premier New Year's Eve celebration. Should you feel the need to go the whole nine yards, why not pay a little extra for a Day and Night pass? You'll be allowed two visits, one for the daytime and one for the evening. My favorite thing about this landmark has to be the fact that it's approximately 1,320 Milky Way candy bars tall. Oh, and I hear it's supposed to be an excellent place to pop the question. DL

ᗕ Experience Music Project

ᗷ *325 5th Ave N*

 877.367.7361

www.empsfm.org

ᗔ *Daily 10a–7p*

Admission: $12–15, free for children age 4 and under

Frank Gehry really must have had fun with this one! If you didn't previously know about this colorful conglomerate, you'll be surprised to find this unique structure at the base of the Space Needle. While I adore spending a few hours exploring the modern music exhibits or hearing a concert at the incomparable Sky Church, I can't help but thinking that Experience Music Project (EMP) exposes this interesting city's sentimental tendencies. What other metropolis allows a rich resident to sit down with the mayor and get his teenage dreams to come true with interactive museum spaces for his geeky obsessions? Paul Allen is an enchanting character, however controversial, and his contributions to the city don't end with this museum, so I thank him for gathering together all the rock memorabilia he could, hiring the finest architect and engineers, and seeing this dream through to its fruition. It is a living place, host to many festivals and fetes; I would say it is the gold at the end of its own rainbow. *SB*

⚐ Nordic Heritage Museum
🚍 *3014 NW 67th St*
☎ *789.5707*
⌨ *www.nordicmuseum.org*
🎫 *Tues–Sat 10a–4p, Sun 12–4p*

Seattle was settled in large part by Nordic people who skillfully sailed over frigid oceans to get to the Puget Sound. In Ballard, the hub of Scandinavian preservation, the Nordic Heritage Museum is a main attraction for community events, perhaps even more so than the permanent exhibits themselves. It is interesting to follow via the installations the journey of these immigrants who came to be the pillars of a new American city, and it is even more interesting to hop in for an artistic Scandinavian film or crash the Nordic Knitting Conference. Looking over the calendar of this active museum, you'll find yourself considering attending events you never thought would be a part of your vacation (or staycation). *SB*

🚌 Pacific Science Center
🚶 *200 2nd Ave N*
📖 *443.2001*
🎫 *www.pacsci.org*
Daily 10a–6p
Admission: $7–14

Thank goodness for science! The language of the natural world has a real-life dictionary carefully explaining many concepts at the Pacific Science Center. Sometimes I forget how much fun science is and how many questions are out there being asked and answered every day. At this monument to the scientific tradition, you can find a world-class planetarium as well as the most recent scans of Lucy's famous skeleton used by archeologists as they continue to search for the past routes of human life. I always wondered why people give "staring off into space" a bad rap—here it is universally regarded as a good thing. *SB*

Museum of History and Industry

2700 24th Ave E
www.seattlehistory.org
Daily 10a–5p
Admission: $6–8, free for children age 4 and under

Museums aren't just big ornate structures stuffed with dusty old rubbish—oh no, they are living things. The Museum of History and Industry (MOHAI) conducts free workshops about how to do historical research, even offering participants the chance to contribute their newfound skills toward unearthing details about Seattle's first world's fair. Sure, there is some great old rubbish hanging around here, too, but the archived photographs and Essential Seattle permanent exhibits are far from boring. Take part in the ever-changing technological advances by first reaching back and understanding their progression thus far. *SB*

Keep an Eye Out for Public Art!

Seattle's revolutionary percent-for-art city ordinance has ensured that funding is set aside for public art. Always free and often welcoming places to sit and read, the following are just a few of the 350-some sculptures around town (for more info, visit *www.seattle.gov/arts/publicart/default.asp*).

Waiting for the Interurban, Richard Beyer, Fremont Ave N and N 34th St

Paragon, Donald Fels, Terminal 107, W Marginal Wy S, Alki Beach

DNA Wave Wall, Vicki Scuri, W Galer St Flyover

Water Weaving Light Cycle, Nobuho Nagasawa, Dale Stammen, and Andrew Schloss, inside Seattle City Hall, 600 5th Ave

Weekend

Fun activities for Saturdays and Sundays, plus yummy spots for brunch

Weekends have a mood all their own. Laze around, relax with your loved ones, or explore something new. Seattleites like to get outside on the weekends, especially during the summer, and enjoy the glorious weather or one of the annual street fairs. A short weekend getaway is an ideal way to see this city. Americans don't get nearly as much vacation time as those from other countries, so take advantage of the weekends and create mini-vacations at these great spots.

$$ Umi Sake House

 2230 1st Ave

 374.8717

www.umisakehouse.com

 Daily 4p–2a

My favorite meal to share with friends if we're eating out is sushi, and Seattle's Umi Sake House was created with just this in mind. My mossback buddies and I gather around crowded tables strewn with stocky bamboo platters of the freshest sushi and most creative rolls. To me, there are few better weekend activities, so I always try to set aside a few extra bucks for a night out sampling sushi with Liz, Nathan, Daniel, and Dax at Umi. Last time we ordered a reasonably priced bottle of Tozai Junmai Nigori sake, and the unfiltered freshness paired perfectly with our crunchy soft-shell crab and silky line-caught salmon sashimi. SB

$ Chace's Pancake Corral

 1606 Bellevue Wy SE (Bellevue)

454.8888

 Mon–Fri 5:45a–2:30p, Sat–Sun 6a–3p

A local Bellevueite was quite excited to take me to this tasty little grease pit. I would describe it as "old-country dirty" in the most endearing way possible. The low prices, creative menu (think hash brown omelet and coconut syrup), and homemade cooking make this place a killer choice for breakfast any day of the week. The menu lexicon can be a bit sexist . . . or not. My "Ladies"

combo was the perfect size, and the cooks were happy to substitute bacon for a sausage patty. I love flexibility. Although the ketchup looked gross, it wouldn't stop me from making the trip to 'burbs again sometime soon. AK

Judy Fu's Snappy Dragon

8917 Roosevelt Wy NE
528.5575
www.snappydragon.com
Mon–Sat 11a–9:30p, Sun 4–9p

This place touches the hearts of my Seattle friends who know and love Chinese food. Everything on the menu is appetizing. Awesome homemade noodles and dumplings, yummy sauces, and fresh veggies, including asparagus, sated my palate. The seafood and meat (prawns and chicken) are tasty and of good quality. And even though the whole lot seemed pretty Americanized, with a name like Snappy Dragon, what were we expecting? All of this consuming occurs in a cute little house in a great little 'hood. Yummers. AK

Portage Bay Cafe

4130 Roosevelt Wy NE
547.8230
www.portagebaycafe.com
Mon–Fri 7:30a–3p, Sat–Sun 8a–3p

Maybe it's because Portage Bay Cafe offers its brunch menu every day that I find weekends here surprisingly less crowded than some of the long-wait eateries dotting Seattle. I shared a bowl of chai and soy milk oatmeal, the black bean and pancetta cake benedict, and the flatiron steak omelet with three hungry friends, still groggy from an EMP concert (see page 85) the night before. Everything was tasty, and although service was slower than my hunger pangs bargained for, the sustainable local ingredients and secret family recipes made for one swell brunch. SB

Dinette

1514 E Olive Wy
328.2282
www.dinetteseattle.com

Sign up ahead of time to claim your spot at one of Dinette's themed communal Sunday dinners to share a family-style feast of seasonal bounty for 36.

Never skip the "toast" course at Dinette if you know what's good for you—
humanely raised charcuterie is tops here, and it's served with zero pretense,
unlike most meat plates around Seattle. Chicken liver mousse and country
pâté, both more rustic choices, are my two favorites. Duck leg confit with
scrumptious parsnip purée (you'll never look down on this pale root again)
and perfectly caramelized roasted Brussels sprouts are sublime. For dessert,
the bittersweet chocolate terrine will do just fine, thank you. Clink moscato
glasses with your neighbors and new friends as you finish your weekend with
an authentic taste of community. SB

$$ Café Presse

1117 12th Ave
709.7674
www.cafepresseseattle.com
Daily 7a–2a

The busy European vibe of Café Presse is carefully calculated by the owners,
the same duo behind Le Pichet (see page 140). For me, it's as satisfying to
run in and out of this place, dressed in chic black boots, trousers, and a coat,
as it is so linger in my vintage velour after hours with a good book. On long
autumn afternoons I come here to catch up on Arsenal's standings or check
in on the German footie scores with a hearty Presse *petit dejeuner* like the
Oeufs Plats with two broiled eggs, sliced French ham, and imported Gruyère
cheese. SB

V 22 Doors

$ 405 15th Ave E
324.6406
Daily 5p–2a

This tiny bistro has a menu bigger than the kitchen itself and lots of homey
vibes echoing between the walls. Come for a weekend brunch—everything
goes well with a mimosa! Plus, the covered outdoor patio is great year-
round. SB

St. Clouds

1131 34th Ave
726.1522
www.stclouds.com

On lazy S-days (I've been calling weekends that since childhood), St. Clouds is a buzz of hungry listeners, taking bites of fluffy omelets and earfuls of live music. Vegetarian not-so-standards include my favorite early bird version of tempeh to date—it's marinated in ponzu sauce and scrambled together with scallions, ginger, and eggs—and a simple yet filling breakfast burrito. Meat eaters with a zest for morning protein will relish the old-school country breakfast. Even when I am not in the mood for a large meal, I come to St. Clouds for its famously delectable coffee cake and a steaming cup of herbal tea. Brunch is served on weekends, and nightly jazz creates a romantic atmosphere to accompany the full dinner menu. *SB*

Earth and Ocean

1112 4th Ave
264.6060
www.earthocean.net
Daily, hours vary

When Earth and Ocean head chef Adam Stevenson took me into his meat locker and I saw the glint in his eye when he pulled out his horse-bone utensil to check the doneness of his coppa, I knew I had just met one inspired guy who loves what he does. And I love what he does. In fact, pitted against even the established talent of other top Seattle charcuteries like Salumi (see page 68), Adam recently came out on top when he added fennel pollen to his salami and special aged spices to his aforementioned coppa. The rest of the menu, and the supernal wine list managed by sommelier April Pogue, is nothing to shake a stick at. Mackerel gets fancy with tender poaching and wasabi-soy glaze, while simple salads come alive with fine cheeses and other elegant dressings. The ingredients are carefully considered before anything enters the kitchen cupboards, and the restaurant frequently offers entire tasting menus featuring specific foraged plants. *SB*

ⅴ Jade Garden

$ *424 7th Ave S*

🏮 *622.8181*

Daily 9a–2:30a

Practically everyone in Seattle has found him- or herself in front of a Jade Garden table at some hour of day or night, and for years it has maintained its thriving Sunday dim sum crowds. I'd still make the trip at 9am sharp to get a good table for the famous congee and fried calamari with Chinese broccoli greens. *SB*

💲 Fremont Sunday Market

🏚 *N 34th St between Phinney Ave and Evanston N*

🗑 *www.fremontmarket.com/fremont*

Year-round, Sun 10a–4p

Inspired by the busy open-air markets of Europe, Fremont's weekly market-place hosts more than 150 vendors along the neighborhood's main drag. My poodle Dutsi and I had a blast winding through the crowded rows of artists, craftspeople, antique hunters, and food carts. We sampled Chicago-style hot dogs at one end of the market, bought a felted dog toy midway, and found three vintage jazz records at a booth before we headed back down to the canal to finish our Sunday stroll. *SB*

💲 Volunteer Park

🏚 *1245 15th Ave E*

🗑 *684.4555*

www.seattle.gov/parks/park_detail.asp?id=399

💡 *Daily 6a–11p*

It might not be a name you come across regularly, but turn the clock back a century and the Olmsted Brothers, significant contributors to American landscape architecture, were hot stuff, as was the news of where and when their next project would take place. The National Association for Olmsted Parks (*www.olmsted.org*) has a complete listing of the special plans laid by these talented siblings—a series of parks and parkways in Louisville, a Buffalo conservancy, and yes, Seattle's gorgeous Volunteer Park. This park contains a series of crown jewels: the historic water tower that becomes quite photogenic when the nearby stand of poplars puts on fall colors, the glass-enclosed flower conservancy, and the Seattle Asian Art Museum (*www.seattleartmuseum.org/visit/visitSAAM.asp*). If you aren't here for a picnic and play on the swings or a stroll around the flowing flora and fauna, stop into the SAAM to see the royal paintings of Jodhpur or a collection of Chinese art from Seattle's perspective. *SB*

Kiddlywinks
Take the kids!

There's a slew of kid-oriented things to do in Seattle for parents of all dispositions: big kid adventures, more pristine shopping sprees, dirty adventures, soft things, and new challenges like learning to swim. Have fun!

 Seattle Children's Theatre

 201 Thomas St
 443.0807
www.sct.org
 Schedules vary, call ahead

Both a school and a regular fixture of Seattle's younger generation of performers, Seattle Children's Theatre is an unpretentious but serious acting resource. Discover a new take on your favorite books (I like to read them before the performance to freshen my memory)—the theater has recently run *A Tale of Two Cities*, *The Wizard of Oz*, and *Goodnight Moon*. *SB*

Schmancy

 1832 2nd Ave
 728.8008
www.schmancytoys.com
Tues–Sun 11a–6p

The fine art of toys has brought back a wave of jealousy for childhood that's been otherwise difficult to muster. I look at Schmancy as a kingdom of the imagination, a colorful universe of characters created in the basements of the Pacific Northwest, on the tatami mats of Japan, and in the plastic molds of Los Angeles warehouses. I buy gifts here for my nephews to perch on their wooden block castles, but I secretly wish I could stash one under my pillow. Shell out $100 for handmade Plush You: SOWA; get Hot Cha Cha

Cha, a two-headed fawn, for half the moola; or pick up some über-cute handmade felt fortune cookies for just $8 with personalized five-word messages sewn in. *SB*

Bootyland

 1317 E Pine St
328.0636
www.bootylandkids.com
Mon–Wed 10:30a–6p, Thurs–Sat 10a–6:30p

Although it seems ridiculous to shell out bundles of dough for your ever-changing children's figures, you don't have to go broke dressing them nicely with the organic hemp and cotton dresses, shirts, and leggings from Bootyland. This Pike and Pine boutique offers an epic collection of kidswear—some recycled, some organic, all sewn by people paid a living wage. Decorate your children with beautiful and fairly priced duds from the cute shop with the red sign. *SB*

Science Art and More

 6417 Roosevelt Wy NE #104
524.3795
www.scienceartandmore.com
Daily 10a–6p

All right, I admit it, when I was growing up I was a science geek, a science dork—whatever you will call it. Telescopes, microscopes, bug wings, and fish eyes entranced me to the point where my mother was asking our local fish monger to save the eyes for my dissecting projects. It was the ability to magnify and see things differently that got me so excited. This palace of educational toys doesn't feel at all like a stuffy classroom. Rather, Science Art and More is a facility for parents, teachers, and lucky kids and their groovy families to find the most enticing gifts. Experimentation with crafts, chemistry, and even creek beds is encouraged! *SB*

Pop Tots

 6405 Roosevelt Wy NE
522.4322
www.poptots.net
 Mon–Sat 11a–6p, Sun 12p–4p

The Children's Museum

When my rocker friend settled down and got pregnant, I was overjoyed to find a Blondie onesie at Pop Tots for her future child. The selection of catchy clothing for kids at this shop is astounding—I didn't realize how many different shoe styles you could find for tiny feet! Organic materials and local designers are in the mix, and the handmade summer outfits for girls are especially adorable. SB

Family Days at Seattle Asian Art Museum

1400 E Prospect St
654.3100
www.seattleartmuseum.org
First Sat of every month, 10a–5p

On the first Saturday of each month, the Seattle Asian Art Museum flings open its doors to families for free. Come and enjoy all the spectacular permanent exhibitions plus featured shows and hands-on projects to further explore traditional arts and crafts. I remember practically growing up at museums when I was a little girl and making treasured keepsakes for my family from the craft kits on offer. SB

The Children's Museum

305 Harrison St
441.1768
www.thechildrensmuseum.org
Mon–Fri 10a–5p, Sat–Sun 10a–6p

I make myself laugh remembering a moment when my honey came home from work to find me curled up watching *Curious George*. I usually pull myself together and ready myself to greet him, but this clever little monkey had me entranced. You can imagine my not-so-age-appropriate glee to discover the exhibit at the Children's Museum featuring science and math installations explained by my favorite cartoon character. Curious George is more like me than I'd like to admit (or the other way around), but whatever the symptoms, this museum is the cure. I love watching children's faces light up as they discover a new truth or world lesson from the kid-friendly shows. There are lots of ways to get involved: summer camps, after-school programs, special performances, and rotating exhibits make this museum a keystone of youthful Seattle. *SB*

Learn

Courses, classes, and seminars of all sorts, and places to take on new challenges

Flexing your brain muscle is a great way to enhance a vacation or a prolonged visit to a new place. Classes are an entrance into the local scene, and you'll unavoidably meet locals. Staying young is a side effect. My grandmother was never bored—at the ripe old age of 82 she took Chinese classes, having no background in the language at all. She always inspired me to listen up and see what I could learn.

Fremont Music School

Fremont Abbey, 4272 Fremont Ave N
501.7415
www.fremontmusicschool.com

Housed in the repurposed Fremont Abbey Arts Center (see page 104), the Fremont Music School offers lessons in many different instruments on a one-on-one basis with a local musician. Schedule a couple of ukulele or guitar lessons in between your landmark hopping, and you'll have an even more authentic Seattle experience. After all, there are a few musicians around here . . . *SB*

911 Seattle Media Arts Center

402 9th Ave N

682.6552

www.911media.org

Mon–Fri 12–6p, and by appointment

Preaching to free the individual artistic voice in a pluralistic way, 911 Seattle Media Arts Center has put together a mishmash of artist-in-residence programs, classes, shows, and collaborative exposés. I'm always psyched when I see the word "diversity" in any mission statement (i.e., "911 Media Arts Center envisions a future where independent voices thrive in a society that fosters diversity, innovation and artistic excellence"), let alone one that hails from an art organization in the middle of mostly white Seattle. It turns out pluralism means more than color here—this community-savvy nonprofit is the keystone of its surrounding neighborhood, bringing creativity to life in whatever form for anyone willing to stop and stick their toes in. *SB*

Richard Hugo House Writing Workshops

1634 11th Ave

322.7030

www.hugohouse.org

Mon–Fri 12–9p, Zine Archive and Publishing Project (ZAPP) open by appointment

My fingers passed over the dusty old typewriters in the annals of one of the West Coast's largest zine archives: the Zine Archive and Publishing Project (ZAPP). I thumbed through a few zines and went straight back to the typewriters—something about Hugo House made me want to do some of my own writing. Lucky for me there's always a top-notch writer-in-residence at "the House." Previous resident Wendy Call, now working on a nonfiction title about globalization in small-town Mexico, imbued her devoted pupils with strength of voice and the technical skill required to beautifully break the rules. Another resident, favorite local poet David Wagoner, most recently author of *Good Morning and Good Night*, teaches here when he's not writing words worth reading over and over. The affordable classes (some are free) are held quarterly and range in topic from cartoon biography to summertime poetry. Local tip: Become a member, immediately if not sooner! (See pages 26 and 53 for more about this special place.) *SB*

Hammer Dulcimer Lessons and Harp Lessons

When I was in my heavy piano practice phase, every time the piano got tuned, I wanted to borrow the felted hammers and make a different sort of music. With private hammer dulcimer lessons I can finally gift myself with the chance. The delicate wooden hammers make an eerily beautiful chime and satisfy my past dream of deconstructing my upright. There are plenty of interesting musical experiences to be had.

The best of Seattle's folk-based music teachers post in the free *Victory Newsletter*, available at many cafes, bookstores, and music shops. Find expert harpist Leslie McMichael at *www.pluckmusic.com* and hammer dulcimer performer Rick Fogel at *www.geocities.com/whamdiddle* after picking up the latest *Victory* edition, and take your fingers for a new kind of spin. *SB*

Northwest Classics Society Classes

Classes often held at 4731 15th Ave NE
860.8784
www.northwestclassics.org

With classes held mostly around the University of Washington campus, the Northwest Classics Society is the backbone of Seattle's literary community, as it pays respect to the forefathers and -mothers of the written thought and the well-conceived word. Share your thoughts about the book of the month at the free book discussion groups, held in Seattle's University Christian Church on the last Monday of every month. Class topics depend on the time of year but some involve studying Latin, reading Homer, and chatting about Plato. E-mail or call ahead as the web site is never very up to date. *SB*

Alki Bathhouse Community Center

2701 Alki Ave SW
684.7430
Mon–Tues, Thurs 1–9p; Wed, Fri 10a–9p

Got $5 to $75 to spare for your creative health? I wish I had the entire summer to wander around the newly remodeled Alki Bathhouse, the most art-centric of Seattle's many active community centers. Enroll your kids in any manner of art camp, each just one week long so they can choose to take several. Fashion

Design for Youth, Urban Art and Reuse, and Pottery Wheel Classes are just a few of the course titles that caught my eye. Of course there are adult classes, too, including a fabulous drawing course so all those "I can't draw" people can prove themselves wrong. I've seen it happen—here you can learn to see with your hands, and you'll be drawing up a storm. *SB*

 The Center for Wooden Boats

 1010 Valley St
 382.2628
www.cwb.org
Daily 10a–6p

South Lake Union, or Tenass Chuck as it was called by the native people, has a certain affinity for wooden boats. Since there were people attempting to cross the shores, wooden crafts succeeded in making the trip. Today you can learn about the modern techniques involved in creating a wooden boat of your own or in restoring an existing ship in need of attention. Learn how to sail on one of the center's open sail days, and then begin conversing with members of this close-knit organization about how you can get involved and where to sign up for classes coming up at the South Lake Union shop. *SB*

Knitting Classes

What is the perfect Seattle craft? Let's think about this for a minute. The often cold and rainy weather induces a strong urge to sit by the fire and a desire to make warm clothing . . . that's it! Knitting! If you don't already know how to knit, you should consider it a survival skill for entry into this city for more than a monthlong period. Men, women, and children, gather around and let the wise knitters of the Emerald City guide you to your newfound passion, creating scarves and sweaters and giving them to your adoring friends and family. Queen Anne, Belltown, Madison Valley, Capitol Hill, and Wallingford all have established knitting communities, centered on their respective yarn holes. Try these great local and woman-owned knitting shops to learn to knit, or brush up your skills so you can churn out more stitches per minute.

Hilltop Yarn and Needlepoint Shop (Queen Anne)

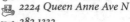

2224 Queen Anne Ave N

282.1332

www.hilltopyarn.com

Mon–Thurs 10a–9p, Fri–Sat 11a–6p, Sun 12–5p

Inside a Queen Anne–style house, this boutique knittery holds the finest fibers and the latest patterns and designs, from both local producers and European fashion houses. *SB*

So Much Yarn (Belltown)

2302 1st Ave

443.0727

www.somuchyarn.com

Mon, Thurs–Fri, Sat 10a–8p; Tues–Wed 11a–5p

The chattiest knitting shop in Seattle, So Much Yarn draws a congregation of corporate wives, newly successful condo owners, and new-to-the-city types working out the kinks in their chic new Belltown environment through the wonders of twisted yarn. Stitch and bitch sessions last until late, especially on nights when classes bring together a boisterous crew of young knitters. Lunchtime sessions on Fridays from noon to 2pm attract suited ladies back from the city's clutches for a lingering creative break. *SB*

Tricoter (Madison Valley)

3121 E Madison St

328.6505

www.tricoter.com

Mon–Wed 10a–5p, Thurs 10a–6p, Fri–Sat 10a–5p

Tricoter is a serious sweater place. Managing to pull away from the amazing button wall, I find myself enamored with the list of patterns, finishing services (for us procrast-a-knitters), and custom designs. This husband and wife enterprise is for knitters and nonknitters alike—all you have to be into to enjoy this spot is a perfectly cozy sweater. *SB*

Stitches (Capitol Hill)

711 E Pike St

709.0707

www.stitchesseattle.com

Daily 11a–7p

The funky selection of fun fabrics, odds and ends, and knitting gear at Stitches is better suited for a nightclubbing costume or a new Mardi Gras outfit than a subtle Seattleite's style, but I welcome the splash of color! Expect boutique prices, but if you don't have the energy to go to the jobbers and discounters on the outskirts of town, you'll be happy to pay a bit extra to have such a rainbow selection before you. *SB*

Bad Woman Yarn (Wallingford)

1815 N 45th St

547.5384

www.badwomanyarn.com

Mon–Fri 10a–8p, Sat 10a–6p, Sun 11a–5p

For a solid middle ground between the more upscale yarn shops and the bargain-basement chains, Bad Woman Yarn is worth the stop on this happening block of 45th. Choose from yarns from around the world, and though you'll be hard-pressed to find something dyed locally, the women behind the counter are far from their proclaimed title. *SB*

Get Inspired

Museums, installations, awe-inspiring exhibits, and anything that aims to enthuse

Seattle is at the core of the Pacific Northwest's art movement, and for generations performing and visual arts have made waves in this seaside city. With Seattle's multitude of top-notch art schools and art teachers and a general sense of high design, getting inspired is practically mandatory just by setting foot here. Film, sculpture, spoken word, and oil painting are alive and well, supported by an infrastructure of art galleries and centers. With open studios crisscrossing the city and a flurry of cutting-edge galleries opening all over town, there's no escaping this city's creative vibe.

Seattle Asian Art Museum

Seattle Asian Art Museum
1400 E Prospect St
654.3100
www.seattleartmuseum.org/visit/visitSAAM.asp
Wed & Fri–Sun 10a–5p, Thurs 10a–9p

One of the most exciting displays of Asian art, both old and new, can be found in the heart of Seattle's Volunteer Park. The Seattle Asian Art Museum is part of the SAM collection, which sponsors all forms of art around the city. A vast array of Chinese ceramics is one of the gems here, but recent acquisitions of Bada Shanren scrolls are also on display, showing off the shift from accurate depiction to emotional context in this art form during the change in reigning dynasties in the late 1600s. Find other prominent Asian artists from a wide range of periods, from Toshiko Takaezu (who worked in the 1950s) to Shen Liang (still painting to this day). There are also American- and Canadian-born Asian artists, and their art often lends an inspiring view of the global relationships. Expect well-curated exhibits full of nuance and symbolism. Come on the first Thursday of each month and you'll get in free, plus check ahead anytime for the schedule of free tours that offer a more in-depth explanation of the works on display. *sb*

Frye Art Museum

704 Terry Ave
622.9250
http://fryemuseum.org
Tues-Wed & Fri-Sat 10a-4:30p, Thu 10a-7:30p, Sun 12-4:30p

One look down the list of the pieces in the Frye Art Museum's permanent collection and any art enthusiast will be taken aback. Modern art is well represented (Fred Machetanz, Millard Sheets, Rosalyn Gale Powell), but so are oils from before 1900 (Gari Melchers, Winslow Homer, Fritz Baer). This special space is almost like a trip to Europe—the art is taken seriously, there is only a donation suggested for admission, and the stately building and perfect lighting give just the right shadow to the slick critics and grungy art students with sketchbooks in tow. *sb*

Neighborhood Art Walks

Seattle has an unbelievable enclave of serious artists who sit in their studios honing their craft, sheltered from the rain. If you want to get the absolute flavor of the Emerald City's art scene, you can take out your red pencil and mark your calendar for nearly every evening of the month. Here's a basic listing of the neighborhood and nearby city art walks—each has its own unique feel and all are worth attending at least once! *sb*

First Thursdays

Openings at Pioneer Square and Seattle Art Museum Area, 6-8p

First Fridays

Bainbridge Island Galleries, 5-8p
Anacortes Galleries, 6-8p, www.anacortesart.com
Belltown Art Walk, 6-8p, 443.6003
Fremont Art Walk, 6-9p, www.fremontseattle.com

First Saturdays

Gig Harbor Art Walk, 1-5p
Port Townsend Art Walk, 5:30-8:30p, 385.0078
Whidbey Island Galleries (Langley), open until 8p

Second Tuesdays
Capitol Hill Art Walk, 6–9p

Second Thursdays
Kirkland Art Walk, 6–8p
West Seattle Art Walk, 6–9p, www.westseattleartwalk.blogspot.com

Second Saturdays:
Ballard Art Walk, 6–9p, 789.1490
Georgetown Art Attack, 6–9p, www.georgetownartattack.com
Kingston Art Walk, 6–8p

Third Thursdays
Edmonds Art Walk, 5–8p, e-mail for more info: scansons66@yahoo.com
Upper Queen Anne Art Walk, 6–8p, e-mail for more info: info@bouncingwall.com
Tacoma Art Walk, 5–8p, 253.272.4258

Third Saturdays
Everett Art Walk, 4–7p, www.everettartwalk.org
LaConner Art Walk, 4–8p

Last Thursdays
Microsoft Art Collection Tours (free, reserve in advance), e-mail for more info: artevent@microsoft.com

Fremont Abbey Arts Center
4272 Fremont Ave N
701.9270
www.fremontabbey.org

The brainchild of local arts leader and band manager Nathan Marion, Fremont Abbey Arts Center is the ideal place to stumble upon a show. Walk the pretty uphill blocks from the Fremont "Center of the Universe," and you'll find this brick church turned community outpost. Theater, music, and spoken word performances round out a regular calendar, interspersed with ongoing activities like music and dance lessons. If you're around for the monthly The Round showcase, you'll be privy to one of Seattle's best underground gigs—a smattering of live painting, choice music, and powerful poetry as simultaneous artistic expression. *SB*

Seattle Art Museum

1300 1st Ave

654.3180

www.seattleartmuseum.org

Tues–Sun 10a–5p, Thurs–Fri 10a–9p

Admission $9–15, free first Thurs of the month

My first introduction to the Seattle Art Museum (SAM) was when I dined across the street and my eyes were glued throughout the meal to the huge glass atrium in my view, wondering just what was hanging from the ceiling of the museum's entrance. After a tasty meal, my friends and I discovered several white 1990s-era Ford Tauruses strung up in the space, each gleaming with neon light rays. If I hadn't already been looking forward to an afternoon checking out the rest of the collections, I was now. The galleries are airy, well lit, and not overcrowded with too much art on each wall. I loved making my way up to the very top floor on the escalators to the back entrance of the African collections—always alive with sound to complement the quiet objects. Watching the traditional dances play out or hearing timeless songs sung to the beat of the drum gives more meaning and insight to each treasure. Clothes and headdresses from Burkina Faso, Cameroon, and the Ivory Coast gave me dreams of being a West African princess wearing one of those colorful feather crowns myself. The first and second Thursdays of the month the museum stays open late for free music and entrance into the galleries, and the first Friday from 6 to 9pm there are special drinks at SAM's restaurant TASTE to go along with the beats of a guest DJ. *SB*

 Western Bridge

 3412 4th Ave S

838.7444

www.westernbridge.org

Hours vary, call ahead

The Trues, the couple who founded and continue to run the large warehouse making up Western Bridge, say that the name refers to the bridge between privately collecting art and sharing it with the community. Their huge modern collection regularly cycles on these walls and includes fabulous light displays by Olafur Eliasson and more great color, light, and space play from Tania Kitchell, Roni Horn, Tauba Auerbach, and Ed Ruscha. Explore this mini-museum in awe of the force Seattle has for hosting discerning collectors. *SB*

Henry Art Gallery

4100 15th Ave N
543.2280
www.henryart.org
Thurs–Fri 11a–9p, Sat–Sun 11a–4p
Admission $6–10, free for under 13, students with ID, and first Thurs of the month

A high-energy art space run by students of the University of Washington, Henry Art Gallery is never boring. Discover exhibits thoroughly exploring the basics of a given art technique, like fixing an image in photography or the process of making an etching. Shows are often composed of artists in residence at the university. One walk around the permanent installations in the sculpture court and the visual wonders in the East and North Gallery wings and I was sure there were a few soon-to-be famous artists showing here. The James Turrell Skyspace, *Light Reign* (a permanent structure), will blow your mind. *SB*

Some Space Gallery

625 1st Ave
425.766.7810
www.somespacegallery.com
Hours vary, call ahead

Founded by two artists and framers, Some Space Gallery is a low-key addition to the ever-growing ring of galleries popping up around Pioneer Square. Most feel corporate, but not this place. Rather, it features lesser-known printmakers, line artists, photographers, and painters who form the pretty collage of exhibitions shown here. From a group show from artists living in Western Washington to the prints of Michael Azzano and Nate Stottrup, there is always something here to catch my eye. *SB*

Seattle Architecture Foundation Architecture Walking Tour

1333 5th Ave, Ste 300
667.9184
www.seattlearchitecture.org
Mon–Fri 9a–5p, Sat 9a–1p on tour dates (check online calendar)

If you are sensitive to your environment, or especially observant, you'll notice after walking a few blocks around downtown Seattle that very few buildings date back before 1900, and those that are nearing a century old are scattered in one particular area, Pioneer Square. If you knew that there was a raging fire in the late 1880s, or that Portland, to the south, was a bustling port before Seattle had even been dreamed up, you'd understand why this is. Learn much, much more from the learned docents at Seattle Architecture Foundation (SAF), one of the most organized and active city structure groups I've seen on the West Coast. Green building tours at SAF are the best way to learn all the ways Seattle is moving toward sustainability. Or opt for Designed for Dining, the three-hour tour that goes behind the scenes of the structures holding the best Seattle kitchens. *SB*

Ambach and Rice

5107 Ballard Ave NW
789.6242
www.ambachandrice.com
Tues–Sat 12–6p, Sun 11a–5p

The floors are just too shiny at Ambach and Rice (which used to be known as OK OK Gallery) for me to ignore the corporate feel of this expressive gallery, but chances are taken on these walls. Maybe not cliffhanger material, but chances are taken nonetheless. A swinging show of dark oil paintings echoing Godzilla taking over a large film-noir cityscape bedecked the walls recently—another well-attended opening for a place that prides itself on discovering great new talents and bringing them to the art market. *SB*

Kubota Garden

9817 55th Ave S
684.4584
www.kubota.org
Daily during daylight hours

The city runs and maintains Kubota Garden, a jaw-dropping perch of a park sprinkled with prized weeping cedars and rare cypresses. This well-maintained landscape overlooks the Cascades when the prickly fronds of Norway spruce part and you peek over a stone garden and a spring-fed pond to catch the view. Come at any time of the day to get inspired by the serenity exuded by this miniaturized landscape, a beautiful emblem of Seattle's cultural and natural history. *SB*

Greg Kucera Gallery

212 3rd Ave S
624.0770
www.gregkucera.com
Tues–Sat 10:30a–5:30p

Yes, it's big and fancy. Local art geeks won't be impressed that I'm including it in this guide. Greg Kucera Gallery plans its shows nearly two years in advance. This gallery isn't the hipster underbelly of the Seattle art scene, and it doesn't pretend to be. It is a great, open space where large, museum-quality pieces are up close and personal. Flip through any of the big catalogs and magazines on an art school campus—you know, the thoroughly flipped-through ones discarded out the back door of the pottery studio near the kiln—and that's where you'll find articles and photos of the artists on display at Greg Kucera. A few months ago I even saw a Gee's Bend Quilters Collective show here, a mini-version of the complete town quilt exhibit I saw at the de Young Museum in San Francisco last fall. Never pay an admission fee and see all the large-scale paintings from modern masters at this luxury gallery. I've never been turned away for gawking. *SB*

Warren G. Magnuson Park

7400 Sand Point Wy NE
684.4946
www.seattle.gov/parks/magnuson/art.htm
Daily 4a–11:30p

Dotting the edges of massive Warren G. Magnuson Park is a fine, if somewhat gimmicky, collection of public art installations. They are especially picturesque overlooking, as they do, the rolling orbs of watery currents making up the Puget Sound. *The Fin Project*, which resembles the dorsal fins of a passing pod of whales and is made of repurposed submarine wings, had much more impact after I picked up on the naval theme and linked it with the history of the parkland. This choice piece of waterfront property used to be a U.S. naval base, and the sculptures here comment on that. There's *Straight Shot*, which allows viewers to peer through holes bored in accurately placed columns as if we were ourselves Navy surveyors working at the old air station. Waltzing along the paths at this gorgeous park wouldn't be the same without understanding the historical context and visualizing the artists' interpretations of a city's answer to misused land. *SB*

Wing Luke Asian Museum

719 S King St

623.5124

www.wingluke.org

Tues–Sun 10a–5p, free first Thurs and third Sat of each month, regular hours
Admission: $5–8

The vastness of the Asian experience and its influence on humanity—from inspiring spring rolls in California to recalling the balance in nature between yin and yang—has evolved the ever-changing fabric on world cultures. The brand-new Wing Luke Asian Museum is home to these converging paths, displaying a major Hawaiian artifact collection one month and bringing it home with a portrayal of Asian American veterans of the Korean War. I am reminded first of all of the culinary contributions of the great Asian continent when I see the ornate, time-honored arts and crafts assembled under this roof. Maybe that's just how my brain is wired, but when you consider such an expansive ethos of beauty and honed skills, it is easy to notice them being transferred from one art to another. Permanent exhibitions detailing the International District community and the journey of Asian immigrants to Seattle and the Pacific Northwest are as informative as they are inspiring. *SB*

Act Out

Seattle has a bustling theater scene, with rotating performances happening all the time. Here are a few theaters to check out if you want to catch a show when you're in town:

Washington Ensemble Theater

608 19th Ave E

325.5105

www.washingtonensemble.org

Intiman Theatre

201 Mercer St

269.1900

www.intiman.org

A Contemporary Theatre (ACT)
700 Union St
292.7676
www.acttheatre.org

Seattle Repertory Theatre
155 Mercer St
443.2210
www.seattlerep.org

Theatre Off Jackson
409 7th Ave S
340.1049
www.theatreoffjackson.org

Create

From beads to seeds, fabric to photos, these spots will surely enable your creative side

I switched colleges my sophomore year to go to art school. I wanted to draw and paint and take photos all day instead of calculating chemical equations and studying political systems. Later, I changed my mind and went back to university, but what I learned from the experience was something that hadn't crossed my mind before: everyone can create beauty, everyone can be an artist. I saw people who had never taken their pencils out of the lines on a steno pad draw impeccable contour figures after just a few months of focused study. Their eyes and their hands had become one unit. With a little drive anyone can contribute to the beauty in the world. I also feel that it is important to maintain a connection with handwork. If you haven't ever tried something like this yourself, the satisfaction of eating something you've cooked or better yet grown and cooked, or wearing a dress you've made or a scarf you've knitted is hard to top. Your hands are the greatest machines.

Pacific Fabrics and Crafts Outlet

2230 4th Ave S

628.6237

www.pacificfabrics.com

Mon–Fri 9a–8p

The biggest and best array of fabrics and all related doohickeys also happens to stock a serious collection of organic cotton, bamboo, and soy cloth. Born From Nature 100 percent organic cotton fleece is the softest way to make a sustainable blankie, and in Seattle you'll need one even if you aren't a kid anymore. On my last visit, I got a few yards of the white sherpa, dyed it teal, and made the plushest edging for my new quilt. Skip regular corduroy for the bamboo version on the rolls here—the cucumber green and grape jelly are summery shades that will give anyone who sews new inspiration. *SB*

Seattle Restaurant Store

14910 Aurora Ave N (Shoreline)

362.4900

www.seattlerestaurantstore.com

Mon–Sat 9a–6p, Sun 10a–4p (closed on Sun June–Aug)

Ever wonder how all those tasty restaurant meals are made? What fancy gadgets Seattle's kitchens are fitted with and where they come from? Get ready for the kid-in-a-candy-store feeling if you are an aspiring chef or a kitchen diva—the Seattle Restaurant Store is a paradise of professional equipment for any and all cooking processes, including super fryers, open-burner stoves, convection ovens, and broilers. Taking a stroll around the showroom here is like going behind the scenes of the restaurant business. Even if you don't have a kitchen to stock, you can be sure you'll want to cook something after seeing this stuff. *SB*

Light in the Attic Records

Send demos: P.O. Box 31970, Seattle, WA 98103

www.lightintheattic.net

This local indie record label records and distributes such artists as The Blakes, Jamaica to Toronto, Noel Ellis, and The Saturday Knights. Light in the Attic's first release, a Free Design record, set the stage for the great tunes that followed. Check out the recordings for yourself and get inspired to record your own album—after all, Seattle is one of the best places to do it. *SB*

The Fiber Gallery

7000 Greenwood Ave N
706.4197
www.fibergallery.com
Mon, Wed, Fri 11a–6p; Tues 11a–9p; Sat–Sun 11a–5p

Earth-Friendly Yarns are the main event at Phinney Ridge's Fiber Gallery. Organic, recycled, vegan, and fair trade aren't just terms for food or clothing—they are also applied to the bright rainbow of threads at this crafty corner store. Join the My First Socks workshop, which includes instruction, camaraderie, and all the supplies needed for weekly two-hour sessions. *SB*

Acorn Street Shop

2818 NE 55th St
525.1726
www.acornstreet.com
Hours vary, call ahead

The grandmother of crafting stores in Seattle, Acorn Street Shop has the warm and fuzzy atmosphere you'd expect from a place with so many wise women inside. You can get your fill of stitching and knitting how-tos, but the real draws for me are the hand-spinning classes and equipment. Nowhere else in the Emerald City can you find such tools for sustainable living. I offer to help during a shearing once in a while, and in exchange I get to take home some bags of wool. Then the carding tools I got from Acorn Street come out and I am one step closer to wearing this fuzzy stuff! *SB*

Georgetown Tile Works

5905 Airport Wy S
767.0331
www.georgetowntileworks.com
Mon 9a–5p, Wed–Fri 12–6p

The best time to see this creative corner of Seattle is the second Saturday of each month, when Georgetown Art Attack is centered around the tile works. Workshop space is designed for anyone looking to make more of clay than a brown ball, and the finished tiles and sculptures are on display in the colorful gallery. Whether you have an idea to re-create Monet's blue-tiled kitchen in your own home or you've never worked with clay and have a hankering for something new, this is your one stop for muddy inspiration. *SB*

Dakota Art Store

6110 Roosevelt Wy NE

523.4830

www.dakotaartstore.com

Mon–Sat 9a–6p, Sun 12–5p

Western Washington's local chain of art supply stores is every bit as serious as my favorite art store in the whole wide world: Pearl in SoHo. No, it isn't the same, but when the helpful employees are artists themselves, who know what it is like to slave away over a canvas for days on end or get cuts messing with decorative papers and not even notice, it is that much closer to artistic perfection. At the Seattle store, and at Dakota's two other locations in Washington, you'll find the highest-quality supplies for those serious about the pursuit of beauty. *SB*

Monkey Love Rubber Stamps

613 Queen Anne Ave N

283.7897

www.monkeyloverubberstamps.com

Tues–Fri 11a–7p, Sat–Sun 12–5p

On any given Saturday at the tables of die-cut papers and shiny glitter, you'll find a gaggle of crafty ladies hovering over their ATCs, or artist trading cards. Come around noon on Saturday to create and swap your creative postcard-sized keepsakes. If you're not there for the ATC swap, you'll still be impressed—an entire wall of rubber stamps has something for everyone. *SB*

Moxie Papergoods and Gifts

3619 California Ave SW

932.2800

www.moxiepapergoods.com

Tues–Fri 10a–7p, Sat–Sun 10a–5p

My mother is crazy about thank-you notes. Since I learned how to write, it was a mandatory task to write a note of gratitude after every occasion, which I soon began to love. Now I make cards for friends and family, every so often gathering up luxe supplies to step up my card style. Moxie is just the place for this: the photo cards, ready to receive an inserted picture, are framed with cool patterns. Textured paper and silkscreen-printed cards and envelopes give me even more reasons to stay in touch via snail mail. Whether it is the letterpress invites or the mod look of the entrance that entices, no letter will be left unsent after a perusal through these papers. *SB*

♲ Paper Delights
2205 N 45th St
547.1002
www.paperdelights.com
Mon–Sat 10a–6p, Sun 11a–5p

The local paperie for pretty party planners in and around Wallingford is Paper Delights, where there are unending ways to send out an invitation. Work with the mother and daughter team to design a note that is just right for your occasion, or stroll around the periphery to pick a premade card with a touch of elegance and whimsy. Treats from Fran's Chocolates (see page 195) are on hand to make a sweet gesture with your stationery. *SB*

Beads in Seattle

Seattle isn't all rain and clouds, but the gracious helping of brisk weather does make for a city of crafty people. Crafty in the best way, of course. Staying inside by the fire, drinking a mug of hot chocolate from Theo Chocolate (see page 194), and beading is a hobby of many handy locals. There are tons of bead stores checkered across town; the following are a few favorites.

✎ Alexander's Bead Bazaar
6307 Roosevelt Wy NE
526.8909
www.alexandersbeads.com
Tues–Sat 11a–6p, Sun 12–5p

Admittedly a bit pricier than the average bead emporium, Alexander's Bead Bazaar is known as the best place for unique treasures, like the African seed beads (not tiny beads, but beads made from colorful seeds) and the Thai silver charms I came away with. No better spot to find the centerpiece for your next necklace. *SB*

☼ Beadworld

9520 Roosevelt Wy

523.0530

www.beadworldnw.com

Daily 11a–6p

Although Beadworld, opened by one of Seattle's craftiest divas, may sound generic, it is anything but. The walls of strands and bowls with treasured charms and trinkets aren't as overwhelming as those at the bigger shops around Seattle, but they have been carefully chosen so there is a higher concentration of irresistible finds. I go crazy over the freshwater pearl collection, which is surprisingly reasonable, and the faceted stones and crystals that make each creation sparkle. *SB*

☼ Fusion Beads

3830 Stone Wy N

782.4595

www.fusionbeads.com

Mon, Wed–Thurs 10a–6p; Tues 10a–7p; Fri–Sat 10a–6p

Fusion Beads is the monster truck of beading, if there is such a thing. An enormous array of all things beading is spread throughout the warehouselike structure. The store's huge online business guarantees lower prices and more selection than any other place in the area (except Shipwreck Beads down in Lacey). *SB*

Roadtrip Recommendation

☼ Shipwreck Beads

8560 Commerce Place Dr NE (Lacey)

360.754.2323

www.shipwreckbeads.com

Daily 9a–6p

Touted as the biggest bead store in the world, this industrial-size space has more aisles than a membership bulk mart. To get to Shipwreck Beads, you will wind through several unlikely business parks, but rest assured, you are going in the right direction. Right when you are about to turn around, thinking you'll never find the place, you'll see a sign, small though it may be, pointing you to the right complex and onto the bead-encrusted sidewalk that will lead you inside. Once you're there, you'll want to grab a rolling cart and peruse the rows of glass, semiprecious beads, and findings. The charm aisle is the pièce de résistance of the store—I spend an hour there and give the entire rest of the store about the same amount of time. Think of any action, talent, hobby, or shape, and you can find a metallic charm of it here. On my last trip, I got a campfire, a hot dog, and an antique sewing machine, all shiny and about the size of my fingernail. The marvel of this epic store is the complete experience. Take a trip to the beading room, complete with TV, remote control, and tables for dozens of bead-happy crafters, and when hunger calls order a Creamsicle milkshake from the better-than-expected restaurant located inside the store. No bead store tops this one. You can purchase discount beads in massive quantities and have a cup of Yukon Chicken soup, made from scratch, all in the same location. This is a great reason to take a trip down the road to Washington's capitol city. *SB*

Buy Me

A unique take on shopping, from artichokes to zippers

Andy Warhol really was on to something when he equated department stores with museums. Indeed, the way to appeal to shoppers is an artful task and well represents our most modern take on design and cultural signing. So whether you have a practical purpose, need a little retail therapy, or just want to gaze at the most up-to-date of museums, these spots should fulfill your aims while also making ripples of positivity across the community by supporting these conscientious enterprises.

I Heart Rummage

Chop Suey, 1325 E Madison
www.iheartrummage.net
First Sun of every other month

The urban crafting rage is nowhere more on fire than in Seattle, and I Heart Rummage is the evidence. The group of ever-changing handcrafters gathers to peddle their wares every other month—and everyone in attendance benefits. Here you'll find cool jewelry, some of which is made from recycled vintage glam necklaces. I picked up a hand-sewn wallet with a map of Philadelphia over the flap, a plastic-coated notebook, three handmade soaps, and a teal glazed soap dish I gave to my mother on Mother's Day (she loved it). *SB*

Jive Time Records

3506 Fremont Ave N

632.5483

www.jivetimerecords.com

Mon–Sat 11a–9p, Sun 11a–7p

Fremont's bright little record shop is a bargain basement for rock 'n' rollers like me. I'm not necessarily looking for the newest band to come out on vinyl, but rather the good oldies to add to my collection, which was started by my parents back in the day. I need to fill out my Moody Blues, Cream, and Otis Redding sections, and that's no problem at Jive Time Records, where I've found all that and more in the $1 bins just outside the shop alone. Once inside, the sought-after Prince album my friend was searching for is quickly unearthed with the help of the friendly owner. *SB*

Raw Threads

5140 Ballard Ave NW, Ste A

782.5112

www.audrise.com

Tues 11a–6p, Wed–Thurs 11a–7:30p, Fri–Sat 11a–8p, Sun 12–5p

With all that ideal indoor crafting weather, it's no wonder Seattle fosters some of the most original fashion, music, and art talents on the West Coast. Raw Threads is a conglomerate of the best indie designers and local handworkers. Cute dresses, fitted tops, funky accessories, and stuff that will make you feel like a proper Pacific Northwest fashion diva abide between these walls. *SB*

REI—Seattle Flagship

222 Yale Ave N

223.1944

www.rei.com

Mon–Sat 9a–9p, Sun 10a–7p

Seattle's epicenter for outdoor gear is REI's flagship store, which opened back in the 1940s. Since then, there have been plenty of upgrades from the clunky hiking boots, static ropes, wooden skis, and oilcloth raincoats. Inside this updated store is a 65-foot climbing wall, free to test out, and even a mountain bike test trail. Classes teaching a plethora of skills and sports plus local hiking excursions originate here, bringing the beautiful Seattle outdoors just a little bit closer. I'm stuck in the paddling section, trying to find a new skirt for my kayak, but I end up with a few discounted watertight sacks as well. A handful of tourists vie for a spot on the climbing wall, but serious gearheads from Washington and Oregon also flock here to talk shop with the knowledgeable staff. *SB*

Show Pony

 702 N 35th St
706.4188
www.loveshowpony.com
Mon–Fri 11a–6p, Sat 11a–7p, Sun 11a–5p

Polaroid photo boxes, hooded scarves from local company Coal, metal cutout doggie bowls, and gorgeous vintage jewelry are the objects of my desire at Show Pony, a new woman-owned boutique and gift shop and an asset to Fremont's shopping scene. The store hosts regular trunk shows with local clothing designers and fun finds from the likes of Jack and Marjorie, Prairie Underground, and Charm School. *SB*

Uwajimaya

600 5th Ave S
624.6248
www.uwajimaya.com
Mon–Sat 8a–10p, Sun 9a–9p

Seattle Chinatown's all-in-one, Uwajimaya Seattle (there are Bellevue and Beaverton locations as well) contains everything from stationery to frozen yogurt—and I am not using the word "everything" lightly. Samurai Noodle, Saigon Bistro, Noodle Zen, and Thai Palace round out the food selections—some traditional street food, some Americanized noodle dishes. Cruise around the endless rows of books and pens while you digest, and finish off with green tea frozen yogurt at Utopia. Oh, yes, this is one place where you are likely to come away with a new gem for your fridge, whether it is strawberry shortcake–shaped magnets or a postcard of Mona Lisa with braces. *SB*

Archie McPhee

1300 N 45th St
297.0240
www.archiemcpheeseattle.com
Mon–Sat 10a–7p, Sun 11a–6p

Recently I have been celebrating bits and pieces of Christmas. One of my new traditions is sending an inflatable fruitcake from Archie McPhee to someone who needs the kind of giggle only a good gag gift can give. There's the "I Heart Big Apple" T-shirt in New York City, the Ghirardelli or Recchiuti chocolate bar in San Francisco, and the action figures from Archie McPhee in Seattle. My favorite is the librarian figurine based on Nancy Pearl, Seattle's favorite book lady. I have friends who are suckers for Beethoven, Jesus, or Jane Austen, and my honey has an Einstein figurine by his alarm clock. The store is a riot; it is a place where laughs are inevitable and stupidity is allowed. Have fun with a Seattle sense of humor. *SB*

Goods for the Planet

525 Dexter Ave N
652.2327
www.goodsfortheplanet.com
Mon–Fri 10a–8p, Sat 10a–7p, Sun 10a–6p

A bona fide menagerie of cool repurposed gifty things backed up by a respectable collection of green supplies for the home, Goods for the Planet is as popular with conscientious neighbors as it is with Saturday shoppers. Toys and clothing are far from the "burlap bag" trend many mistake for green fashion—they are as chic as can be. The prices aren't bargain basement, but that does ensure that each object comes from a place where the planet was taken into consideration and the workers were paid a living wage. You can bring batteries and old cell phones to the store for recycling, too! *SB*

Kobo

814 E Roy St
726.0704
www.koboseattle.com
Mon–Sat 11a–6p

The Japanese artist aesthetic has caught on in a major way around the Pacific Northwest. Nowhere is this trend more evident than between the tall walls of

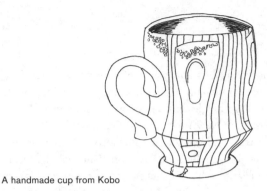

A handmade cup from Kobo

Kobo, my favorite place to go and gawk for an afternoon. This gallery space mixes together works from Japanese design houses and local talents, and folk creations from the United States and Japan. I can't help desiring the Enfu pop-art wall hangings and the fantastic repurposed wood creations by Helga Winter, who has found a magical way of turning green madrona wood into flawless bowls and beautiful objects. There are never two identical adventures to Kobo, and although prices are steep for many of the items, you can be sure that the artists get paid well for their work. Kobo stocks some fun, less expensive art objects, too, so those needing to go easy on their wallet can still bring some of this fabulous Seattle icon home. *SB*

ⓒⓞ **Tall Grass Bakery**

Ⓥ *5907 24th Ave NW*

☎ *706.0991*

Daily 9a–7p

My favorite loaf in Seattle comes from this little bakery in Ballard. Hominy bread, made with crunchy white corn grits, is staring me down, willing me to take it home. The surprisingly dark Avery's Pumpernickel and comforting Whole Wheat and Honey are other top choices, unless you make it in early on a Thursday when the 100 percent spelt loaves are sold right from the oven. Spellbinding Coconut-Almond Granola and many other Tall Grass Bakery breads can be found around town at food shops and farmers markets, but it's a treat to go to the source of these almost completely vegan delights. At least to wink at the bakers. *SB*

Not a Number Cards and Gifts
1905 N 45th St
784.0965
http://notanumbergifts.com
Mon–Thurs 11a–7p, Fri–Sat 11a–8p, Sun 11a–6p

I try hard to keep my desk free from clutter. When it's in its ideal state, there are few objects remaining on its shiny wooden surface: a wooden pencil holder, my desktop computer and compact speakers, and my black poodle wind-up toy from Not a Number Cards and Gifts. At this unique shop, I've also found some perfect cards for sticky situations, a button of the Dalai Lama for my father, and a postcard of a "fruits" girl from Tokyo for my girlfriend Becca. There are lots of giggles awaiting you through these doors—hysterical gifts, notes, and point-less-yet-oh-so-necessary kitsch like my beloved poodle toy. *SB*

Dusty Strings
3406 Fremont Ave N
634.1662
www.dustystrings.com
Mon–Sat 10a–6p, Sun 12–5p

Without even facing the storefronts on Fremont Avenue, you can tell there is a music store of some sort on this block just by watching bus riders disem-bark. There are always a slew of passengers wearing "Hey, dude, where's my mandolin?" T-shirts or carrying guitar cases over their left shoulders. Dusty Strings contains anything but—it's a lively music shop known for great repair work and good buys on quality used instruments. Discover more about local music lessons, newly forming bands, or a nearby ukulele meet-up after you're done getting a shiny new set of strings. *SB*

Blackbird
5410 22nd Ave NW
547.2524
http://helloblackbird.blogspot.com
Mon–Fri 9a–8p, Sat 9a–9p, Sun 9a–7p

This all-in-one men's store was designed for real guy-guys who also want to look nicely stylish. Find classic men's clothing, get your hair trimmed in the store, or find a fancy raincoat so you can still pull off your sultry-cool look in the wet weather. Even girls can get into the boutique atmosphere at Blackbird—at least I'm never wanting for interesting things to look at while my honey is getting a new 'do. *SB*

Pets and Poodles in Seattle

Despite the city's near-perpetual wetness, there are just as many die-hard dog owners in Seattle as in Los Angeles. Of course, here Ballard bulldogs get dressed up in appropriate polar fleece dog jackets instead of rhinestone-studded collars, and fox terriers from Fremont don't approve of their owners painting their nails, but you can still style your pooch in this outdoorsy city. I applaud these pet parents for putting up with the mud and muck caused by regular rainfall, and just the same I understand that life without a dog is no life at all. Here are some great spots around town to wash, feed, brush, and treat your best friend:

Bark Natural Pet Care, 5338 Ballard Ave NW, 633.2275

The Feed Bag Pet Provisions, 516 Pike St, 322.5413

Great Dog, 11333 Roosevelt Wy NE, 526.1101

MudBay, 815 E Thomas St (and other Seattle locations), 322.6177

Railey's Leash and Treat, 513 N 36th St, 632.5200

Three Dog Bakery, 1418 1st Ave, 364.9999

Urban Beast, 217 Yale Ave N, 324.4400

 La Tienda Folk Art Gallery

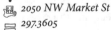

2050 NW Market St

297.3605

www.latienda-folkart.com

Mon–Fri 10:30a–6p, Sat 10a–6p, Sun 12–4:30p

Finding unique gifts from reliably fair-trade sources is easy at La Tienda Folk Art Gallery. I'm inspired by the handiwork of traditional cultures and hopeful that I can support it in some way by purchasing jewelry, ornaments, and more from this stocked store. *SB*

Violette

212 1st Ave S

652.8991

www.violetteboutique.blogspot.com

Mon–Fri 10a–5p, Sat 11a–5p, Sun 12–4p

Rico and Oliver, the owner's two black standard poodles, greeted me on my first visit to Violette, a cuddly micro-enterprise with dresses made to ring in the spring and cashmere sweaters to protect against the winter chill. Flowing lavender skirts and pretty tops fill the space, each made by hand from recycled leather and cloth. I wanted to take home all the dresses and plan tea parties to wear them to—hopefully the poodles could come, too! I left with a new gray hat to cover up my cold ears and an idea to come back and have Beth create something unique for me from one of her many Eko Chic ideas she's hatched in the back of the store. *SB*

Les Amis

3420 Evanston Ave N

632.2877

www.lesamis-inc.com

Mon–Wed 11a–6p, Thurs–Sat 11a–7p, Sun 11a–5p

Hot stuff. Shiny red shoes, sharp A-line skirt, romantic ruffled blouse. Walk outside, pass the Fremont rocket ship, and then go past the market, the gym, the art gallery. Take the bus downtown. Pretend I'm in Paris. Have a coffee at Belle Epicurean with a copy of *W* to thumb through. Walk out, magazine under my arm. Stroll by the water. Thanks, Les Amis, for the outfit, the feeling, the entire afternoon. Shiny red shoes. Hot stuff. *SB*

Velouria

2205 NW Market St

788.0330

http://shopvelouria.tripod.com

Mon–Wed 11a–6p, Thurs–Sat 11a–8p, Sun 12p–6p

Handcrafted clothing by independent designers is the name of the game at Ballard's Velouria. Don't be deceived by the name—this cool clothing shop is not stuck in a 1970s flashback zone. The peach-colored store has hoodies, sweaters, hats, gloves, jackets, scarves, and T-shirts—a whole wardrobe of handmade clothing. A couple of times a month Velouria hosts community activities like after-hours trunk shows or fashion shows. I am most enamored of the carefully sewn ties, the dresses by Holly Stalder, and the jewelry by Amy Tavern. *SB*

Truly Organic

4112 NE 103rd Pl
930.6713
www.truly-organic.com

This online retailer of simple, basic cotton clothing follows the conscientious business model by ensuring all its operations are sustainably maintained. Organic cotton fibers are fairly traded, dyes are handmade, and workers at all stages of the process are paid a living wage. Find Truly Organic's line of fine garments online, even though the business is based in Seattle. *SB*

Community Charge Cards

www.pugetsound.cc

Smart, smart Seattle. I love the shop-local ideas that keep pouring out of this city as if the floodgates just opened and all the community businesses spoke up. Puget Sound Community Change is the group that integrates citizens and merchants on a deeper level. Sure, you can go and support your independent businesses, but in Seattle you can do so with the ease, reliability, and savings that the big chain stores try to enchant you with. Start by enrolling for a free community card online, and then bring it with you and have the cashier swipe the card at any participating business. Some 120 merchants are involved at the time of this writing, and the list keeps growing, but if you're not sure, just ask. Then you can decide whether to keep your savings (a small percentage of your total purchase) or give it away to the community-based nonprofit or school of your choice. New, specially designed cards are available for donating all your rewards to PCC Farmland Trust, Co-op America, or ArtsFund (see page 229). Happy local shopping! *SB*

Pike Place Market

Pike Place Market

The best of Seattle's famous marketplace

When people the world over think of Seattle, I'd be willing to wager that the throwing of the fish in Pike Place Market comes to mind as a close second to the Space Needle. Full of color and absolutely packed on summer weekends, this historic market was originally created to sell onions, of all things. But these weren't your average white onions from the grocery store—Washington's Walla Walla onions were expertly farmed by skillful Asian Americans who owned and worked the market. Unfortunately, the market has no Asian or Asian American–owned businesses currently. Nonetheless, it is a regular stop for some local home chefs who are careful to watch how everything is priced and weighed out. There are as many ways to experience this American landmark as there are stalls and crafts-people in it, so dive in with a healthy flexibility and go with the flow when navigating the narrow hallways. There was never a livelier place in such a picturesque location. (For complete business listings and historical information, visit www.pikeplacemarket.org.)

The Pink Door

1919 Post Alley

443.3241

www.thepinkdoor.net

Mon–Thurs 11:30a–10p, Fri–Sat 11:30a–11p, Sun 4–11p

The minute the clouds peel away from the mountains, I am heading toward the deck at The Pink Door. Having been meaning to go ever since I heard about Julia's magical birthday experience there, Nathan, Perrin, and I happened to find this Pike Place porch by chance on a late-night restaurant search party. We came through the tiny faded pink door off the alley, went straight for the porch, and gathered around a plate of green salad—and not just any green salad. This one had everything green and simultaneously everything interesting I'd often wished was on my salad: twice-cooked and shelled fava beans, crisp haricots verts, delicate mâche sprouts, and more. The traditional Italian soup collection was hard to resist, and even though we were barely bothered by the breeze, it was still nice to have soup steaming up our faces as part of the atmosphere. During the later hours the porch has fewer guests; during cabaret performances you'd better have reservations. If you are low on funds, just savor a Fernet Branca on the rocks and look out, like I have done, over the Olympics from a perch right above Seattle's tastiest icon. *SB*

Savor Seattle Food Tours

888.987.2867

www.savorseattletours.com

$$

Gather at the elevated area in Seattle's Best Coffee for a chance to have Angela in your ear—literally. This food diva, the daughter of a restaurant owner and the niece of a chef, has designed a great tour of Pike Place Market, from which you are sure to come away with new knowledge and secrets of the market, as well as new interests and culinary persuasions. Admittedly, it is a little hard to get used to wearing the earpiece speaker while walking around a crowded landmark trying to follow the girl with the slick black hair and the pink umbrella. Don't eat anything before launching on this tour—you'll taste donuts, smoked fish, several special beverages, dried cherries, and even a treat from Seattle celebrity chef Tom Douglas. *SB*

Market Heritage Tours

774.5249
www.pikeplacemarket.org
Weekday tours (schedule varies, so call ahead)
Cost: $7–10

The Pike Place Market's own historical tour begins inside the market and indulges attendees with the time-honored secrets of the bustling city centerpiece. Snack on a goodie from the market—a donut if you've got a sweet tooth or some salmon jerky if you want savory. Sign up ahead of time to secure your spot in the tour group and hear all the market lore from your guide. *SB*

DeLaurenti Specialty Food and Wine

1435 1st Ave
622.0141
www.delaurenti.com
Mon–Sat 9a–6p, Sun 10a–5p

Right around the corner from the famous Post Alley gum wall at the market's far end is an epicurean gem, DeLaurenti Specialty Food and Wine market. I was in a rush for the Bainbridge Ferry and grabbed a salad and sandwich to go from this gourmet grocer. In no other city have I had such a tasty meal purchased and taken away in such a hurry. When I returned to linger, I had a prolonged conversation about race in Seattle and the state of gentrification over an incredibly fresh display of olives in all shades and sizes. I took with me a few sweet delights—some boxed shortbread cookies for later and a lavender iced tea to sip as my bus buzzed down the roadway. *SB*

Beecher's Handmade Cheese

1600 Pike Pl
956.1964
www.beechershandmadecheese.com
Daily 9a–6p

Food science was never so intriguing as in the story of Beecher's famous cheese. I came into the shop on a busy summer afternoon, and the smiling man behind the counter made it look easy to find the time for a full explanation. Beecher's process is unique, as the cheese makers rinse and separate the milk fats and curds in such a way that two distinct products are derived: a rich and creamy curdlike crumble and a tantalizing slicing cheese, the Flagship Reserve, which is the shop's best-seller. There are loads of other choices—books and sugary things in addition to cheese and deli items—but I say if you've come this far, you owe it to yourself to try Beecher's claim to fame. *SB*

Apple Cider and Cheese Fondue

Here's a recipe using Beecher's Flagship Reserve cheese to share with friends and warm you up if you get a chill.

Serves 4 to 6

12 ounces Beecher's Flagship cheese, grated
12 ounces Beecher's Just Jack cheese, grated
2 tablespoons cornstarch
1¼ cups hard apple cider
4 teaspoons freshly squeezed lemon juice
1 teaspoon freshly ground pepper
Sliced baguettes from Le Panier (see page 132) or another local bakery
Washington apples, washed and sliced into bite-size wedges

In a medium bowl, toss the cheeses and cornstarch together until the cheese is fully coated. Set aside.

In a fondue pot over medium heat, bring the apple cider and lemon juice to a simmer. Slowly add the cheese, stirring after each addition to fully incorporate the cheese. Once the mixture is smooth, sprinkle with the pepper and serve with the baguette and apple slices.

Note: Do not let the fondue boil, as that may cause the cheese to separate and become stringy.

Pike Place Fish Market

 86 Pike St
800.542.7732
www.pikeplacefish.com
Mon–Sat 6:30a–6p, Sun 7a–5p

The image of ruggedly handsome men clad in golden-yellow rubber jumpsuits throwing large salmon is iconic Seattle. In reality, the event comes across as a little hokey, and on summer weekends the dense crowds of tourists drown out any possibility of this being a necessary event. But even if it's a worn-out spectacle replaced by conveyor belts behind the market, it's still fun to get a whiff of the fresh fish and listen to the corny jokes these showmen have come up with over the years as their popularity grew. Since 75 percent of the ocean's fish have been overharvested, I opt for species that are tasty yet low on the trophic scale, such as mackerel, which is smoked and sold as delicious kippered snacks here. In fact, the mackerel is my primary reason for repeat Pike Place Fish Market visits—I am an addict of the stuff. SB

Original Starbucks

1912 Pike Pl
448.8762
www.starbucks.com
Mon–Fri 6a–7:30p, Sat–Sun 6:30a–7:30p

Although this much-visited Starbucks location is touted far and wide as the original location, it is in fact the third. (The flagship spot moved around several times before landing in its present spot across from the main market building.) But for romantic purposes, I am willing to overlook this fact since it contributes to the tips buskers get while performing outside, and it is a quaint location to have started an international phenomenon. While I have my quips and qualms with Starbucks's worldwide expansion, if you want to hear a great local street musician and pay your respects to the cranial capitalism propelled from the many industrious entrepreneurs in Seattle, I say go for it. By the way, the organic Serena blend isn't named for me, but it's pretty darn good in a French press. SB

MarketSpice

85A Pike St
622.6340
www.marketspice.com
Mon–Sat 9a–6p, Sun 9a–5p

I am a kid in a candy store inside this shop. It was lucky I was low on moola and on the Savor Seattle tour of Pike Place Market (see page 125) when I first was introduced to MarketSpice. Named for the famous orange- and cinnamon-spiced MarketSpice Tea, there is no end to the exotic ingredients found in the jars, bins, and packets at this chef's wonderland. I purchase hard-to-find spices and salt in bulk, always shocked at how reasonable the prices are considering this shop is located right in the middle of Seattle's most trafficked tourist destination. Cute tea sets and loose-leaf teas are ideal for a tea party, and if you're planning one, don't hesitate to invite me! *SB*

Piroshky Piroshky

 1908 Pike Pl

441.6068

www.piroshkybakery.com

Sun–Fri 8a–6:30p, Sat 8a–7p

Seattle's original Russian-style piroshki shop is right across from Pike Place Market's main corridor. Read the family story on the wall while you wait for your beef and cheese or celery, potato, and cheese piroshki to arrive in your hands, wafting a steamy, delicious aroma. *SB*

Turkish Delight

 1930 Pike Pl

443.1387

Daily 10a–5:30p

Recalling my childhood reading of *The Chronicles of Narnia* and *A Wrinkle in Time*, I had extra zest for the taste of Turkish delight. Try some of this exotic candy and other foreign treats at this eclectic stand that looks like it would be more in place in a Hobbit town. *SB*

Daily Dozen Doughnut Company

 93 Pike St

467.7769

The twirling, squirting, rolling, flipping donut machine at Daily Dozen Doughnut Company is as fun to watch as the end product is delicious. Hot cinnamon-sugar mini-donuts are the best order. Come when the market is nearing closing time and Daily Dozen usually has loads of donuts to give out for free—no such thing as a day-old donut here! *SB*

Tenzing Momo

 93 Pike St

623.9837

www.tenzingmomo.com

Holy food from Himalayan recipes is cooked fresh daily at this Nepali-Tibetan restaurant and take-out counter. After a ferry ride back from Bainbridge Island,

I easily get a craving for a hot plate of meat *momos* with Sriracha sauce—lovingly know as rooster sauce in these parts. *SB*

The Crumpet Shop

1503 1st Ave
682.1598
Mon–Fri 7a–5p; Sat–Sun 7:30a–5p

It is hard to choose a filling for my crumpet: sharp cheese and egg crumpet, plain toasted with proper marmalade or schmeared with ricotta cheese, scattered with blanched almonds and drizzled with local honey? There's no rule that says you have to order just one! One thing is certain: these are real cranny-laden crumpets and the Lady Grey tea is just like my British-schooled grandmother used to make it. *SB*

Lowell's Restaurant and Bar

1519 Pike Pl
622.2036
www.eatatlowells.com
Daily 7a–close

Provided you don't arrive at the height of the summer tourist season or the holiday-giddy December shop-a-thon, eating at Lowell's Restaurant and Bar is a delightful Seattle experience. Gorgeous views of the city fringes meeting the teal Puget Sound water, comfy seating, and a thorough menu with excellent local fish dishes are my top three reasons to find a window-side table here. *DL*

Copacabana Cafe

1520½ Pike Pl
622.6359
Mon–Sat 11:30a–4p, Sun 11:30a–5p

This Peruvian-inspired Bolivian cafe has an inspired menu with spicy salsas to go on almost anything. But who cares about the food when the Pisco Sour, a perennial cocktail favorite, is as strong and brightly flavored as any Seattle party crowd would want it to be? Although there are usually more tourists than natives, Copacabana always has a good mix of interesting personalities swilling its fantastic cocktails. *DL*

Le Panier

1902 Pike Pl

441.3669

www.lepanier.com

Mon–Sat 7a–6p, Sun 7a–5p

Very crusty French baguettes are the main affair at Le Panier. If you didn't already have a reason to ride around on a cruiser bike equipped with a front basket, now you have one—to show off your fresh loaves! SB

Re-Find

Take another look at what's been passed over . . . ahead is a treasure trove straight off a train from the past

There are enough DIYers, history buffs, and reuse freaks in Seattle to sustain a healthy selection of stores specializing in resale. While away your time mulling over old record collections, perusing previously hinged doors, and purchasing a vintage treasure from one of the thrift stores. Use what we've already got circulating around the country rather than something brand new—if it's new to you, it's just as exciting!

Red Light

312 Broadway E, 329.2200

4560 University Wy NE, 545.4044

www.redlightvintage.com

Daily 11a–6p

A serious light is shed on decades of Seattle closets at this trendy vintage resale shop. Think corseted Victorian gowns, hot pink 1980s prom dresses, casual beatnik sweaters, and an array of vintage baubles that will make your head spin. Yes, you could find your next Halloween costume here, but it's equally feasible you'll find your next hot-date outfit. SB

Antika

8421 Greenwood Ave N
789.6393
www.antikaantiques.com
Daily 11a–6p

The Kortans, the couple who've owned this shop for more than a decade, sure do know their stuff when gathering together treasures of the past. The furniture here is one of the best bargains in town—many pieces were made from rare woods in previous centuries. Find bulk containers for kitchen staples and plenty of colorful mixing bowls to spruce up your home, or get a vintage cocktail mixer for your martini-swilling friends. *SB*

20twenty

5208 Ballard Ave NW
706.0969
www.myspace.com/twenty_twenty
Mon–Sat 11a–7p, Sun 11a–5p

Skip the picking over part of most thrift store conquests—20twenty has collected all the best vintage finds in one place. In addition to old-time typewriters, great sunglasses frames, and a smattering of dated duds, there are repurposed treasures like notebooks bound with old book covers and inexpensive T-shirts screen-printed with Polaroid cameras. Score! *SB*

Earthwise Architectural and Building Salvage

3447 4th Ave S
624.4510
www.earthwise-salvage.com
Daily 9:30a–5:30p

A visit to Earthwise Architectural and Building Salvage is like seeing the city turned inside out. The aim of this decade-old store is twofold: to preserve elements of historic Seattle structures and to repurpose usable discarded materials. I bring my camera and snap photos of bathtubs lined up, rows of doors, and buckets of fixtures, and then purchase a spoon-shaped drawer pull to pocket for some other day. *SB*

The RE Store

 1440 NW 52nd St
297.9119
www.re-store.org
Mon–Sat 9a–5p, Sun 10a–5p

More than just a place to find great deals on lightly used building materials, the RE Store blends with the community by inviting the public to free how-to workshops and participating in fundraising efforts to help with neighborhood improvements. A trip here is like snooping around in Seattle's attic. *SB*

Second Use Building Materials

 7953 2nd Ave S
763.6929
www.seconduse.com
Daily 9a–5p

With by far Seattle's largest assemblage of house parts, both insides and outsides, Second Use Building Materials is ideal for anyone with a creative sense of adventure. Here are a couple of Second Use games I've come up with: $5, 10 minutes in the store, and 15 minutes to create something from your purchase; and find and photograph as many teal objects as possible within a 20-minute visit. *SB*

Insurrection

 8403½ Greenwood Ave N
 782.5752
www.insurrectionvintage.com
 Tues–Sat 10a–6p

The classic vintage styles gathered together inside Insurrection are quite a sight to behold. Cowboy boots that look like they are straight from either a French fashionista's closet or a cattle field in Texas push my desire buttons—especially since they are worn-in just the right amount. Oh, the colors, the stitching! There's more of it in the vintage shirt section, but the tones turn to brown and black in the motorcycle jacket section. If you ever dreamed of finding a jacket of the style worn by James Dean, this is your spot. *SB*

Atlas Clothing

1419 10th Ave
323.0503
http://atlasclothing.net
Mon–Thurs 12–7p, Fri–Sat 12–7:30p, Sun 12–6p

Atlas Clothing has the vintage world on its shoulders, or at least that's the way it's depicted on the bright yellow sign outside the store. Head through the dark red doorway, which may or may not be tagged with graffiti, and find yourself squeezed among more circular clothing racks than should fit in the space. Fun sale racks make for exciting evening-out outfit finds like the lime halter top I dyed a darker shade of green to make a smashing cocktail top. Expect typical vintage markups from the thrift stores but significantly better selection and an ample selection of bargains on shoes and accessories. *SB*

Private Screening

3504 Fremont Pl N
548.0751
www.privatescreeningseattle.com
Mon, Wed–Sat 11a–6p; Sun 11a–6p

Where can you find an 1880s print entitled *Circus Maximus*, a hand-embroidered hanky, and a petal-pattern Mexican agate brooch all under one roof? Private Screening, of course—the city's pickiest vintage treasure chest. Search here for specific vintage items. The knowledgeable staff is more organized about antiquing than you'd expect. *SB*

Lifelong Thrift Store

1017 E Union St
957.1655
www.lifelongaidsalliance.org/thriftstore
Mon–Sat 10:30a–7p, Sun 12–5p

It seems most everyone in this city has a treasured T-shirt, bag, or pair of jeans acquired from the choice collections at Lifelong Thrift Store. If there is such a thing as a famous thrift store, this is it. For some reason, the donations given to this AIDS-fundraising shop are especially representative of Seattle style. *SB*

Deluxe Junk

♻ *3518 Fremont Pl N*
🏛 *634.2733*
🚌 *Fri–Mon 11:30a–5:30p*

From Bakelite bracelets for $1 through to egg-shaped lounge chairs for $1,000, Deluxe Junk runs the deluxe gamut. If you're like me and can't live without several typewriters, then you can certainly set your heart on one found here. I ended up with a priceless stack of school photos from the 1950s all signed with notes to someone named Cristy—I can't wait to use them in a future art project. Don't expect things to be organized; after all, the word "Junk" in the store's name means something. The workers are friendlier here than at any of the other antique places I have been around the city, and the prices can be both astoundingly reasonable and painfully out of reach. *SB*

♻ Ecohaus

📷 *4121 1st Ave S*
⚓ *315.1974*
🖥 *www.ecohaus.com*
📁 *Mon–Fri 8a–6p, Sat 10a–5p, Sun 11a–5p*

Another cool spot for those with visions of future building projects, Ecohaus is the foundation of the new Seattle. As green ideas swell, and more and more construction involves the goal of LEED certification, places like this with repurposed materials and new nontoxic or otherwise low-impact supplies are even more important. Even if you are just passing by, stop in to check out the savviest solutions for sustainable structures. *SB*

Casual Night Out

Dining and delighting in a relaxed atmosphere

There is always a time when you just want to kick back and have a relaxed evening out. The state of Washington is blanketed with rich natural beauty, with ridges of snow-peaked mountains hemming in epicenters of international culture and dining. Go out, but go in comfort, with the divine purpose of repose. Good eats and good laughs galore lie ahead.

BalMar

5449 Ballard Ave NW

297.0500

www.thebalmar.com

Mon–Wed 5p–2a, Thurs–Sun 4p–2a

With low lighting and high-flying cocktails, BalMar is my favorite place for happy hour in Ballard. Each day from 5 to 7pm, house drinks and assorted pints go for far less than usual, and I can sit and watch the DJ set up, catching glimpses of her secret records as she gets ready for her set. If you arrive at BalMar in the early evening, you'll be pleased to find friends and neighbors assembling here. The friendly vibe is hard not to catch. *SB*

Zayda Buddy's Pizza

5405 Leary Ave NW

783.7777

www.zaydabuddyspizza.com

Daily 11a–close

Oh golly, gee whiz! Zayda Buddy's Pizza gives me the annoying urge to practice my horrible Minnesota accent. It's hard to resist at least one "You betcha!" once you behold the forceful collection of Midwestern beer: Stroh's, Grain Belt Premium, Blatz, and more. Order a pizza pie, let your hair down, and try not to begrudge your friends poking fun at one of America's favorite dialects. *SB*

Cafe Flora

2901 E Madison St

325.9100

www.cafeflora.com

Mon–Sat 11:30a–2:30p, 5–10p; Sun 9a–2p, 5–9p

Inside the twinkling atrium beside the bubbling fountain, you can dine comfortably even in the midst of winter. But the bounty of the colder months will still be brought to your table. You can order fried ginger-yam ravioli with a julienne of Asian vegetables or wild mushroom and hazelnut farro as hearty entrees, together with a bottle of biodynamic Pacific Northwest pinot and a sweet finish of tantalizing vegan carrot cake (you won't believe it's dairy free)—there are few better casual nights out to be had. Whether you're here

Cafe Flora

to catch up with a relative, meet a new friend, or indulge in the romance of dinner and a sinking sun, Cafe Flora conforms to your needs. *SB*

Ayutthaya Thai Restaurant

727 E Pike St
324.8833
Daily 11a–2:30p, 5–9:30p

Accessible, convenient, delicious, and fast are the four corners of Ayutthaya Thai Restaurant's kitchen. In the midst of a Pike and Pine adventure that's more focused on music, art, or people watching than on dining, I am grateful to find reliably good Thai food to fill me up in between getting sung to at Caffé Vita (see page 44) and learning how to take proper care of sex toys at nearby Babeland. The curries are sublime although admittedly a bit Americanized. I order the pineapple fried rice and chicken satay as staples and the vegetable curry with fish sauce to balance out the meal. *SB*

Ezell's Famous Chicken

501 23rd Ave, 324.4141
11805 Renton Ave S, 772.1925
www.ezellschicken.com
Mon–Thurs 10a–10p, Fri–Sat 10a–11p

Famous for greasing up the faces of hungry Seattleites, this Central District staple is one of the last places with real home-style Southern cooking. Everywhere else I go, there seems to be a squeaky-clean glass panel in between me and my fried chicken, mashed potatoes, and slaw. Since I'm a dark meat lover, I get the two-piece dinner with thighs for under $10, served with homemade sides and a generous helping of friendly service—more bubbly than at other eatery in the Emerald City. There's a reason Ezell's Famous Chicken is a cult classic, and I think it has as much to do with the atmosphere and experience as it does the spicy, flaky skin and juicy meat of the chicken. *SB*

Tom Douglas

www.tomdouglas.com

He's a master of Pacific Northwestern culinary identity, but what does Tom Douglas really do? He runs a handful of restaurants, produces a brand of meat and fish rubs, and has spread the word about seriously good food in America's upper-left corner. His cookbooks and TV appearances have contributed a sparkling characterization to the otherwise geeky image of Seattle, although he's not the only major food player on the map here, far from it. Here are his current projects:

Dahlia Lounge and Bakery, 2001 4th Ave, 441.4540

Etta's, 2020 Western Ave, 443.6000

Lola, 2000 4th Ave, #B, 441.1430 (part of Hotel Andra, see page 206)

Palace Kitchen, 2030 5th Ave, 448.2001

Serious Pie, 316 Virginia St, 838.7388

Cookbooks: *Tom's Big Dinners: Big-Time Home Cooking for Family and Friends* (William Morrow Cookbooks, 2003) and *I Love Crab Cakes! 50 Recipes for an American Classic* (William Morrow Cookbooks, 2006)

Rub with Love spice rubs, *www.tomdouglas.com/store*

Le Pichet

1933 1st Ave

256.1499

www.lepichetseattle.com

Mon–Thurs & Sun 8a–12a, Fri–Sat 8a–2a

As soon as I beheld this cozy bistro, I could feel a warmth emanating from within as well as some impossible-to-ignore aromas. Simple, organic food is served to mostly two tops, and the subtle elegance shines through even standard French preparations of fish and vegetables. Start with an entrée (remember, in France that's what the first course is called) of cold-cured duck on a bed of avocado, watercress, and pistachio salad or Spanish sardines wrapped in smoked ham with walnuts and ricotta. For the main affair, I can't resist calling ahead to order a whole chicken, which takes an hour of individual prep time. I swear the *moules frites* here are passing along subliminal messages: "Eat at Le Pichet, eat at Le Pichet." Since the menu changes with the passing of the seasons, you will always be surprised at the tasty offerings, but do try to save enough room for dessert—the chocolate creations are irresistible. *SB*

 Musashi's

 1400 N 45th St

633.0212

Tues–Thurs 11:30a–2:30p & 5–9p, Fri 11:30a–2:30p & 5–10p, Sat 5–9:30p

It's small, it's often crowded, it's cheap, and it's covered in corny movie posters. What is it? Musashi's, Wallingford's favorite hole-in-the-wall sushi eatery. Come with a small wad of cash, dress warmly so the wait on the outside benches doesn't chill you, and then squeeze into your table for plastic platefuls of fresh and tasty sushi. *SB*

 Vegan Garden Restaurant

 1228 S Jackson St

726.8669

http://vegangardenrestaurant.com

Mon–Sat 11a–9p

Followers of Vegetarian Bistro, a favorite veggie dine-out spot before it closed in 2008, will happily settle for Vegan Garden Restaurant, as long as they aren't spooked by fake meat. Ignore the references to chicken and beef in the menu descriptions—everything in this kitchen comes from plants, including the tofu and lotus root "fish." Golden rolls with pineapple sauce and bamboo-shoot vermicelli are my standby orders—I like to ask the cooks to chop my crispy spring rolls and put them right on top of the steaming soup before bringing it to my table. Yum! Don't expect a fancy atmosphere or an especially winning ambiance—just come for the healthy and affordable meals that will satisfy your picky vegan friends and meat-loving pals alike. *SB*

Piecora's New York Pizza

1401 E Madison St
322.9411
www.piecoras.com
Mon–Thurs 11:30–11p, Fri 11:30a–12a, Sat 12p–12a, Sun 10a–10p

Good pizza has to be crispy and have texture but be bendable enough to eat folded in halves or thirds. Also, as far as I'm concerned, you can forgo the toppings other than a moist tomato sauce and a good helping of stringy mozzarella. At Piecora's New York Pizza I can fold my pizza to my heart's desire, and no one bats an eyelash when I order plain cheese. Of course, the Sweet Italian, with sweet fried peppers and Italian sausage, and the Brooklyn, with pepperoni, black olives, and fresh mushrooms, are both supremely tempting when I've been walking up and down the streets of Capitol Hill all day. If I come in before 4:30pm my order is dependable: the slice and salad deal for under $7. Eat in with a gaggle of friends before an outing in the neighborhood—I've found Piecora's especially accommodating to larger parties, and there's a pretty full American-Italian menu to choose from if you're not in the mood for pizza. *SB*

Quinn's Pub

1001 E Pike St
325.7711
http://quinnspubseattle.com
Mon–Fri 11a–3p, 5p–12a; Sat 11a–3p, 5p–1a; Sun 5p–1a

When you turn on a light in a room, do you notice the quality of the light? When you feel the heat from a fireplace, do you pick up on variations in the sensation of warmth? If you can notice such subtleties, then the glow of Quinn's Pub will give you a special kind of excitement. Perched in the Pike and Pine crosshairs, this restaurant with the feel of a local pub is full of something in between warmth and light created by the lively conversations and jubilant atmosphere inside. An order of wild boar sloppy joes and a wet sandwich layered with house-made sausages later, your belly will be full and your mind at ease—at least that's the effect this friendly joint had on me. *SB*

West Five Lounge and Restaurant

 4539 California Ave SW

935.1966

www.westfive.com

Sun–Thurs 11a–12a, Fri–Sat 11a–1a, happy hour daily 4–6p

This quintessential Seattle eatery is all Pacific Northwest, all of the time. Gorgeous Astral Mac 'n' Cheese, dreamed up with five different cheeses, is a home run, especially after sharing a pitcher of some local IPA with your buddies. The entire menu echoes Americana; bacon-wrapped meat loaf, Cajun rice and beans, and sloppy joes made with hormone-free organic ground beef all have a place on it. The last time I visited West Five Lounge and Restaurant, I wanted something lighter and found the organic Cobb salad made with deviled eggs and ripe tomatoes to be perfectly satisfying. Huddling around drinks and comfort food at West Five in my studded leather bar chair, I can begin to imagine a scene I'd like to direct in a movie one day, where a man in black appears with a gun below the big lighted crown at West Five and everyone along both walls of the restaurant swivels in sync as he turns to run away. *SB*

$ Abbondanza Pizzeria

 6503 California Ave SW

935.8989

 Tues–Fri 11:30–2:30, 4:30–9:30; Sat–Sun 12–3p, 4:30–10:30

While it's true that East Coast pizza has a hard time making the trip west, Abbondanza Pizzeria re-creates the gooey cheese and thin and simultaneously crisp and chewy crust with real abandon. The result is a reliably good family pizza joint that doesn't try too hard, with an atmosphere just like the pizzerias I remember from my childhood. Order pasta for a change—there are some 10 sauces to choose from on this tasty bargain menu. *SB*

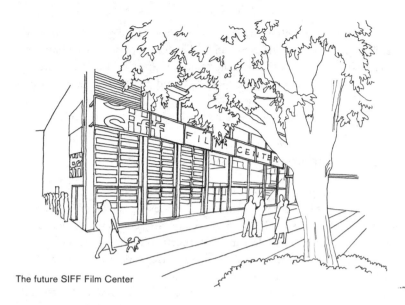
The future SIFF Film Center

Film Buffs

Movies a-go-go

A night out at the movies is a mandatory pastime in these parts. Seattle's culture is silver-screen oriented, so skip the big movieplex and head for an art house theater to see an old favorite or a new great from across the world. The Emerald City's favorite theaters frequently host the annual array of citywide film festivals, so you get a good mix of brand-new movies and art house flicks, classics, and foreign cinema throughout the year. Keep your noise to a minimum, and let the show begin!

SIFF Cinema

321 Mercer St, McCaw Hall
www.seattlefilm.com
Check web site for current show times

In addition to putting on the country's largest international film festival, Seattle International Film Festival (SIFF; see page 146), SIFF Cinema hosts year-round independent national and foreign films at McCaw Hall. If you still need proof that Seattle is a cinema-savvy place, then get in line for showings like *L'Origine de la Tendresse* and other film shorts from up-and-coming French directors like Olivier Bourbeillon, Felipe Canales, and Alain-Paul Mallard. The new SIFF building breaks ground any minute (at presstime), which will house all of the best events, films, lectures, and classes that make Seattle such a film buff-ready town. It's hard to leave with a resource like this, no joke. *SB*

Landmark Cinemas

781.5755

www.landmarktheatres.com/market/seattle/seattle_frameset.htm

It seems to me as if Landmark Cinemas is Seattle's big capitalist cookie monster, and all the city's art house theaters are tasty cookies destined for his mouth. Egyptian Theatre, Harvard Exit Theatre, Guild 45th Theatre, Metro Cinemas, Neptune Theatre, Seven Gables Theatre, Varsity Theatre, and Crest Cinema Center are all Landmark owned. Why should I care? Landmark keeps prices moderate, hosts loads of local filmmakers and film festivals, allows each space to remain unique and original, hires locals, and screens some pretty darn cool movies. It's just that the big business structure is a little too efficient to directly benefit Seattle as all the theater-goers out here should be able to do. And much of the money gleaned from artsy cine-geeks gets recirculated to an office on the other coast. So there are pluses and minuses, but I still end up in the lines at the brick-ensconced Harvard Exit and art deco Metro Cinemas, hyped to see the show. *SB*

Crest Cinema Center, 16505 5th Ave NE (all shows $3)

Egyptian Theatre, 805 E Pine St

Guild 45th Theatre, 2115 N 45th

Harvard Exit Theatre, 807 E Roy St

Metro Cinemas, 4500 9th Ave NE

Neptune Theatre, 1303 NE 45th St

Seven Gables Theatre, 911 NE 50th St

Varsity Theatre, 4329 University Wy NE

911 Seattle Media Arts Center Film Events

402 9th Ave N
682.6552
www.911media.org
Tues–Sat 12–6p

This ideal community arts agitator has lots of things going for it—worthwhile workshops, filmmaking gear and facilities, and the list goes on—but my favorite among them are the open screenings. The second Monday of each month, Greg Gould hosts a sort of filmmaker open mic night for the digital media arts. Take what you've recently made or even what you finished just hours before in 911 Seattle Media Arts Center's very own editing suite and show it to real live people. Then talk about it afterward. Sound fun? Just show up at 8pm or check the 911 Seattle Media events calendar for the next film-eriffic get-together. *SB*

Cinerama

2100 4th Ave
441.3653
www.cinerama.com

We forgave the art house cinemas around town for being owned by Landmark, and now it's time we forgave historic Cinerama for being one of the AMC gaggle. In this case, "historic" means dating back to 1963, but then again, it was only around 1900 that there was a city to speak of on the Puget Sound. Nonetheless, Cinerama has been fully restored and the three-panel films shown here are as unique a moviegoing experience as I can dream up. 70mm films are hard to come by in the age of digitalization, but these super high-resolution reels are worth the trip. *SB*

Northwest Film Forum

1515 12th Ave
www.nwfilmforum.org

Northwest Film Forum is more than the host of several of Seattle's premier film festivals: it's a holistic resource for anyone interested in filmmaking. Learn the skills—from crafting a story and researching for a documentary to using the latest filmmaking technologies—and set yourself loose on the city armed solely with a spark of creativity and a video camera. Then see what happens . . . *SB*

Seattle Film Festival Calendar

January

Children's Film Festival, *www.nwfilmforum.org/go/childrensfilmfest/cff seattle.htm*

February

Northwest Asian American Film Festival, *www.nwaaff.org*

Post Alley Film Festival, *www.postalleyfilmfestival.com*

Seattle Human Rights Film Festival, *www.shrff.org*

Science Fiction Short Films Festival, *www.siff.net/cinema/seriesDetail. aspx?FID=92*

March

Irish Reels Film Festival, *www.irishreels.org*

April

Seattle Arab and Iranian Film Festival, *www.arabfilm.com/festivals.html*

Seattle Jewish Film Festival, *www.seattlejewishfilmfestival.org*

National Film Festival for Talented Youth, *www.nffty.org*

Langston Hughes African American Film Festival, *www.langstonblack filmfest.org*

Seattle Polish Film Festival, *http://polishfilms.org*

Georgetown Super 8 Film Festival, *http://georgetownsuper8.com*

May

Seattle International Film Festival (through mid-June), *www.siff.net/festival*

Hazel Wolf Environmental Film Festival, *www.hazelfilm.org*

Translations: The Seattle Transgender Film Festival, *www.threedollarbill cinema.org/08/translations*

June

Seattle's True Independent Film Festival, *www.trueindependent.org*

July

Fremont Outdoor Movies, *www.fremontoutdoormovies.com*

August

South Lake Union Cinema on the Lawn, *www.cinemaonthelawn.com*

Movies at the Mural, *http://www.seattlecenter.com/events/festivals/detail. asp?EV_EventNum=41*

West Seattle Sidewalk Cinema, *http://sidewalkcinema.com/sc_wp*

Movies on the Pedestal, *www.moviesonthepedestal.com*

September

One Reel Film Festival (part of Bumbershoot music festival), *www. bumbershoot.com*

Port Townsend Film Festival, *www.ptfilmfest.com*

Tasveer Independent South Asian Film Festival, *http://isaff.tasveer.org*

October

Seattle Lesbian and Gay Film Festival, *http://threedollarbillcinema.org*

Local Sightings, *www.nwfilmforum.org/go/localsightings*

November

Couchfest Films, *www.couchfestfilms.org*

Blue November MicroFilmFest, *http://blue-november.com/microfilmfest.html*

2D or Not 2D Animation Festival, *www.plexipixel.com/2dornot2d*

December

Critics Wrap, *http://fryemuseum.org/program/magic_lantern*

Imbibe

Where to sip and swill with a local feel

Drinking, ah drinking. It is so wrong, yet it is so right. I go for places that offer mocktails and cocktails; it is rare that I am down for too much alcohol, but that doesn't mean I can't appreciate it. I love a good whiskey or bourbon; I just can't take more than one drink most of the time. But don't mind me, go and prove you're more robust at one of these ideal spots, and if you don't drink at all, no worries, most serve creative nonalcoholic bevvies next to their strongly intoxicating ones.

King's Hardware

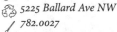 *5225 Ballard Ave NW*
782.0027
www.kingsballard.com
Mon–Fri 4p–2a, Sat–Sun 12a–2a

It's called King's Hardware, but get this—it's a bar! If this seems like the naming equivalent of hiding signless in a secret back alley, don't worry, King's Hardware isn't that elitist. Nor is it hiding. The place gets so packed on weekends that crowds overflow onto the sidewalk and even onto the street, making this hipster stronghold highly visible. From 10 blocks away.

King's Hardware actually was a hardware store at one time, and when the new owners bought it and converted it into a bar, they just . . . kept the name. Slightly odd, but then again, they do serve some stiff drinks, so maybe "hardware" makes sense after all.

This bar's excessive popularity can make it a pain to visit, but it also makes it a great place to meet people. This place is the epicenter and headquarters of Ballard's young indie crowd, but it never feels exclusive. It's hard to be pretentious when there's a giant plastic swordfish mounted above the bar. *IM*

Tini Bigs

 100 Denny Wy
284.0931
www.tinibigs.com
Daily 4p–2a

Swanky cocktails and Seattle go hand in hand, especially at this Lower Queen Anne bar that caters to locals. I flirted with a Spanish Tini with dreamy coffee and Kahlúa on a recent trip, finding it refreshing to my palate. I also had a sip of an Aloe Tini, and I finally was ready for the ultimate Washingtonian's drink: the Washington Apple, done right at Tini Bigs.

I was let in on one of Tini Bigs's many drink secrets: Dry Fly vodka, the only spirit legally produced in the entire state of Washington. As a result of the strict rules allowing spirit production only from locally grown ingredients (high five, government!), potato-derived vodka in the eastern part of the state is the only way to go. Enjoy responsibly, as always! *SB*

Classic Dry Fly Martini

3 ounces of Dry Fly gin or vodka

Dry vermouth atomized into a chilled martini glass

A marble-size piece of dry ice (found at finer grocery outlets), placed in the martini glass

Stir or shake the gin with ice, then strain into the martini glass. Garnish with blue cheese–stuffed olives.

Black Bottle

 2600 1st Ave

 441.1500

www.blackbottleseattle.com

Daily 4:30p–2a

Come as you are—all are welcome at the low-key Black Bottle gastro-tavern. Ease into the evening with a sip at this comfortable hangout, filled with all manner of downtown Seattle employees and unemployed artists. Reasonable prices on both tasty grub and selective, mostly organic wines add to my captivation with this homey spot. Order Columbia Valley's Zefina Zinfandel to go with an order of grilled lamb and sumac hummus or beer-and-mustard-braised local sausages. Vegetarians will be smitten with the Portobello Grilled and Butter Bean Salad and my see-food diet was well taken care of with Fresh Sardines Namban and a simmering bowl of Mussels Marseille-Style. Nothing on the food menu is more than $12, and the wines are chosen with an eye for both sustainability and dynamic taste. *SB*

The Saint

🏛 Can Can

94 Pike St (downstairs)
652.0832
www.thecancan.com
Daily 4:30p–close

In Pike Place's underbelly lies the 1920s-era Can Can, where the drinks and the ambiance reflect times gone by. If you've got enough courage to try the real wormwood-influenced absinthe, Green Hours featuring French absinthe discounts are Tuesday through Sunday, 4:30 to 6:30pm, and all night Wednesday. Other strong drinks are available, but I find I am happy with salmon carpaccio or beet salad, each $9 from the Cabaret Overture section of the menu, and a little dessert wine to go along with the show. On weekends, Can Can offers an unbelievable four-course dinner to go with the 7:30pm showing—for example, cream of pumpkin soup, spiced walnut and Gorgonzola salad, honey-dijon seared chicken breast, and dessert for just $25. Let Fiona Minx entrance you, or watch the fancy dance steps of Rainbow while you take in this underground lounge. *SB*

The Saint

1416 E Olive Wy
323.9922
www.thesaintsocialclub.com
Daily 5p–2a

The alcohol derived from agave cactus, better known in these parts as tequila, has a serious fan club in Seattle. The Saint in Capitol Hill is where the stuff is explored thoroughly—the menu is long and diverse in a way that surprises most first-timers who didn't previously know about tequila's dynamicism. Decorated as a temple to Spanish romance with lit candles and alluring photographs, the Saint is a place I can come alone and not feel awkward to leave my main squeeze at home; the crowd is not all couples batting their eyelashes back and forth at each other. I order a $5 margarita made with the top-notch tequila of the day at happy hour and some mole-drenched nibbles. Coming here early to get the personal attention of the savvy bartender and great deals on drinks and grub is the best way to experience this little slice of cactus. SB

Barolo Ristorante

1940 Westlake Ave
770.9000
www.baroloseattle.com
Mon–Thurs 11:30a–10:30p, Fri 11:30a–11p, Sat 4:30–11p, Sun 4:30–10:30p

Italian red wine flows freely at Barolo Ristorante, Seattle's upscale take on Romanesque wine tasting. I came with five friends celebrating a recent graduation, and we sat under a flowing glass chandelier at the far end of a regal dining table. We ordered several muscly Italian reds—a bubbly Lambrusco to start, followed by some universally adored Barbaresco, and then a round of old world–style Barolo with flecks of pulp still remaining. The food was far better than we anticipated, but then again, these fabulous reds have a way of elevating every simultaneous experience. I favored the grilled calamari and the oily ravioli stuffed with fluffy ricotta and truffle shavings. Service is as you would expect from a first-generation Italian eatery: curt and brisk if you act hurried and awkward, and overfriendly and highly conversational if you've chatted with the waitress or know one of the staff or owners. SB

Big Time Brewery and Alehouse

4133 University Wy NE
545.4509
www.bigtimebrewery.com
Mon–Thurs 11:30a–12:30a, Fri–Sat 11:30a–1:30a

Why order a bottle of suds shipped from halfway across the world when Seattle has microbreweries like Big Time Brewery and Alehouse? Famous for its effervescent ales and ideal pub grub to go alongside, this community watering hole is a favorite for a reason. I like the relaxed atmosphere that pervades this scene—it is one of the few places where the "Seattle stare" is lifted and talking to strangers is commonplace. SB

Linda's Tavern

707 E Pine St
325.1220
Daily 4p–2a, happy hour 7–9p

I know people whose parents met at Linda's Tavern back in the early 1970s. I know people who come here to gossip over a pitcher of beer and punk rock music. I come here to people watch from the picnic bench–like tables and survey the sunset from the secret back patio with a plate full of crispy fries. This is an iconic watering hole in the Emerald City, one where simple pleasures and the native laid-back scene are exemplified. Come early for breakfast fare or later for happy hour specials. SB

Owl 'n' Thistle Irish Pub and Restaurant

808 Post Ave
621.7777
www.owlnthistle.com
Daily 11a–2a

It's not far-fetched that you'd find a pretty darn authentic Irish pub in the heart of Seattle. The mossy lushness of the Pacific Northwest does bear a certain resemblance to the green knolls of Ireland. Owl 'n' Thistle even has its own house band and a slew of regulars who like to join in singing songs on blustery Friday evenings. Warming up is easy in the cozy clutches of this pub, and there is a menu of wholesome edibles to go along with a stout and a gig or two. Duck under the brick and crisscrossed panes by the golden owl sign, and you'll enter something similar to what I imagine a Hobbit hole is like. SB

The Capitol Club

414 E Pine St
325.2149
www.thecapitolclub.net
Daily 5p–2a

This swingin' tapas bar and watering hole is many things to many people. I like that there's a balcony, and I'm a little startled to have found candied bacon in one of the specialty cocktails, but overall a fondness is easily fostered even after one visit here. My honey and I arrived at the Capitol Club late on our last visit and were happily surprised to find food specials from 10pm through to midnight. We devoured a plate of roasted red pepper and chicken empanadas and some balsamic-glazed, bacon-wrapped dates with our pair of Basilicos (Stoli Blueberi with lime, basil, and soda water). No, we didn't go out on a limb and sample the Chocolate Bacon Martini. Maybe next time . . . SB

The BottleNeck Lounge

2328 E Madison St
323.1098
www.bottlenecklounge.com
Mon–Wed, Sun 4p–12a; Thurs–Sat 4p–2a

Sunday. Ten dollars in my pocket. Go to BottleNeck. Order the Bloody Mary and the grilled cheese special. Regain ability to form complete sentences. The BottleNeck Lounge is a great neighborhood bar, home to a slew of doggie-named drinks and the aforementioned Sunday meal deal. Local art on the walls and regular live music sets sweeten the deal. SB

Elysian Brewing Company

1221 E Pike St (and two other Seattle locations)
860.1920
www.elysianbrewing.com
Mon–Fri 11:30a–2a, Sat–Sun 12p–2a

Woodsy, warm, and welcoming, Elysian Brewery Company's main pub in Cap Hill is large enough to fit a night full of neighbors and small enough to make each pint glass clink feel personal. Try brews named for mythic creatures—Perseus is a mean porter, Zephyrus is the house pilsner, and Cyclops is Elysian's version of barley wine. Sitting at a round table under the candle-heavy chandelier, watching bartenders whiz back and forth behind the large wooden counter, I am reminded of the pub communities in England. Each of my roommates there had his or her own special spot with a certain vibe. I can image this location being many people's go-to bar, even with so many of them in the area. The Tangletown location by the sports stadiums is another great place to sample this pure Seattle beer. *SB*

$$ Sambar

425 NW Market St
781.4883
www.sambarseattle.com
Tues–Thurs 5:30p–12a, Fri–Sat 5:30p–2a

Bruce and Sara, the couple behind this tiny martini bar, know how to brush on a coat of sophistication like my mother washing her canvas. The high-falutin cocktails—think muddled herbs, fruit infusions, small-batch liquors, and house-made liqueurs—complete the modern Zen feeling of Sambar. My favorite drink here is the classy French 75. If you come with a stylish partner, order the crispy fries, as thin as shoelaces and curved just slightly to scoop as much aioli you need them to. Squeeze in early if there's more than one of you—only a handful of people max out this place completely. Le Gourmand (*www.legourmandrestaurant.com*) next door is an excellent place for a complete meal once your mouth starts watering. *SB*

Oliver's Twist

6822 Greenwood Ave N
706.6673
www.oliverstwistseattle.com
Sun–Tues 5p–12a, Wed–Sat 5p–1a

The incredible combinations at Phinney Ridge's Oliver's Twist have kept me from feeling pub boredom even after going to four other spots that same night. After all, one great pub after another can get old without the odd tomato cappuccino and grilled cheese sandwich or garlic-truffled popcorn in the mix, eh? Don't worry, the cappuccino is a lovely bowl of frothy tomato bisque, and the truffle oil scattered on the freshly popped corn kernels rockets this snack to being an epicurean delight. A comfortable lounge atmosphere makes this a great situation to be stuck in with a few friends. All you need is a hungry belly and some juicy conversations to get into. *SB*

Barking Dog Alehouse

705 NW 70th St
782.2974
http://thebarkingdogalehouse.com
Mon–Fri 11a–10p, Sat–Sun 11a–11p

The Barking Dog Alehouse is home to the most wonderful selection of local beers on draft, sold at just $3.50 a pop during happy hour, weekdays 4 to 6pm. Bridgeport Ebenezer Winter, Elysian Dragontooth Stout, Snoqualmie Steam Train Porter, and Hales Cream Ale are just a few of the brews in this award-winning assemblage. Stay for dinner and you won't be let down—between the tofu fries, roasted vegetable ravioli, and lemongrass crème brûlée, you'll forget that you originally came to the Barking Dog in search of beer. *SB*

Blue Moon Tavern

712 NE 45th St
675.9116
http://bluemoonseattle.blogspot.com
Daily 12p–2a

With a live music calendar locals cling to, zero cover charge, and a fair share of neon, Blue Moon Tavern works its magic on the Seattle indie scene. This is a raucous scene to be sure—one night you may find a half-nude guitarist crowd-surfing near your head, and the next night you may encounter two gals in pigtails wearing short skirts and playing ukuleles. Needless to say, there's never a dull moment, but there are loads of great local brews on tap and a good chance you'll be hearing and seeing something worth writing home about. *SB*

Listen

Any auditory experience you can imagine, from open mics to musical performances—it is all here

Well-strung notes can carry every shade of human emotion. I like to close my eyes and let my other senses go when I catch wind of some magical melodies. My mother used to say you can't listen with your mouth open, but some of these places promote listening while you eat scrumptious tapas or sashimi. Whatever your ears perk up to, it is essential to enjoy sounds and indulge in listening as often as possible. I encourage trying a genre of music or a type of performance you wouldn't usually look for—stretch your ears' horizons!

Singing in the Rain: Song Time in Seattle

Various locations

Seattleites spend months indoors, either to wax cerebral in solitude or to band together with others staying out of the rain. More often than not, this results in singing, for what better way to pass the time in a storm than with a shared song? When you find yourself in need of a tune, look up one of the many renowned choirs in the Seattle area for a concert or casual performance.

Vocalpoint! Seattle (*www.northwestchoirs.org*) are some of the most recognized boys' and girls' choirs on the West Coast. **Tudor Choir** (*www.tudorchoir.org*), **Renaissance Singers** (*www.therenaissancesingers.com*), **The Esoterics** (*www.theesoterics.org*), and **Opus 7 Vocal Ensemble** (*www.opus7.org*) bring back the sounds of the past, from Gregorian chants to classical choral works. **Columbia Choirs of Metropolitan Seattle** (*www.columbiachoirs.com*), **Seattle Peace Chorus** (*www.seattlepeacechorus.org*), and the **Seattle Lesbian and Gay Chorus** (*www.slgc.org*) perform a mix of popular favorites and traditional pieces. **Seattle Choral Company** (*www.seattlechoralcompany.org*), **Seattle Opera** (*www.seattleopera.org*), and **Tacoma Opera Association** (also *www.seattleopera.org*) put on a number of operas and operettas throughout the season.

I like sitting with my eyes closed on a pew in Saint Mark's Cathedral for a free Sunday Gregorian chant performance for evensong. The organ is silenced on its perch overlooking the veiled city, and only the meditative voices of the singers resound between the cold stone walls of the cathedral. Whatever your vocal performance preference, look up one of these groups when you're in town and you'll find something more interesting than chatting online to pass the rainy hours. *SB*

The Sunset
Tractor Tavern

 5433 Ballard Ave NW, 784.4800, www.sunsettavern.com
5213 Ballard Ave NW, 789.3599, www.tractortavern.com
Hours vary by location, call ahead

Ballard's two keystone pubs exist for music. The walls were built to hold in tunes, the beers are served so music lovers and their unsuspecting friends will stay quenched, and every night some kind of music is the center of this neighborhood's universe. Tractor and Sunset are very different—Sunset caters to my punk-loving friends who are brave enough to go up for Rockaroke, where a live band backs your karaoke classics, and Tractor is geared toward a low-key night of twang or Celtic strings. Sunset is cozier than Tractor, and Tractor is folksier than Sunset, but both focus on bringing good sounds to Ballard every day they are open. Grab a pint or a frat-days shot called the Washington Apple, and get ready to jam out Ballard style. *SB*

Seattle Women's Jazz Orchestra

www.swojo.org
Various locations and times

Some of the finest musicians in the region are members of this eclectic jazz group, which plays all over the state of Washington. Check out a performance of original music by Vern Sielert or Jill Townsend, or something arranged by Al Farlow, all regional composers. There are many different types of jazz sounds, even within a single concert. *SB*

Nectar

 412 N 36th St
632.2020
www.nectarlounge.com
Schedules vary, call ahead

Fremont's Nectar is an ideal spot to catch some hip-hop beats or local reggae sounds. The unique space comes complete with a bamboo-lined patio area, covered for rain protection, which welcomes you into the main lounge filled with art, colored lights, and good company. Happy hour specials aren't devoid of music like at some other bars—many DJs and indie bands set up early here. *SB*

Neumos

 925 E Pike St
709.9442
www.neumos.com
Schedules vary, call ahead

The Seattle music scene just wouldn't be the same without Neumos. Come to see local rockers take to the stage, like the X-Ray Eyes or Hey Marseilles, who have a poetic revision for modern classical music. There's also traditional Moroccan music and cool kids like AC Newman of New Pornographers fame. Buy tickets in advance at Rudy's Barbershops or at Moe Bar, adjacent to Neumos. *SB*

The Vera Project

Warren Ave N and Republican St (Seattle Center)
956.8372
www.theveraproject.org

Music is for everyone, young and old. If you are a youngster, skip out on your parents' museum-hopping day and go to the Vera Project for a rock 'n' roll class or to peruse the art galleries. A yearly calendar is full of shows, and all ages are always welcome—in fact, many of the bands are composed of "underage" members. Vera is one of Seattle's treasures, and locals are loyal. Download a podcast and listen to some Vera sounds before trekking to this city on the Sound (pun intended) to get in the know about the newest local groups. *SB*

Seattle Playlist

Here is Jamie Freedman's superb starting point for authentic, multi-dimensional, local music—some sounds to get you into the real Seattle music scene, including different genres and time periods. It isn't meant to be encyclopedic, just a taste for some of our favorite auditory pleasures homegrown in the Emerald City. (We also un-recommend Kenny G, a Seattle local who should be mentioned, not necessarily listened to, unless elevator music is your thing . . .)

1. The Banyans: "Neon Heat"
2. The Lonely Forest: "Julia's Song"
3. Arthur & Yu: "1000 Words"
4. Fleet Foxes: "White Winter Hymnal"
5. The Kindness Kind: "The Lusk Letter"
6. Damien Jurado: "Gillian Was a Horse"
7. Rosie Thomas: "Pretty Dress"
8. Daniel G. Harmann: "Beer from a Bottle"
9. Seattle Pro Musica: "Laus Trinitati" (Hildegard Von Bingen)
10. Soundgarden: "Down in a Hole"
11. The Jimi Hendrix Experience: "Foxey Lady"
12. The Ventures: "Walk Don't Run"
13. Blue Scholars: "The Ave"
14. Seven Year Bitch: "The Scratch"
15. Infernal Noise Brigade: "Ja Helo"
16. Death Cab for Cutie: "I Will Possess Your Heart"
17. Band of Horses: "The Funeral"
18. Alice in Chains: "Angry Chair"
19. The Mazeltones: "Romania/Seattle"
20. Nirvana: "Smells Like Teen Spirit"
21. Heart: "Barracuda"
22. Judy Collins: "Who Knows Where the Time Goes?"
23. Quincy Jones and His Orchestra: "Straight No Chaser"
24. Natalie Portman's Shaved Head: "Iceage Babeland"
25. Queensrÿche: "Anybody Listening?"
26. Screaming Trees: "Nearly Lost You"
27. Sir Mix-a-Lot: "Baby Got Back," also "Seattle Ain't Bullshittin'"
28. Vic Meyers: "Wishing"
29. Common Market: "Tobacco Road"
30. The Postal Service: "Such Great Heights"
31. Big World Breaks: "Prayers in Trinidad"
32. Sun City Girls: "Space Prophet Dogon"
33. Orkestar Zirkonium: "Zece Prajini"
34. Pearl Jam: "Even Flow"
35. Foo Fighters: "My Hero"
36. Picoso: "Escuchame Mama"

Jamie Freedman dives into each and every music scene in which she finds herself. She is an ethnomusicologist who has lived and traveled all over the world. Jamie is a musician herself, writes for www.examiner.com, and helps organize Rock 'n' Roll Camp for Girls. Check out her blog for new tunes and shows at www.alwaysmoretohear.com.

High Dive

513 N 36th St
632.0212
www.highdiveseattle.com
Schedules vary, call ahead

My first introduction to Seattle was a nighttime drive on the highway north from Olympia and a show by the Hungry Pines at High Dive. I parked, got my hand stamped, and before I knew it I was totally involved in the local scene. It was interesting. I drank a pint of Sierra Nevada and bobbed my head with the rest of the serious, timid crowd. Everyone seemed zoned or totally entranced with the music. Either way, one thing was clear to me: this was authentic Seattle. The bathroom was tagged and doodled, I met a guy at the bar who was playing at High Dive in the nights to come, and I couch surfed on the drummer's futon. High Dive is essential. *SB*

Sound Ensembles: Classical Music Groups Around Seattle

Whether you prefer bells or basses, pianos or piccolos, there's no shortage of ensembles playing concerts around the Puget Sound. Here are some groups you might want to look into and catch a show while you're in town:

Seattle Pro Musica
www.seattlepromusica.org
An exceptional choral ensemble.

Rainier Symphony
www.rainiersymphony.org
A fine community orchestra.

Mostly Nordic Chamber Music
www.kser.org
www.nordicmuseum.org
A wonderful series of classical concerts.

Early Music Guild of Seattle
www.earlymusicguild.org
Inspiring performances of medieval, Renaissance, and Baroque music.

High Dive's neon sign

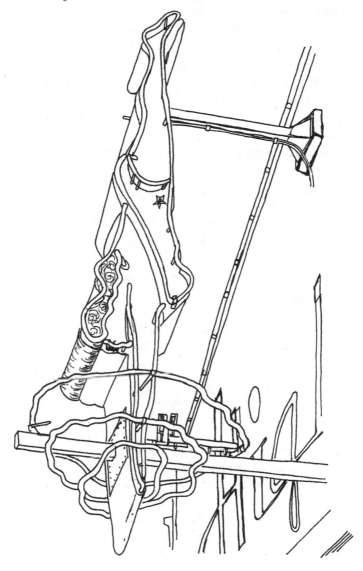

Seattle Philharmonic Orchestra
www.seattlephil.com
A major American orchestra directed by Adam Stern.

Seattle Symphony
www.seattlesymphony.org
The preeminent Seattle orchestra, conducted by Gerard Schwarz and supported by the Seattle Symphony Chorale (*www.seattlesymphonychorale.org*).

Seattle Baroque Orchestra
www.seattlebaroque.org
A professional orchestra featuring Ingrid Matthews and Byron Schenkman, with many recordings.

Bells of the Sound
www.bellsofthesound.org
A veteran handbell choir that performs in the greater Puget Sound area.

Seattle Youth Symphony Orchestra
www.syso.org
An advanced youth orchestra with summer programs and regular concerts.

Northwest Sinfonietta
www.nwsinfonietta.org
A chamber orchestra performing the works of classical masters.

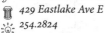 ## Lo-Fi Performance Gallery

429 Eastlake Ave E
254.2824
www.thelofi.net, www.myspace.com/percussions
Schedules vary, call ahead

My first visit to Lo-Fi Performance Gallery was on a First Friday art walk, when I sneaked in to wet my whistle and see what the sign on the door meant ("deep funk, boogaloo, raw soul, sleazy disco, jazz breaks, rare boogie"). I was glad to find this hip mix inside the small, rosy-lit space. The groove was on, the vibe was hot, and the audience was into DJ Greasy and DJ David James for real. In the following weeks, I attended more shows, most notably Stop Biting Tuesdays with hip-hop, trip-hop, downtempo, and soul. Find local DJs spinning their faves here almost every night. *SB*

Boxed Music in Seattle

Each type of recording has a distinct following—the vinyl freaks, the geeks still trying to resurrect the 8-track, the mixtape addicts, the CD fans with those narrow organizing towers, the iPodded ones wearing earbuds 24/7 . . . you follow. Here's where to find boxed music in whatever package you like:

Sonic Boom Records
514 15th Ave E (and other Seattle locations)
568.2666
www.sonicboomrecords.com
Prides itself on stocking the best local and indie label CDs

Bop Street Records
5219 Ballard Ave NW
297.2232
www.spiralvinyl.com
A Seattle legend for vinyl diggers and "random find" enthusiasts

Easy Street Records
20 Mercer St (and other Seattle locations)
691.3279
www.easystreetonline.com
Offers new releases and little-known new album treasures in addition to used CDs and records

Benaroya Hall
 200 University St
215.4800
www.seattlesymphony.org/benaroya
Schedules vary, call ahead

Seattle is known for its varied performing arts ensembles, but it's shocking to think that the city once lacked the proper venues to support them all. Before the opening of Benaroya Hall, Seattle's symphony, opera company, and ballet were forced to share the Seattle Center Opera House, which was booked solid 360 days a year. The Seattle Symphony increased its subscribers by 50 percent and gained national attention in its first season after the move, and it has since increased its presentations from about 100 a year to nearly 220. That and the ensuing community support for the Seattle Symphony and its new home serve as proof that this venue has had a profound role in the revitalization of Seattle's downtown. DL

🏛 Columbia City Theater/Hendrix Electric Lounge
/ *4916 Rainier Ave S*
$$ *723.0088*
www.columbiacitytheater.com
Schedules vary, call ahead

Not to be confused with the Columbia City Cinema around the corner, this hybrid business is the Lincoln Town Car of clubs. It's plush and snazzy but can have the distinct side effect of aging you. I go anyway because the drinks are strong, the concerts are usually great, and the parties are hopping. SB

/ The Triple Door
V *216 Union St*
$$ *838.4333*
www.thetripledoor.net
Daily 4p–2a

Oddly enough, the owners of fancy-pants Asian restaurant Wild Ginger (see page 170) are also the parents of the Triple Door, where some of Seattle's best local acts take the stage. There's music from many genres—strange new sounds from Brooklyn, drumming and electronica from Japan, and indie rockers from down the street. The Musicquarium is a relaxing place to hear great sounds and slurp choice wines from a long local list. SB

Spectators
Sit back and watch this

Major league sports and exciting sardine cans can be found here!

☞ Jimmy's on First
1046 1st Ave S
204.9700
www.jimmysonfirst.com
Mon–Sat 6:30a–11p, Sun 7a–11p

As I've said before, baseball is a paradigm that continually reminds me of America's strong points: it's a beacon of hope in troubled times. So I am happy

Safeco Field, home of the Seattle Mariners

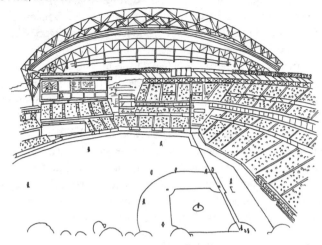

to find any place that can bring the baseball experience to life, in all its greasy American goodness. Jimmy's on First—a part of one of my favorite local chain hotels in Seattle, the Silver Cloud Hotel–Stadium—is one such gem. During the baseball season, especially after games, the place is all sardines, but come on a night in early spring and your meal here, served amid a baseball-loving crowd with a classy touch and some memorabilia, will ring in the season right. Start with the fried calamari, never chewy, or some of the chef's favorite crostini and house-made artichoke dip. The heaping portions make Jimmy's a good place to split an entrée and double up on dessert; I can't leave without the old-school ice cream sundae, a tough find in this rainy city. The prices are reasonable, the ambiance is friendly, and the sporty mentality is omnipresent. This is the place to get ready for game day, even in the off-season. SB

$$ Seattle Mariners Baseball

 Safeco Field
 1250 First Ave S
346.4000
http://seattle.mariners.mlb.com

Even though I am not—I repeat, not—a Mariners fan, this team has saved my life on two occasions, and for that I am eternally grateful. First, when I was a senior in high school, having been expelled Toby Wolff–style from an East Coast prep school, I found myself finishing up grade 12 in Vancouver, BC. I was going through trauma of several sorts, and having a real, live baseball team within a few hours' bus ride made me feel whole and sort of happily American at the time. Then it happened again when I lived in a northern Kyoto village with a kind yet timid Japanese woman, recently out from her parents' nest. We got into a gifting war, wherein she would constantly gift me, and out of duty I'd gift back, ad infinitum until I decided to move out. It was then that one of Japan's superheroes became my own: Ichiro, and with him, the Mariners. TV got me out of a terrible emotional rut on the other side of the world.

So here I am finally experiencing a game in person in Seattle. The stadium is within a few blocks of downtown, so the whole day has been a proverbial smash hit. There are respectful fans, yummy overpriced garlic fries, and all the excitement us American baseball lovers can't get enough of. *SB*

Seattle Thunderbirds Ice Hockey

Games: KeyArena at Seattle Center, 305 Harrison St
Practices: 14326 124th Ave NE, Kirkland
425.869.7825
www.seattlethunderbirds.com

On a mission to bring high-caliber ice hockey to the Pacific Northwest, the Seattle Thunderbirds are one of the founding teams of the Western Hockey League. The silver, blue, and white uniforms flash on the ice in a whirl of manly grunts, cackling crashes, and speedy shots. Watch the team cream the Portland Winter Hawks or the Spokane Chiefs—even though the league has only a handful of teams, there are still plenty of games a season (36 home games in fall and winter), and the tickets don't cost as much as those for NHL games. Other than to see the guys in action, I go for Cool Bird, the 7-foot-tall corny mascot who, try as he might, can never seem to score a shot. If you can't make it to a game at the arena, you can listen to one on 1150AM KKNW radio or see it on local TV. *SB*

☀ Rat City Rollergirls

KeyArena at Seattle Center, 305 Harrison St
www.ratcityrollergirls.com

Seattle's Rat City Rollergirls are mean queens in the rink! A match against rival team Grave Danger or Sockit Wenches provides an extreme kind of riveting excitement that can only come from watching girls with long sticks on speeding skates. Each team member has her own personality and distinct style in the rink. Just don't expect a calm performance—these ladies are angsty! *SB*

⚓ Seattle Seahawks

Qwest Field
800 Occidental Ave S
888.694.2957
www.seahawks.com

Back when the Seattle Seahawks called the Kingdome home, Seattle fans earned the title of "12th Man" for their raucousness, once instigating 11 false starts by the New York Giants. Qwest Field may or may not retain the Kingdome's status as one of the loudest stadiums in the NFL, but loyal fans will forever be recognized with their very own retired jersey, number 12. Although the Seahawks are not known as one of the most successful franchises, the team has a number of Western Division titles (both NFC and AFC, strangely enough) and an NFC championship under its belt. The Seahawks' lone Super Bowl appearance was a regrettable loss to the Pittsburgh Steelers in 2006; I'd like to see a rematch in the not-too-distant future. Seahawks fans, prepare your larynges. *DL*

☀ Seattle Sounders FC

Qwest Field
800 Occidental Ave S
877.657.4685
www.soundersfc.com

This is not the first soccer team to carry the name "Sounders." The name dates back to 1974 with the original team of the North American Soccer League and again in 1994 with the Sounders of the United Soccer Leagues First Division. Minority owner Drew Carey, who knows the importance of fan involvement, leveraged the creation of the Seattle FC Association, allowing members to vote in the election of the team's general manager and to weigh in on other team decisions. Anything that makes me feel like more than just a quota is a good thing. *DL*

Seattle Storm

Key Arena
305 Harrison St
217.9622
www.wnba.com/storm

The Seattle Storm basketball team is barely a decade old, but these ladies have shown what they're made of, reaching the playoffs in five consecutive seasons and going all the way to the top in 2004. When the Storm hits the court to the hard-rock riffs of AC/DC, you know the other team is in for a world of hurt. The Storm brings a new, festive meaning to the time-out, as team members often encourage fans to rush the court for a mock conga line. *DL*

Dress Up

Don your shiny shoes and head out to one of these fancy places—not all come with a huge price tag

There are those occasions when you just have to dress up, when something inside you wants to put your best foot forward and go all out. Seattle has a definitive ritzy side, all done up and tied with a bow. But this is the West Coast we're talking about, so a laid-back attitude comes into play even in these posh places. If you are looking for the best food, or just an opportunity to take your new dress shoes out on the town, these places are your best bet. Not all of them require big bucks, though some places are pricier. Remember, drinks are usually the culprit in amping up your dining bill, so if you are careful in that department, you can make the more expensive places affordable. Washington is big on visible food safety, so don't be surprised if your menu has health suggestions and warnings on it; even the delectable duck burgers at Tilth, cooked a little rare, get a friendly reminder on the menu. Don't be alarmed if you're not accustomed to seeing this—it's just another example of classic Washingtonian communication methods.

Nishino

3130 E Madison St, #106
322.5800
www.nishinorestaurant.com
$$$ *Mon–Sat 5:30–10:30p, Sun 5:30–9:30p*

Just off Lake Washington Boulevard, Nishino sits bedecked in Seattle finery—a restaurant happily stuck between local creativity and classic Japanese techniques. Don't expect the kind of authentic hole-in-the-wall ambiance of the International District sushi joints here; this lovely eatery is casual but romantic and regal. Large oil paintings hang down almost to the tabletop, and an open, neighborly feel pervades this place even though it is clearly fancy. Stemless martini glasses came to our table filled with seaweed in fanciful shapes, marinated raw fish, and chunks of organic avocado. Skate tartare arrived shrouded in thin fried taro chips, and sashimi plates with three fresh fish of the day were simple but sublime. Nishino is all about the elegance of Japanese cuisine and the unparalleled ingredients found in and around the Puget Sound. *SB*

Crush

2319 E Madison St
302.7874
www.chefjasonwilson.com
Sun–Thurs 5:30–10:30p, Fri–Sat 5:30p–12:30a

If you have a crush on the bounties of the Pacific Northwest, then you'll soon transfer your affections to Crush the restaurant. Chef Jason Wilson is as serious about the weightlessness of his parsnip flan as he is the sustainability of the smoked salmon caviar and aged maple syrup that top it. The starched white interior, mixed with whimsical arrangements of branches and shiny black detailing, give this place an obvious pomp and circumstance that almost doesn't fit with the energy of the food—the menu is all about flirting with local foods, not getting snooty about them. I always order gnocchi when it's on the menu, as the chanterelle and poached egg–topped noodle pillows rival those of San Francisco's famous chef Traci des Jardins. A supernal wine list gets me back into a fun mood—one look over the domestic section and I know I'm sticking with the Columbia and Willamette valleys, the best of each of which is poured at Crush. *SB*

Volterra

5411 Ballard Ave NW
786.5100
www.volterrarestaurant.com
Hours vary, call ahead

Named for the Tuscan village where Chef Don Curtiss and his wife, Michelle, were married, Volterra is enchanted with wisps of authentic Italy. From Ballard, the trip there would be long and arduous, so I make it with only my taste buds. The fava bean tart and the seared scallop antipasti deserve to be eaten outside on the patio in the dappled sunlight. On winter evenings, warm yourself with wild mushroom polenta, eggplant pouches, and wild boar tenderloin. Chef Don is concerned with local ingredients but also with the buzz of his fame and the romance of his past—all key ingredients for a shining star in the competitive Seattle culinary scene. *SB*

Wild Ginger

1401 3rd Ave
623.4450
www.wildginger.net
Mon–Sat 11:30a–3p, 5p–12a; Sun 4–11p

Entering the high-ceilinged expanse of downtown Seattle's Wild Ginger, I was taken away by the exotic aromas from the kitchen and the happy hum of diners. Although I noticed a slightly corporate feel as I was seated in a row of neat booths coated in crisp linens, I got more comfortable once my frilly mango daiquiri came. If I were here with my parents when I was 10 years old, I would have begged them to order me a virgin version. The seven-page dinner menu was hard for me to navigate hungry, so I munched on some veggie Buddha rolls while I pored over the pages, finally picking Monk's curry with eggplant, sweet potatoes, and peanuts in a spicy vegetarian curry sauce, and the young mountain lamb slathered with garlic and black pepper sauce from the satay menu. I had to avoid a pile of dishes with shrimp, mahi mahi, and tuna, all of which are scarce and none of which are sustainable, but the other offerings were so stellar I soon forgot my frustration. Vegetarians, vegans, and meat eaters will all be able to dine together, and even though the chic, big-city vibe has accumulated in this Seattle eatery, it is affordable enough for a mouthwatering midweek meal. *SB*

Tilth Restaurant

1411 N 45th St
633.0801
www.tilthblog.wordpress.com
Hours vary, call ahead

Welcome to Maria's house! Tilth Restaurant is an extension of Maria Hines' passion, influence, dreams, and talent. The mossy green home holds a close team of cooks and kitchen helpers who carefully plate oblong spoonfuls of creamed vegetables and gingerly carry bottles of new Beaujolais or Firehouse Red from Columbia Valley's Tamarack Cellars to and from the mostly sulfite-free wine cabinet. Maybe Maria was envisioning her next recipe while she was scaling rocks in Thailand, but whatever extreme inspiration she gets condenses and congeals before she dons her white chef jacket and creates a dish for the first time. Most of my menu picks are vegetarian: perfectly cooked Lacinato kale, carrot and pine nut risotto, and the decidedly nonvegetarian slow-cooked pork cheek. Avocado mousse, Meyer lemon–almond cake, and chocolate ganache cake made with Theo Chocolate (see page 194) are a representation of my favorite desserts, but the sweets menu changes as frequently as the main courses, so don't get wedded to one item. I stick with house-made sarsaparilla soda or kombucha to finish my meal lightly. Scan the menu carefully—each farm and artisanal producer is proudly listed as another emblem of Tilth's commitment to sustainability and slow food. SB

Rover's

2808 E Madison St
325.7442
www.rovers-seattle.com
Tues–Thurs 6–9:30p; Fri 12–1:30p, 5:30–9:30p; Sat 5:30–9:30p

Thierry Rautureau of Rover's is known as the Chef in the Hat because he's always sporting a fedora, even when he's explaining to me his prize creation: scrambled eggs with lime crème fraîche and white sturgeon caviar. Good thing there has been a strong effort, especially in Southern California, to keep up white sturgeon populations so I can enjoy this treat. Thierry and his loyal, creative team support many foragers, traditional farmers, line fishers, and artisanal producers, but once you are seated behind this Madison courtyard, it is hard to think of anything else but appreciation and delight for the Rover's experience. Kusshi oysters with seared leeks, muscovy duck breast with grilled foie gras, intricate beet and goat cheese tartlets . . . the poetic plate names blur into one delicious memory. My night at Rover's was a romance of the senses. *SB*

Union

 1400 1st Ave
838.8000
www.unionseattle.com
Daily 5–10p

Big round tables, little square booths, and high reddish ceilings make Union an inviting canvas for the food to bring alive. Gleaming white-rimmed dishes covered my table. After only a few minutes at Union, I was amazed at the great service and at the originality of the feast before me and my dining partners. We fought over bites of rabbit ravioli and tender calamari, wrestled to steal the last nibble of creamy buffalo mozzarella, and played rock-paper-scissors to decide who finished off the seductively simple Manila clams and linguine. In the end, we were all stuffed anyway, but the meal was one to remember—a bona fide celebration of Seattle culture and local ingredients right in view of the explosive exhibits at Seattle Art Museum (see page 105). *SB*

Brasa Restaurant

2107 3rd Ave
728.4220
www.brasa.com
Sun–Thurs 5–10:30p, Fri–Sat 5–11p

Some say sleek and airy Brasa Restaurant has already had its heyday, but I say it's still in it. Fantastic squid ink risotto that would be the envy of even Venetians, pork belly with poached eggs and truffle-honey syrup, beef tenderloin with puréed potatoes and crisp Walla Walla onions . . . my mouth waters just reminiscing about my romantic dinner at Brasa with my honey. We indulged, I admit, but it was glorious. I had a Clear Creek pear brandy for dessert and fed him bites of poached pear with house-made vanilla ice cream. *SB*

$$$ Canlis

2576 Aurora Ave N

238.3313

www.canlis.com

Mon–Wed 5:30–10:30p, Thurs–Fri 5:30–1a, Sat 5p–1a

After meeting Outkast's Andre3000 and Seattle news magazine host John Curley at the premiere of *Battle in Seattle*, I capped an already amazing day with a perfect meal at Canlis. Terry, our server, informed us that we'd be in the hands of chef after asking if we had any preferences or dietary restrictions. Mark Canlis, third-generation owner of the restaurant, and a bottle of his specially made Canlis Cuvée arrived at our table as the amuse-bouche plates left. (My dining guest and I had practically licked clean the plate of fresh corn and pea purée, which was decorated with a baby corn tassel from the chef's garden before the stalk turned any shade of green. Sweet and tender!) He was kind and soft-spoken, as gentle and elegant as the atmosphere he and his two brothers maintain at Canlis. His personal stories and attentive nature were glorious. Then the hearts of palm arrived. And the butter-doused halibut. By the end of the meal some seven courses later, I felt as if I had been read aloud a novel in food. Despite the dress code, there was a relaxation attained at Canlis that is hard to describe without experiencing it for yourself. Make reservations and walk across the threshold, past the ancient Japanese stone wheel, into a palace of food overlooking Gas Works Park (see page 30). Pick a big night for such a special meal. *SB*

Lark

926 12th Ave
323.5275
www.larkseattle.com
Tues–Sun 5–10:30p

If King Mustard and Queen Quince reigned over a kitchen, it would have to be Lark. This comfortable (as in quaint and elegant) Capitol Hill eatery has chosen the finest of ingredients, and if he doesn't make his own from scratch, the chef gets them from a local artisan purveyor. King Mustard invited his cousin Marcona Almond to the table, and with her she brought Prince Marinated Olive. I was imagining stories with these key players on my plate as I dined. Lavender and rosemary sunchokes, ribollita of white beans and kale, locally grown farro with black trumpet mushrooms, Penn Cove mussels with dill and horseradish sour cream, foie gras terrine with kumquat-vanilla marmalade, and beef short rib ravioli with yellow foot chanterelles are my favorite menu items, although there are frequent fluctuations in what's on offer from season to season. Bring someone who's both deserving and impressionable, and you'll be in for some tasty memories. *SB*

Boka Kitchen and Bar

1010 1st Ave
357.9000
www.bokaseattle.com
Hours vary, call ahead

Chef Angie Roberts really gets excited around farms and fisheries. After tasting her inventive cuisine, I imagined that she bottles up this joy and sprinkles it on each plate she checks before it leaves the kitchen. The woodsy feel of the long bar with cushioned stools is distinctly Northwestern, and fine liquors are as local as possible, like a vodka from Eastern Washington. But Boka Kitchen and Bar serves three meals a day and caters to a night crowd. And while the restaurant stays busy, the staff juggles shifts rather flawlessly. I try to make it for happy hour in the shiny red heels I got from Les Amis (see page 123)—there are super food and drink specials. Sugarcane-skewered crab cakes, perfect roast chicken, local salmon, seared scallops, and desserts elevated to an art form make Boka one of the elite Seattle eateries. *SB*

Portage

2209 Queen Anne Ave N
352.6213
www.portagerestaurant.com
Daily 5p–close

Vuong Loc, the wizard in the Portage kitchen, is sincere and endearing. One bite of his food and you'll feel it. The classic French method he is driven to perfect with his premium Seattle ingredients is a smash hit with fine-cuisine novices and food reviewers alike. Start with fennel potage canopied with foraged mushrooms and a salad of baby Chioggia (red-and-white-striped beets) and golden beet gratin topped with niçoise olives and Roquefort mousse. The truffled potato risotto that came with my seared diver scallops gave me shivers up my spine, like the first time I heard *Don Giovanni* live. For our main courses, we shared the stuffed lamb chop, which I'd heard was a house special, and the irresistible-sounding duck confit cassoulet. Although there was a little more salt than I would have liked in some of the dishes, I was smitten with the careful wine pairings, the balanced service, and the excellent technique with which the food was prepared. *SB*

Veil

555 Aloha St
216.0600
www.veilrestaurant.com
$$$ *Tues–Sat 5–10p, lounge until 2a*

Veil is almost too hot for me to handle. The über-cool ambiance, leather cubist chairs, and sexy private booths make for an enticing lounge, and that's before you even see the menu. Updated American cuisine is at its best under Chef Shannon Galusha's hand. She uses the freshest organic ingredients and almost completely sustainable seafood like diver scallops from Sailor Girl and shrimp from off the coast of San Diego. I'm partial to the soups at Veil, an unlikely edible considering the atmosphere but nonetheless delicious, like the corn bisque with Dungeness crab and summer cherry tomatoes. I also have to recommend the crème fraîche–lobster mac and cheese and the butter-poached ling cod. These delicacies are served to drum and bass and downtempo beats, in a clublike ambiance with a chic, big-city attitude and a slew of strong cocktails to match the pulse of the evening. *SB*

Joule

1913 N 45th St
632.1913
www.joulerestaurant.com
$$ *Sun–Thurs 5–10p, Fri–Sat 5–11p*

I have to say I am always a little critical of self-proclaimed fusion restaurants, but even going into Joule with a negative bias, I was astounded at the conceptual creativity with which each dish was built. Mussels, spinach, grapes, and carrots go into one of the signature salads, a great way to start off the elegant Korean-French-American meal. I adored my zucchini pancake with shrimp and smoked chili sauce and my honey's crispy pork belly, with surprisingly good pickled leeks. We savored the leftover sauces in our dishes with baguettes slathered with seaweed butter, and I even topped one bite with the coleslaw from our wild boar rib entrée from the Sparked section of the dinner menu. Although it was hard to envision wanting to take another bite of anything, we sat and talked about our day on Bainbridge Island before splitting the "Joule Box," a selection of petite desserts like ruby grapefruit brûlée. *SB*

Stay Up Late

Where to find midnight snacks, 24-hour businesses, and casual late-night drinking, dining, and dancing

Staying up late to dance, dine, and relax is something everyone does at least once in a while. Here are the best places around to get in touch with your nocturnal side.

Waid's Haitian Cuisine and Lounge

1212 E Jefferson St
328.6493
www.waidshouse.com
$$ *Daily 12p–2a*

Waid's is Seattle's Haitian love shack. If I didn't know any better, I'd think it were the very love shack that the B-52s were singing about, but once I handed

Chapel

over my 10 bones and got inside, I realized this was much more exotic. The island comes to Seattle, and the heat is actually kept high enough to simulate something like the tropical weather in Haiti. At least with a couple authentic Haitian liquor shots and a sip of my friend's coconut mojito, I was pleasantly warm and ready to get on the spacious dance floor. Waid himself often hangs at the bar and chats up the many fans of his special venue/bar/kitchen/ concert hall. On Friday nights, the dance floor is lit red; couples swinging to excellent Latin rhythms and international drum beats. If you come early, order huge plates of delicious *taso*, grilled goat with blackened peppers; sample *lambi*, conch meat in curry sauce; and dip addictive taro chips into a side of spicy chili curry. I agree whole-heartedly with Waid, who maintains, "all love." If you see him roaming this fun-filled space, ask if he's got any Ballatine in back, a very special Haitian rum. *SB*

Chapel
$$ 1600 Melrose Ave
447.4180
www.chapelseattle.com
Sun–Thurs 5p–1a, Fri–Sat 5p–2a

When my rosemary chicken hot pot came to the table and I smelled the wafts of caramelized D'Avignon sausage and sauerkraut, I couldn't believe it was nearing one in the morning. Chapel—a cavernous 1920s funeral home turned nightclub—was still hopping like nobody's business, just like there had never been a night before and there wouldn't be another after. Delicious eats are made from local, organic stuff. But it is the fab desserts and a rich, diverse bar menu that make this church-cum-bar a superstar on any Seattle night. *SB*

$ Twilight Exit

2514 E Cherry St, enter through alley
324.7462
Mon–Fri 11a–2a, Sat–Sun 4p–2a

A bar of all trades, Twilight Exit is a perfect place for those nights when you've got some friends coming into town and aren't sure what to get into. Its new incarnation on Cherry Street has upped the ante on both beer and food. Pinball, cheap beer, foosball, and a rockin' jukebox sure do have a way of entertaining me and my buddies after a day hiking all around town. We chop it up over a game of pool until our heads are mashed up. Don't blame us—the beer is really cheap (and goes great with the chicken-fried bacon)! *SB*

Dick's Drive In

111 NE 45th St (and other locations)
632.5125
www.ddir.com
Daily 10:30a–2a

This Seattle institution wins the fast food race—order a burger (plain or deluxe, no special instructions are accepted) and it'll be hot in your hands before the minute is up. Organic beef and potatoes are used for salty, greasy delights—I know of few places that can so easily satisfy mobs of stumbling, tipsy locals on grub that's this conscientious. The shakes are the most delicious menu item—strawberry is my go-to here, but an entire meal of a deluxe burger and fries tacked on will still run you under $6. Everyone making your shakes gets company benefits and better pay than the average burger flipper, not to mention the long list of community efforts to which this three-generation business donates: soup kitchens, homeless youth resources, food banks, and even community forums where locals can add their two cents about the city budget, public transit, or other important topics. Munch one, munch all! *SB*

The Five Point

415 Cedar St
448.9993
www.the5pointcafe.com
Daily, open 24 hours

Five Point is not for frills or fancy, but for late night grub and cheap drinks. This place has been serving concert-goers since the Seattle music scene has been on the map, and with breakfast available all the time, and on the cheap, it will remain a go-to spot for greasy, satisfying grub and a bit of gritty community feel for many years to come. Be a part of the scene and comfort your hungry belly while immersed in incessant noise, a lingering smoky atmosphere, and all manner of music fans. *SB*

13 Coins Restaurant and Night Owl Lounge

125 Boren Ave N
682.2513
www.13coins.com
Daily, open 24 hours

This 24-hour restaurant and lounge is "absolutely fabulous," although I don't think that Patsy and Edina from classic BBC program would ever show their faces here. Sit on high pleather chairs that swivel around the diner counter, or a booth enclosed with the same deep brown "pillowing" extended well up the walls. Simple waffles with ice cream can be a lifesaver at 3 am, if you can make up your mind between the hearty pasta dishes, the wonderful croissant sandwiches, or the surprisingly beautiful berry-granola parfait, served like an ice cream sundae. Zesty Bloody Marys are my favorite (best enjoyed piano-side in the lounge) if you're here to keep the night going, or order herbal tea to wind down. It is rare to find such an exquisite throwback, and this one is well loved for good reason. *SB*

Pamper

Shelters from the hustle and bustle, simple enjoyments, and all things feel-good

Part of the whole pampering process is good, hot comfort food. The classic is chicken soup, but I look for spots that avoid adding too much salt as a substitute for slow-cooked flavor. Overdoing the salt is bad news for the body—instead of pampering, you get dehydration! So in this chapter, I've paid special attention to not only the in-the-moment effects, but also the aftereffects. Here is a selection of feel-good foods, restful spaces, and, of course, spas and salons to refresh, re-energize, and restart your engine.

 ## Ummelina

 1525 4th Ave
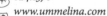 *624.1370*
 *www.ummelina.com*
Sun–Thurs 10:30a–7p, Fri–Sat 8:30a–9p

Ummelina is a very special little hideaway. Up a narrow escalator in what looks like another downtown mall entrance, the first hint that there's pampering to come is the sweet smell wafting from this spa's entrance. The hand-blended fragrances and body products are made from high-quality organic ingredients, many inspired by old-world wisdom. Not sweet like grandma's old lilac room spray, but warm with spruce, nutmeg, lavender, and rose essences—a musky lightness that readies the air for your pleasure. You can choose from an array of almost bizarre-sounding treatments that include various water features, baths, and steam rooms, but I suggest sticking to the more straightforward massages and facials. Each starts with tea and a cozy sit in the peaceful common area where my feet experienced quite possibly the best part of the event—the foot rub. Every aspect of this woman-owned business is carefully considered, both in terms of care and value. The organic products made with time-honored healing recipes finish the job. Take some home to pack away for you next journey—Ummelina's facial wash and moisturizers are a girl's best friend on the road. *SB*

Vida Spa

2125 Terry Ave
888.865.2630
www.vidawellness.com
Call for an appointment

Located just across from the elegant Pan Pacific Hotel, Vida Spa and its holistic Ayurvedic spa philosophy are a dream come true. I started my journey in a cozy resting area with comfortable chairs, a modern fireplace, low lighting, and all the tea and organic almond-apricot trail mix I could want. I read one of the tabletop books to get a better idea of the three main Ayurvedic body types and discovered I was a vata kapha dosha (you are usually two). Once called in, I was treated with the utmost care, with several phases of treatments for my entire body. I lay in a cedar box that allowed for my head to rest outside, while essential oils and steam wrapped my whole self inside. Then I was dusted with fine perfumed pumice and my skin was left glowing. Getting back to my room across the open-air walkway was one big blur—I was so elevated from this magnificent treatment that I floated on a cloud for days afterward. *SB*

Zovo Lingerie

46612 26th Ave NE
525.9686
www.zovolingerie.com
Mon–Sat 9:30a–9p, Sun 11a–6p

Frustrated with the dire situation of underwear shopping in her native Seattle, Zovo Lingerie owner Victoria decided that every time she found a great bra, cute panties, or luxurious pampering products, she would make note until she had a store stocked with only the best. Now she has created a Zovo line of basic underwear and bras, plus comfortable pajamas you'll look forward to wearing at the end of a long day. The mercerized cotton undies are affordable, luxurious, and made with care and quality by well-paid workers. Shop the store to envision yourself as the goddess you are, not to impress anyone else—at least that's how I approach this undergarment treasure chest. *SB*

Hong Kong Noodle House

414 8th Ave S

332.1881

Hours vary, call ahead

Low in sodium and high in healing, the perfectly delicious congee of Hong Kong Noodle House soars above those I have tried at other eateries along the International District's congee trail. This restaurant's version is flavorful without the salt, made plain or with tender beef, squid, or chicken. I can get over a cold, swim a mile, and then run up the stairs of the Space Needle after a big bowl. OK, maybe not the Space Needle part, but this savory soup does have an amazingly positive and energizing effect. *SB*

Swoon Boutique Spa

1422 E Pike St

323.0106

www.swoonspa.com

Tues–Fri 10a–7p, Sat–Mon 10a–6p

It is amazing all of the little things we can do to be green—things you'd never think of doing to contribute to the greater good. I never thought that waxing my legs could be related to sustainability, but then again, I may have skipped over a few pages in that Ayurvedic beauty book I read. As it turns out, sugaring your legs according to an age-old Indian method takes the petroleum, the chemicals, and the other trash out of the waxing process, plus the results last almost twice as long. The first few sugaring experiences I had at Swoon were a little painful, I won't lie, but the more I have sugared, the less it has twinged. I love the smooth results, and Swoon gets all the credit for spreading the sugaring method around Seattle and for turning me on to it! Manicures and pedicures include mini-massages complete with organic aromatic oils, and the polish selection is hard to top. The skillful pamperers at Swoon have some great local music and restaurant recommendations as I also discovered, so being talkative while you are greening your beauty regimen may well pay off. *SB*

Hothouse Spa and Sauna

1019 E Pike St
568.3240
http://hothousespa.com
Wed–Mon 12p–12a, last entry 11p

The closest thing to a Japanese *sento* in Seattle is Hothouse Spa and Sauna. It is also the easiest way to transform a rainy afternoon. Pay $12, plus $1 for your locker, for unlimited access to the healing spaces inside. You'll find a square hot tub spacious enough to comfortably fit a handful of women, several showers lining the far wall, steam rooms and saunas, and cold rinse showerheads as big as a sunflower in August. Women and men are separated completely, with identical spaces dedicated to each gender. There is a cozy stretching space, and jugs of cool lemony water are available to refresh you while you relax. Add a 15-minute massage for just $25, and three hours will blissfully disappear. *SB*

Frenchy's Day Spa

3131 E Madison St, #103
325.9582
www.frenchysdayspa.com
Mon 9a–5p, Tues 9a–8p, Wed–Sat 9a–6p, Sun 11a–6p

Full of chatty local women, Frenchy's Day Spa is always abuzz with activity. It's housed in an unlikely strip of shops on Madison Street, but the first time I went inside Frenchy's I felt as though I had entered a gracious, sweet-smelling living room. Sure, there may be a lot going on, but that's how they like it; peering over at a jewelry trunk show while my nails dried convinced me of this more-is-better philosophy, at least in this instance. I had a wonderful French manicure, complete with paraffin hand wraps that gave my skin the kid-glove feel, and I was off to opening night of the Seattle International Film Festival (see page 143). I even got a great pho suggestion (see Green Leaf Vietnamese Restaurant, page 184) from my highly skilled stylist. *SB*

Vain

2018 1st Ave, 441.3441
5401 Ballard Ave NW, 706.2707
www.vain.com
Hours vary, call ahead

Widely known as the edgiest, most popular salon in Seattle, Vain now has two locations, started from just one chair in the back of a boutique with Victoria at the helm. She has since taken her place among Seattle's style elite, keeping an eye on her protégés and hair artists as well as on customer satisfaction. Deeply rooted in the arts scene, the Ballard location always has a wild new show hanging on its walls, and above the Belltown salon are artist studios subsidized by Vain. Haircuts are affordable, but it's hard to be seen as a walk-in, so call ahead and expect to be cute and conscientious by the time you leave. *SB*

Green Leaf Vietnamese Restaurant

418 8th Ave S

340.1388

http://greenleaftaste.com

Daily 10:30a–10p

Recommended by Vietnamese Americans and mossbacks alike, Green Leaf's pho transcends soup in my opinion. The clear, slow-cooked broth is both flavorful and bright, and each bowl is carefully laden with tender meats, crispy bean sprouts, and *ram rau*, Vietnamese coriander. When I was feeling a bit under the weather, three bowls of Green Leaf's soup made me better within two days. *SB*

Dandelion Botanical Company

5424 Ballard Ave NW, Ste 103

545.8892

www.dandelionbotanical.com

Daily 10:30a–7p

I'm a tried and true foodie—a person who appreciates all kinds of culinary adventures. It isn't often that I find myself surrounded by so many new and foreign flavors, given that I go the extra mile to be versed in all things edible. But a trip to Dandelion will stretch even my cooking creations—what to do with borage flowering tops, bladderwrack, local San Juan Island kelp, or sargassum? And that's before I get to the collections of Chinese and Ayurvedic herbs and healing powders. The interconnectedness of food and body is taken to another level at Dandelion—a place where the senses can adventure in new and different ways. If you have a plan to make your own cosmetics, then this is a great place to start—equally so if you're here to find a gift for someone picky. Even my choosiest friends are smitten with the pottery and teas I've rustled up from the collections at Dandelion. *SB*

Dahlia Spa

 1422 31st Ave S
 322.1770
www.dahliaspa.com
Call ahead for an appointment

I'm gaga for the facials at Dahlia Spa. I originally trekked over to the spine of the Mount Baker neighborhood for some talked-about hot cocoa at Sweet and Savory (see page 194) next door. I couldn't help but poke my nose into inviting Dahlia Spa, and after my ravishing chocolate drink, I soon found myself returning for a last-minute facial appointment. My skin was glowing from the professional touch and natural products, and I received at least four compliments specifically on my complexion by the close of the day. Massages and other pampering possibilities are also on offer, so next time I'll be back for more. *SB*

Valentine's

7912 Greenwood Ave N
706.6303
www.valentinesseattle.com
Tues 11a–7p, Wed–Fri 10a–8p, Sat 9a–6p, Sun 11a–5p

Valentine's is a classy barbershop in the Greenwood neighborhood that's known for its special care of men. Whether for a picky sophisticate, an unsure professor, or a burgeoning rock star, the affordable cuts, combs, shaves, and trims at Valentine's will spiff up any male. The elegant ambiance, every bit masculine, makes man-pampering an exciting experience rather than one that inspires fear of metrosexuality. *SB*

Serena's Tea Treasure Hunt

Warming up with a hot pot of tea is a necessary ingredient of Seattle life. It's no wonder there are some great teahouses in this city, each with its own vision, unique tea selection, and ambiance of rejuvenation. Here are some of my favorites:

The Tea Gallery

700 5th Ave, Level 6 N
382.8141
www.myteagallery.com
Mon–Fri 7:30a–4p

Offering only the finest teas and little else, this simple, quiet spot has zero residue of the coffeehouse craze. The herbal varieties of rooibos are some of the best I've tried to date.

Floating Leaves Tea

1704 NW Market St
529.4268
http://floatingleaves.com
Mon & Wed–Sun 11a–7p

Unlike the pricey boutiques surrounding Floating Leaves Tea, the atmosphere inside feels unpressured and soothing. The helpful staff members know each of the teas on the menu like the back of their hands, to the point that you could ask them for a tea for a neurotic overachiever, a stressed-out musician, or a worried new-to-town Seattleite. Whatever your need, they'd hand you the perfect blend.

The Teacup

2128 Queen Anne Ave N
238.5931
www.seattleteacup.com
Mon–Thurs 10a–8p, Fri–Sat 9a–6p

This pretty little Queen Anne teashop doesn't look like much from the outside, but once you enter you might think you're in a tea pharmacy. Behind the sleek wood-paneled counter are walls covered in rows of glass jars, each neatly labeled. Hourglasses are on every table to ensure proper brewing time if you're drinking your jasmine buds there, and there's every color of tea cozy under the sun.

Remedy Teas

345 15th Ave E
323.4832
www.remedyteas.com
Daily 7a–11p

Taking the pharmacy look even more literally than the Teacup, at Cap Hill's Remedy Teas, the teas are numbered in long, lean containers hung along the back wall. The counter showcases the featured tea of the day, which you can sample for free, and a tempting window of locally baked goodies and snacks.

Miro Tea

▤ *5405 Ballard Ave NW*
☎ *782.6832*
www.mirotea.com
Mon–Sat 8a–10p, Sun 8a–8p

Steeped in authentic Japanese style, Miro Tea's counters, made of slivered logs, are covered with tempered glass teapots, clearly labeled jars, and lots of modern chairs to lounge in. Mandarin White is my go-to flavor. Here you also can find handmade crepes to go with your tea. Delish!

Electric Tea Garden

((ᵖ)) *1402 E Pike St*
▤ *568.3972*
http://electricteagarden.com
Tues–Sat 2–10p

Electric Tea Garden is indeed plugged in. Regular DJ sessions spun live from the Cap Hill digs are even aired on Live365 online radio (*www.live365.com*). Enter Electric Tea House with an open mind, and you'll find artists and activists drinking gunsmoke black tea, lavender-rose white tea, and more. You never know what conversations will be sparked over these brews.

Teahouse Kuan Yin

1911 N 45th St
632.2055
www.teahousekuanyin.com
Mon–Thurs 9a–10:30p, Fri–Sat 9a–12a, Sun 9a–10:30p

Rather than trying to be the cool kid in town, Teahouse Kuan Yin is unapologetically homey and comfortable—and its teas are also attitude free. I first heard of Kuan Yin because of its famed selection of *pu-erh* teas. The organic Black River Mountain tea aged from 1997 is $9 for 2 ounces, or find something ever more rare in the organic Golden Melon *jin gua cha*, which is formed into a ball called a *tuo* and sold for $40 apiece. This is some special tea, and Kuan Yin is a great neighborhood lounge spot to boot. Books and games are ready for you if you want to stay for another pot. *SB*

Sweet Tooth

All things sweet converge here—these are the best places to discover your soft spot for sugary treats

Even the healthiest of us crave a sugar rush every so often, and satisfying that craving is a task Seattle's bakers, chocolatiers, pastry chefs, and dairy gods and goddesses have heartily taken up. Pack your toothbrush and brush in between licking ice cream cones, munching handmade caramels, and seducing your senses with a truffle-smothered cupcake. I figure as long as I keep walking, swimming, riding, and doing whatever else I drum up in the Get Active chapter, also heeding my dentist's advice, I can enjoy all the wonders herein.

 Cafe Besalu

5909 24th Ave NW
789.1463
Wed–Sun 7a–3p

$$

When a cafe is open only half the week for a few hours a day and has lines running out the door onto the sidewalk, you know something special is going on. Cafe Besalu is tiny, it's hard to find a seat, and if there's any music or ambiance at all, it's drowned out by the crowd, but people come here from all over Seattle to experience the best French pastries you can get without a passport. Pretty much everything you see here was baked hours or minutes ago, and the staff constantly replenishes the display case with pastries and croissants fresh from the oven. Even after eating here several times a week for a few months, I'm still blown away by the Gruyère and caramelized onion pastry and the various fruit Danishes and tarts made from fresh seasonal fruits like apples, pears, plums, and apricots. Most of these treats are based on Besalu's crowning achievement: the perfect croissant dough. It flakes and crackles in your teeth just before melting on your tongue like heavenly manna. If you try to prolong this dream by taking some goodies home, be prepared for disappointment. Like a passionate summer love affair in Paris, these pastries won't survive in captivity, and within a few hours they will mysteriously go flat and stale. So live in the moment, savor the delicate magic of virtuoso bakers, and just come back again another day. *IM*

Molly Moon Ice Cream

917 E Pine St, 708.7947
1622½ N 45th St, 547.5105
www.mollymoonicecream.com
Daily 12–11p

Molly Moon wants to talk with you about ice cream, and the ice cream parlors (one in Wallingford and another in Capitol Hill) start the conversation by inviting you to recommend your own flavor ideas. That's one of the ways the list has grown and changed to include strange and delicious concoctions like pomegranate-curry sorbet, rosemary–Meyer lemon, and cardamom. The classics are incredible too—strawberry is probably my favorite, but "scout" mint, vanilla bean, and coffee (made with Espresso Vivace's brews, see page 44) are stellar. Balsamic-strawberry and ginger are two others you should wish for, after all, the menu here changes regularly and is always evolving. *SB*

Cupcake Royale

2052 NW Market St (and three other locations)
782.9557
www.cupcakeroyale.com
Mon–Thurs 6:30a–10p, Fri–Sat 7:30a–11p, Sun 7:30a–10p

Bite into a ravishing Red Velvet cupcake, an almost vermilion cocoa cake with cream-cheesy icing; dive into a buttercream-covered classic cupcake; or select any of the other options on Cupcake Royale's zippy pink menus (printed on recycled paper, of course)—you won't be disappointed. This proud member of Seattle's effective Green Scene recycling program is happily host to more *New Yorker* mags and books with dog-eared pages than Macs, though they do creep through the cracks. My friend and I like sitting at the window (yes, sometimes toting our Macs) and admiring Ballard's impressive shoe and sunglasses collection from this ideal spot of street runway. Today a man with $450 Chanel Stunna shades and a naïve but pointy smile chats with us and recommends a cup of Serene, the utterly tantalizing herbal tea blend that makes fast friends with my vanilla lavender cake, since I am not in the mood for more caffeine. Stumptown coffee (from Portland) is French-pressed by the experts at Café Vérité (inside the same location and at others around town), and on weekday afternoons there are enough tables available for poring over whatever reading you've got in tow. *SB*

((ρ)) Mighty O Donuts
2110 N 55th St
543.0335
www.mightyo.com
Mon 6a–1p, Tues–Fri 6a–5p, Sat–Sun 7a–5p

I had to run two blocks in fat, syrupy rain to get from my car to Mighty O Donuts, so it was especially comforting to walk in the door and be immediately enveloped by soft light and the warm, motherly smell of fresh donuts. Mighty O offers a rotation of delicious fair-trade coffees and a wide variety of handmade donuts. I had the Cocoloco, a chocolate cake donut covered in cinnamon sprinkles. I forgave it some slight dryness for the complex, dense flavor created by the all-natural organic ingredients used. It felt like I was eating actual food instead of a white puff of processed flour and partially hydrogenated motor oil. The vibe here is family-friendly but not too watered down. The table of three toddlers didn't seem to notice the local photography on the walls featuring scantily clad pinup girls buried in piles of hot, sexy donuts. *IM*

Simply Desserts
3421 Fremont Ave N
633.2671
Tues–Thurs 12–10p, Fri–Sat 12–11:30p, Sun 12p–6p

Located on my vote for the most aggravating pedestrian intersection this side of the Rockies, Simply Desserts is a saving grace if you've had to wait through five lights to cross the street! Rolling up their sleeves and getting serious about cake seems to be the bakers' MO here, and the elegant, distinct finished product reflects that. Stop in after a solid rummage through the antique den or the bookstore to either side of Simply Desserts, and then snag a slice to go for a lucky friend. Mexican Chocolate, Bittersweet Hazelnut, and Carrot are my top three picks, but if you are a cheesecake maven, I recommend this shop's lemon version. Each cake is beautifully made, as if from another era altogether, from natural ingredients. Triple Chocolate Brownies are just $23 a dozen, making them the ideal sinful treat to bring to any get-together where you need to show up with your hands full. *SB*

The Erotic Bakery

2323 N 45th St
545.6969
www.theeroticbakery.com
Mon–Sat 10a–7p

If it's not clear what you're looking for around Seattle, or if you're feeling a little lost and in need of a totally surprising discovery, then come to the Erotic Bakery. Marzipan has never had so much naughty fun. You'll find all shapes and sizes of the "fun" parts of the body in various flavors. Cakes and cookies get dressed up with edible phallic decoration—it's hard not to buy at least one gag gift when you're perusing the displays. Gawking is allowed, because these look-alike sweets taste as good as they look, and they look so real you have to be 18 to enter the store. *SB*

Trophy Cupcakes

1815 N 45th St
632.7020
www.trophycupcakes.com
Mon–Fri 8a–8p, Sat 8:30a–8p, Sun 8:30a–5p

Newsflash! I found the stairway to heaven and your ticket to ride costs a mere $3! Jennifer Shea, a dietician by trade, has turned her hands to sweets, making her dreams and the dreams of those lucky enough to find her shop come true. Enter the renovated historic schoolhouse in Wallingford, and if you're anything like me you'll be planning your next birthday party and wishing you were a kid again. I come on Monday or Wednesday for the Hummingbird, a banana-pineapple-coconut cake slathered with perfect cream cheese icing. The daily cupcake menus are a delight; each cake is named with the same kind of creativity that goes into making these luscious goodies. Be sure to check out the University Village branch as well. *SB*

Dilettante Chocolates

538 Broadway Ave E
329.6463
www.dilettante.com
Mon–Thurs 10a–12a, Fri–Sat 10a–1a

Sugar rush! Dilettante is the prom queen of Seattle's sweet shops—dressed up in finery with a touch of airhead in her personality and always perfectly coiffed locks. In short, Dilettante looks so good it deserves the prom queen crown. Founded by a third-generation chocolatier, Dana Davenport, this shop's aim is to create supreme cocoa good enough for royalty. Signature dragées and flavored truffle crèmes are as lovely as they are dainty, but my favorites are the deluxe truffles filled with secret buttercreams and covered in fine robes of chocolates in all shades. Pick up a four-piece box for little more than $5 and you'll have pocket change for a fine coffee (roasted in-house from fair-trade beans) to go with it. You can find Dilettante at the Sea-Tac airport if you forgot to visit while you were in town. *SB*

Top Pot Doughnuts

2124 5th Ave, 728.1966
609 Summit Ave E, 323.7841
6855 35th Ave NE, 525.1966
www.toppotdoughnuts.com
Mon–Fri 6a–7p, Sat–Sun 7a–7p

If I were blindfolded and spun around three times, and it was dark out, I'd still be able to find my way to the nearest Top Pot Doughnuts. That's because each spotless location fries up fresh donut batches through the wee hours, allowing the tantalizing, if slightly displeasing, aroma of frying oil to escape these magical kitchens. I say "magical" because the concoctions at Top Pot look more like they belong in a cartoon with wizards waving magic wands than in my belly. I am no donut connoisseur, but if I were, I would be a regular here. Ballerina-pink sugar rings, coconut-flecked Feather Boas, and cruller twists fill the large glass cases—the decision process alone is a fun adventure in the depths of your psyche. "What donut is my soul in the mood for?" I ask as I wonder how my belly would recover from another Bismarck (a custard-stuffed, chocolate-glazed donut). I settle on a maple-glazed cake donut, which tastes as filling as I remember the Bismarck to be, but it has just the right spice hidden in the recipe to complement my morning coffee and reading. I dove into *The Omnivore's Dilemma* while sitting below the 5th Avenue location's slanted glass panes—my only dilemma now is who to share the rest of my donut with. *SB*

Chocolati Café

1716 N 45th St
633.7765
www.chocolati.com
Daily 6:30a–11p

Embracing American invention takes on new meaning at Chocolati Café, Wallingford's handmade chocolate shop. Fortune cookies, conceived in Los Angeles, have traveled north and in the process have put on some clothes for the cooler weather—chocolate clothes. Each handmade cookie is dipped and drizzled with the stuff, making the future seem that much sweeter. Find chocolates in funny shapes like wrenches and umbrellas, or opt for some cocoa to warm you inside and out. *SB*

Tour de Chocolat

Start: Chocolate Box, 108 Pine St
427.2515
www.sschocolatebox.com
Schedules vary, most tours 8:30a–11:45a
Cost: $69

If you are ready for a real trip through Seattle's sweet underbelly, then you simply must sign yourself up for this sugar endurance test. Start at Chocolate Box downtown, where you can see myriad chocolates from Washington State, then gather up with the group, hop on the van, and get ready to learn everything there is to know about chocolate in Seattle. Theo Chocolate hosts the most educational aspect of the adventure since it buys cocoa in its unprocessed, untarnished form: the whole pods. You'll watch each step in the chocolate-making process and taste the results of a completely sustainable chocolate production. Then Fran's Chocolates will mesmerize your taste buds with its famous salted caramels (Fran's was one of the first places to make them in this country), and you'll be off to your next stop. Mixed into the tour is a lot of good learning and some sightseeing; on the sunny day I took the tour, we stopped at the height of Queen Anne for an epic view and some factoids from our courteous driver, Ed. *SB*

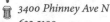 **Theo Chocolate**

 3400 Phinney Ave N

632.5100

www.theochocolate.com

Mon–Fri 10a–6p

Theo Chocolate is a real Seattle highlight. The inspiring business model, created to sync farmers, traders, factory workers, and chocolate makers into a mutually beneficial circle of commerce, has motivated other local businesses to think about their impact on the planet. Theo takes it slow—the company knows the farms where the beans are grown and knows what to do with those beans, which is more than I can say for most chocolatiers, who work only with smooth and finished bars. Take a tour to get behind Theo's process, or just hop into the shop (located at the front of the factory) to taste the only chocolate bar I've ever had that was flecked with croutons (yes, 3400 Phinney Chocolate's Bread and Chocolate Bar really exists, and not just in my imagination). *SB*

 Sweet and Savory

 1418 31st Ave S

325.2900

www.sweetandsavoryseattle.com

Tues–Fri 6a–2p, Sat–Sun 7a–2p

Welcome to Paris . . . I mean, welcome to 31st Avenue S, Seattle! Sweet and Savory is a little chip of France wedged into one of Seattle's idyllic hilltop neighborhoods, with the hot chocolate and creamy quiche to prove it. A tiny cup and saucer will come to your table, and you may be put off, thinking you'd be treated to a heaping mug of chocolate viscosity, but the portion is just right, trust me. This is sipping chocolate, best accompanied by a window seat, a croissant, and *The Paris Review*. After you forget you're in America, head out for a stroll—the houses and gardens on either slant from the main street are a sight to behold, especially when the clouds part on the emerald waters below and the snowy peaks reveal themselves. Regulars clutter the counter under rows of hanging baskets and chitchat over accordion music. *SB*

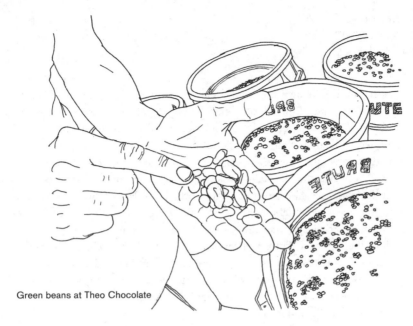
Green beans at Theo Chocolate

⚯ Fran's Chocolates

2626 NE University Village St, 528.9969
1325 1st Ave, 682.0168
www.franschocolates.com
Hours vary by location, call ahead

If Theo Chocolate is the construction crew, Fran's Chocolates is the interior designer. Named for the original chocolate diva Fran Bigelow, whose exceptional skills have made her creations world famous, this is the chocolate for which Seattle is best known. Gray Salt Caramels are the reason to visit Fran's, and even though you can find these at other shops around town, the exquisite jewelry store of a showroom gives the sweet taste something extra fancy. If you see chocolate as an art form or as a beautiful moment of blissful enjoyment, you'll be on the same page with Fran. Her Double Chocolate Figs—supple dried figs filled with smooth ganache and coated in rich dark chocolate—are a dream for fruit lovers, and the many fine truffles are impeccable, but nothing can steer me clear of one of her caramels if I'm within eyeshot. *SB*

Hiroki

2224 N 56th St
547.4128
www.hiroki.us
Tues 12–4p, Wed–Fri 12–9p, Sat–Sun 9a–9p

Each nation has its own take on sweets that somehow underscores aspects of the culture like a little window into the country. In America our desserts are often sloppy or oversized, a conglomerate of the melting pot we are, sprinkled with some gluttony for good measure. In Mexico the pastries are brightly colored, passionate, and very seasonal to go along with all the annual festivals. In Japan there's a dainty, manicured, and well-organized perfection when it comes to sugar. This cake stays in the lines. Japan's sweets have also been inspired by the nationalities that have visited its shores, so you'll see tiramisu, Bavarian cake, and cheesecake on the same menu, all neat and tidy. I adore the light and fluffy Princess Cake and the crème chantilly–stuffed cream puffs at Hiroki. Mousses here defy gravity, and even the piecrust isn't weighed down. I sit and sip tea while taking tiny bites from my Opera Cake. If I had my way, I'd be wearing a skirt and have brought some Emily Dickinson to complete the mood. *SB*

Serena's Gulab Jamun Adventure

The sweetest dessert I have ever had (aside from peanut brittle maybe) is *gulab jamun*, the donutlike delicacy from Northern India. Light, doughy balls made from low-fat cheese and a special blend of flour are fried and served doused with chilled cardamom syrup. Because of their fragrant sweetness and intensely uplifting effect, I think they are the perfect sweet treat for Seattle, and many authentic places in town serve them.

Kalia Indian Cuisine

8518 Greenwood Ave
782.7890
www.kaliacuisine.com
Hours vary, call ahead

Kalia Indian Cuisine offers Bollywood movie viewing during your *gulab jamun* feast. Get a good seat and order a double dose—you'll become a fan quickly! Kalia is a great hangout in Seattle for its relaxed authenticity mixed with good food and dessert, of course.

🏨 Bengal Tiger East Indian Cuisine

🅥 *6510 Roosevelt Wy NE*
💲 *985.0041*
🍴 *www.bengaltigerwa.com*

You'll find the cheesiest incarnation of these sweets at Bengal Tiger East Indian Cuisine. Made with curds and whey, a little like cottage cheese, this version is less sweet than others but every bit as tantalizing—and so is the large vegetarian savory menu.

🏨 Mehak India Cuisine

🅥 *12327 Roosevelt Wy NE*
💲 *632.5307*
🖋 *http://mehakindia.com*
   Daily 11a–10p

The Pakistani-style cooking at Mehak Indian is finished off with *gulab jamun* just like these other spots, but *kheer*, a rice pudding with almonds, also appears on the sweets menu. You can choose your "donuts" to come warm or chilled here. I like them steaming hot when I need a quick escape from the icky weather—just be careful not to burn your tongue! *SB*

Stay In

The best takeout and take-home activities in town

Sometimes I try to pack too much into a day. By evening, all systems are not go. But taking in the town can be done inside, too. Many great restaurants specialize in to-go food and delivery, and some are more suited to take out, so you can choose one of those low-energy nights to have an in-hotel or in-home dinner. While you're at it, why not rent a flick, grab a board game, and make a cozy night of it?

🏨 Bottleworks

📠 *1710 N 45th St, Ste 3*
♻ *633.2437*
   http://bottleworksbeerstore.blogspot.com
   Sun–Wed 11a–8p, Thurs–Sat 11a–9p; Tastings: Mon 5–7p

With the most exciting selection of beer I have seen since traipsing across Germany, Wallingford's Bottleworks is a resource for those with suds on the brain. I love just admiring the various bottles, each with a different shape, size, color, and label. Once I stopped in on a Monday between 5 and 7pm and found a free tasting in progress, so I joined in and discovered a new dunkel, or dark, wheat beer I could never have previously imagined. Chat with the friendly shopkeeper, who's also behind Brouwer's Cafe, and you'll take home some great brew from near or far. Bottleworks is a great place to stop before crashing any Seattle house party. (I'm not encouraging anything . . .) *SB*

Julie's Garden

 81 Yesler Wy

 223.3690

www.julies-garden.com

Mon–Fri 10a–9p, Sat 11a–7p

Julie's Garden serves Chinese takeout minus the MSG and the charge for delivery. I call and order vegetarian pad thai, mixed beef pho, and cold condensed milk coffee, and I'm ready for a cozy night in. Now all I have to do is decide whether I'm going to keep writing for the evening or take a movie break and invite a buddy over to share my Julie's feast. *SB*

Annapurna Cafe

 1833 Broadway

320.7770

 www.annapurnacafe.com

Hours vary, call ahead

Down a narrow flight of stairs, underneath the commotion of Cap Hill and the community college towering above, Annapurna Cafe is a low-ground hideout with flavor as tall as the mountains that this spot is named for. I prefer ordering my *momos* (the spinach variety are completely green here) and Himalayan curry with sweet peas, potatoes, and Tibetan herbs for delivery or takeout. Mango Mazza with stir-fried *paneer* cheese, mango cubes, carrots, and mushrooms, and the Gyatak Bowl with special wide Tibetan noodles are two other must-trys in my book. Never did I imagine it would be so easy to stay in for a feast of Himalayan proportions. *SB*

Gary's Games and Hobbies

8539 Greenwood Ave N

789.8891

www.garysgamesandhobbies.com

Mon–Tues 9a–5p, Wed–Sat 9a–8p, Sun 12–5p

I'm a low-tech gal most of the time, and I relish long hours spent mulling over books and puzzles and card games late into the night. Find all your go-to games at Gary's, plus some great fun you never knew existed; this is the place to start your in-home, or in-room laze. Card games come to life here as well, just ask one of the helpful employees and he or she will straighten you out on any rules you forget. *SB*

Padrino's Pizza and Pasta

2357 10th Ave E

322.6300

http://seattle.padrinospizzapasta.com

Daily 11a–3a

With prettier pizza and loads more proper-meal options than other delivery places in Seattle, Padrino's Pizza and Pasta will bring gourmet chicken and spinach pizza or a heaping portion of salmon fettuccine to your door. This is the only way I get real food when I am on a writing binge, past deadline, and needing to consume something without having to lift a finger. Salads, sandwiches, calzones—they're all at my door until 3 am. Thank goodness I was turned on to this spot! *SB*

MAD Pizza

1314 Madison St, 322.7447

3601 Fremont Ave N, 632.5453

4021 E Madison St, 329.7037

1263 Thomas St, 587.6800

www.madpizza.com

Sun–Thurs 11a–11p, Fri–Sat 11a–12a

Just the thought of the cheesy slices of MAD Pizza makes me want to order one right here, right now. The four Seattle locations make delivery in your area almost 100 percent assured; there are few places in the city where MAD won't drop off an order. Pizza names like Mad Life Crisis and Prozac Pie jest at the high depression rate around this rainy city, but I'll take a slice of either

anytime. The Mad Life Crisis contains pesto, mozzarella, feta, Roma tomatoes, and Jamaican jerk chicken, and the Prozac Pie is covered in pepperoni,
Italian sausage, olives, mushrooms, and loads of mozzarella. MAD's got great
options for picky eaters, vegans, and vegetarians, and the salads are as trium-
phant as the thoughtful pizza pies. *SB*

Pronto Pizza and Pasta

3208 W McGraw St

283.5910

Daily 10a–3a

When it comes to the late night pizza delivery department, my experiences
with Pronto Pizza and Pasta have been, shall we say, interesting. Each time
I've ordered a pizza from Pronto, I've been at a different Seattle home, but
I got the same delivery gal. She knew I was up to something by the time we
had seen each other three times. There is such a large number of possibilities on the menu that I had to keep coming back for more to get the whole
picture. I'm not accustomed to having a range of options such as a vegetable
calzone, flaky halibut, handmade tortellini, and humongous salad arrive at
my friend's door for our supper, but then again, I'm still discovering a lot
about this city. It's excellent to have such a great service, and the family-run
business that offers it has been a pillar of the community for years. *SB*

Video Rental Alert

Seattle is the setting for many television shows and movies, and not
just *Frasier* and *Sleepless in Seattle*. Rent some of these flicks and
try to pinpoint the locations—come on, it will be fun.

Tugboat Annie (1930s, hard to find); Sydney Pollack's *The Slender
Thread*; Jerry Schatzberg's *Sweet Revenge* (MGM Classic); a mishmash of 1970s cinema like *The Last Convertible*, *The Changeling*
(the Peter Medak original), and *Cinderella Liberty*; Taylor Hackford's
An Officer and a Gentleman (1981); John Badham's *WarGames*
(1982); *A Year in the Life* (the series began in 1985); *Starman* and
David Mamet's *House of Games* (both 1986); one of my favorite
goofy John Cusack flicks by Cameron Crowe, *Say Anything* (1988);
Backtrack (1988); *The Fabulous Baker Boys* (1989); David Lynch's

Fire Walk with Me, Cameron Crowe's *Singles*, and the TV show *Face of a Stranger* (all 1991); another classic Cusack, *Better Off Dead*, in 1992, and in that same year, Nora Ephron's *Sleepless in Seattle*, George Sluizer's *The Vanishing*, Michael Switzer's *With a Vengeance*, and Joyce Chopra's *The Danger of Love* (what a busy year for the Seattle film office!); Bertolucci came in 1993 to film *Little Buddha*; 1994 brought *Threat of Innocence*, *Mad Love* (unless you adore Drew Barrymore, you can skip this one), *Disclosure*, *Born to Be Wild*, and *Medicine Ball*; *Prefontaine* with smokin' hot Jared Leto, *Mr. and Mrs. Smith* (the TV series), and Disney's *The Sixth Man* came out in 1996; *Frasier* started (much to my chagrin) in 1997; and *The Real World: Seattle* and *Ten Things I Hate About You* solidified the teenage-appeal of Seattle culture in 1998; *Get Carter*, *The Leonard Cohen Afterworld*, and *Chaos Theory* were filmed just before the century changeover; and so far, the hits in the 2000s hailing from the Emerald City have been *The Ring* and its not-as-good sequel *The Dark Horse*, *The Last Mimzy* (blech), *Battle in Seattle* (must-see), *Into the Wild* (must-read and must-see, but read first), and the 2008 Coen brothers' flick, *Burn After Reading*. (More Seattle cineriffic info is at *www.seattle.gov/filmoffice*.)

Video Stores

Here are the best locally owned video stores to find the cult, art, mainstream, mindless action, Hallmark ending, and thought-provoking classic movies you've ever dreamed of, plus the ones you always forget to rent. Most of the following have easy rental policies that allow access to locals and travelers alike:

Scarecrow Video
5030 Roosevelt Wy NE
524.8554
www.scarecrowvideo.com

Rain City Video
464 N 36th St, 545.3539
719 NW Market St, 783.8367
www.raincityvideo.com

Island Video

3711 NE 45th St, 527.2300

3109 E Madison St, 323.1725

7216 Greenwood Ave N, 297.1020

Belltown Video

2500 3rd Ave

443.5435

www.belltownvideo.com

Reckless Video

8915 Roosevelt Wy NE

524.4473

www.recklessvideo.com

Volunteer

Fun, quick, and easy ways to help the city flourish

Lending a hand—giving a few hours of your time toward the greater good—has an amazing positive effect on both you and the surrounding community. My experiences in various world cities were always enriched when I met locals through a volunteer effort, and there is a plethora of ways to get involved in Seattle, whether you live here or are just traveling through.

ArtWorks

923 S Bayview St

292.4142

www.urbanartworks.org

Connecting young artists with professional opportunities in their creative fields is crucial work, in my opinion. When we are given a chance to use our passions in our employment, then we can truly contribute what we are meant to give to the world. Volunteering in various capacities at Seattle's ArtWorks makes for an interesting time no matter what, and it offers an inspiring way to give back. sb

YouthCare

694.4500
www.youthcare.org

Every day, YouthCare ensures that more youth have a roof over their heads. Through various support programs and facilities, this 30-year-old project is dedicated to helping homeless, abused, or abandoned youth. *SB*

Reel Grrls

Events at various locations
323.0693
www.reelgrrls.org

A wonderful program for girls to get behind the camera instead of in front of a TV, Reel Grrls hosts events, fundraisers, and film screenings to display the projects of its talented students. *SB*

Vera Project

Warren Ave N and Republican St (Seattle Center)
956.8372
www.theveraproject.org

This youth-run music and arts center engages community members in creating music and sharing in artistic means of communication. This plays out with a series of music shows presented by the group and volunteers. Since local bands are so big in Seattle, and its audiences are among the country's most attentive, lending a hand to the Vera Project is guaranteed to lead to some musical discovery at the very least. *SB*

Lifelong AIDS Alliance

1002 E Seneca St
328.8979
www.lifelongaidsalliance.org

With a calendar full of creative fundraising events, a retail thrift store (with great some great finds; see the Re-Find chapter, page 132), an ever-popular Gay Bingo night, and a complete program of AIDS care services, Lifelong AIDS Alliance is a necessary resource for the Seattle community. You can easily become a part of this organization's important work by signing up online—just follow the volunteer link from the main page of the web site. *SB*

St. Clouds Homeless Cooking Project

1131 34th Ave
726.1522
www.stclouds.com/NewFiles/community.html
Each month St. Clouds restaurant sets aside ingredients and human resources to set up a soup (and more) kitchen for the homeless and those in need of a hot, free meal. Sign up to volunteer with the organization by calling the restaurant. Look for themes like the annual Bread for Water Cedar River Watershed fundraiser or the Dine for Darfur event when the Homeless Cooking Project is not on. Come back after your volunteering escapades for a luscious meal or late-night snack in the restaurant (*www.stclouds.com/newfiles.latenight.html*). SB

Arboretum Foundation

2300 Arboretum Dr E
325.4510
www.arboretumfoundation.org/volunteer/volunteer.cfm
If you want to learn more about plants and trees without forking over your last pennies for a workshop, or you want to make new friends with similar botanical interests, volunteering for the Arboretum Foundation is a must. Help maintain Washington Park Arboretum's grounds, assist with special events like the display at the Northwest Flower and Garden Show, or pot plants donated to the collection. The Arboretum offers a range of activities at all skill levels and time commitments, so get ready to get some dirt under your nails, which is secretly my favorite annoyance. SB

Phinney Neighborhood Soup Kitchen

Calvary Lutheran Church, 7002 23rd Ave NW
783.2244
www.phinneycenter.org/programs/soupkitchen.shtml
Mon 12p
Each Monday at lunchtime, this unassuming Seattle church is transformed into a dining hall of epic proportions, serving up to 2,000 hot meals to those in need. Help cook, serve, and clean up to make this charitable meal continue to be possible now and in the future. SB

Fremont Abbey Arts Center

4272 Fremont Ave N

701.9270

www.fremontabbey.org

Fundraising projects, children's art activities, community outreach projects, and underground concert setup—it's all in a day's work as a volunteer at Fremont Abbey Arts Center. Check the web site for the correct e-mail address or give Fremont Abbey a ring on the old telephone to inquire about current volunteer opportunities. *SB*

First Place for Kids

Various locations

323.6715

www.firstplaceschool.org

Having just celebrated its twentieth anniversary teaching children who are either homeless or low income, First Place for Kids is a pillar of Seattle's philanthropic community. Volunteer your time to help at the school in many capacities. *SB*

Planned Parenthood of the Great Northwest

2001 E Madison St

328.7734

www.plannedparenthood.org/ppgnw/volunteer-opportunities-23160.htm

It's no joke that over 700 volunteers give their time and attention toward helping women safely take care of their health and feminine needs. Join their forces by filing out the simple online form and giving the group an idea of your availability –Planned Parenthood takes short- and long-term helpers. *SB*

Arts Corps

Various locations

www.artscorps.org/enlist

Encouraging a healthy mix of imagination, reflection, and discipline, Arts Corps brings creativity to young Seattleites of all backgrounds. Come help this organization get art back into the classroom by team-teaching with other dedicated volunteers and community members. Or assist outside of the classroom at fairs, special events, and wherever Arts Corps could use a helping hand. You'll just need to fill out a volunteer inquiry form prior to participation. *SB*

Lodge

Every place to rest your noggin

Hotels

Seattle boasts a slew of fine hotels, running the gamut from princess palace–esque to simple, affordable, and clean. Most are in the downtown area.

Hotel Andra

2000 4th Ave

448.8600

www.hotelandra.com

No detail in my new favorite boutique hotel is overlooked. And when I'm aiming to stay in style, I expect that my wishes will be the staff's commands. Just sitting in the orange-splashed lobby makes my writing machine turn on—I am inspired by the cool candleholders, the luxe seating by the mod fireplace, and the colorful crowd pouring in and out of the big glass doors.

On a recent trip to the Emerald City I was saved by Hotel Andra's hospitality—saved from the rain, from my granola craving, and from my need for a big cozy bed on which to rest my overtraveled body. A bride-to-be down the hall, flanked by her giggling bridesmaids, told me about the great breakfast downstairs at the Tom Douglas restaurant, Lola (see page 139), and I quickly ordered some, with the staff accommodating my request even though it was midday. Andra is a swank place, comfortable even for the choosiest guest, but not priced so high as to be exclusive of lower-budget travelers. If I had my way, I'd come back with a gaggle of girlfriends to stay in the suite, eat Lola's handy room service, and stay up all night swapping stories on the soft comforters. SB

Arctic Club Hotel

700 3rd Ave

340.0340

www.arcticclubhotel.com

In the heart of the city, where more "mature" travelers like to stay, the Arctic Club Hotel is a first-class transformation from a historical men's club into an event destination or a luxe stay. Learn something new about the hotel's namesake every day, like how many sled dogs it takes to pull a male walrus (hint: it's more than 50), in the History of Arctic Expeditions exhibit. Unfortunately, the rooms facing 3rd Street are not soundproofed, so I recommend requesting another unless you've got earplugs handy.

Executive Chef Thomas Kollasch of the on-site restaurant Juno creates menus with a focus on organic and eco-friendly ingredients; each dish is a stylish taste of the season. Good food combined with the hotel's Northern Lights Dome and over-the-top rococo details make for a splashy place for a wedding or other big event. *IB*

Warwick Seattle Hotel

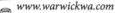
401 Lenora St
443.4300
www.warwickwa.com

Stand in your nightie at the floor-to-ceiling glass sliding doors, take in the magnificent views of the Space Needle, and unwind in the heated swimming pool, whirlpool, and sauna in the Warwick Seattle Hotel's fitness room. Internet access and parking are both add-ons (at $11 and $27, respectively), so don't be surprised at checkout. The French-style Brasserie Margaux is more formal than the Brasserie Margaux Bar (both inside the hotel), which features casual tapas and a tasty happy hour. The Warwick is just steps away from some of my favorite central Seattle attractions. *IB*

The Roosevelt Hotel

1531 7th Ave
261.1200
www.roosevelthotel.com

This is a dog-friendly family hotel and romantic getaway spot all in one, with bed-and-breakfast possibilities right in the heart of town. The Roosevelt Hotel is a short distance from both of Seattle's hub hospitals, where families can stay close with special hospital stay packages. It also offers the Cupid in the City package, an ultimate evening of romance including a Whirlpool Suite, rose petals scattered on the bed, two martinis or one appetizer in Von's Grand City Café, champagne and chocolate upon arrival, valet parking, and a noon checkout time. Oh, baby! *IB*

The Fairmont Olympic Hotel

208 Seattle

 The Edgewater

2411 Alaskan Wy, Pier 67
800.624.0670
www.edgewaterhotel.com

With panoramic views of the Elliott Bay waterfront, this urban wilderness hotel has pine furniture and rustic river-rock fireplaces, plus it's right on Pier 67. There are no avoidance goals when you choose to stay at the Edgewater Hotel. Restaurant Six Seven in the hotel is all about incorporating fresh fish and local ingredients, offering a great dining experience surrounded by regional beauty. Winter, summer, and special occasion packages are available for couples and families. *IB*

Alexis Hotel

1007 1st Ave
888.850.1155
www.alexishotel.com

The Alexis Hotel is a work of art, and you can sleep there! These 121 perfectly luxurious rooms are just one block from the Seattle waterfront, and Alexis Hotel is on the *Travel and Leisure*'s "Best 500 Hotels in the World" list for good reason. A complimentary hosted wine reception in the lobby "living room," wireless Internet access, a fitness center, and a 24-hour private steam room to release any aches or tension—how much better does it get? *IB*

The Fairmont Olympic Hotel

411 University St
621.1700 or 888.363.5022
www.fairmont.com/seattle

Long before Fairmont became one of America's most luxurious hotel chains with palace-like accommodations scattered from coast to coast, this Seattle landmark was hosting opulent balls for famous pioneers and characters. Around every corner is another story, another intriguing piece of history (all of which can be uncovered in the book about this location that's available from the concierge). The Italian-Renaissance style of this large hotel is evident inside and out, with elegant patterns and stylish details often overlooked at other hotels. The beds are tremendously comfortable, so don't be surprised if you find yourself sleeping in during your stay, especially when room service is so tempting. Among the many choices you can order hand-painted chocolates, alderwood-smoked salmon eggs benedict, rack of Willamette Valley lamb, and wild huckleberry crème brûlée. There's an organic kids menu as well as other eco-friendly details: the hotel uses recycled water and composted food scraps to nurture the plentiful plants and floral arrangements in the rooms, lobby, and outdoors. If you book ahead online you can find special web-only discounts, and sometimes room prices come in well under $200—astonishing given how you'll feel like royalty while staying there. My room had huge windows looking out on all the Downtown action and an über-comfy chaise lounge where I read myself to sleep. Don't forget to check out the beautiful wading pool, workout facilities, and spa options available to all guests—no other place I've stayed in the city can match them. The lap of luxury is a great place to be sometimes, and it's fully accessible at this favorite Seattle hotel. SB

Crowne Plaza Hotel Seattle
1113 6th Ave
464.1980
www.cphotelseattle.com
The Crowne Plaza Hotel Seattle is full of surprises. Aside from the fact that each room comes with a handy, if somewhat laughable, sleep kit (complete with meditation CD and lavender spray), this hotel has actually won multiple awards and recognition for its oil recycling and composting programs. The hotel chain creates a surplus of fuel after all its own service vehicles are tanked up just from the waste created in day-to-day operations. You'll find lots of groups and business travelers staying at this especially tall downtown location. It has a workout room, two separate breakfast service areas, and great views if you're OK with long elevator rides to the higher floors. SB

Ace Hotel
2423 1st Ave
448.4721
www.acehotel.com
A totally original idea for a hotel, Ace Hotel has standard clean white rooms that act like a canvas for my vacation. They come equipped with cable TV, large windows, and high ceilings, with the toilet and bath down the hall and hip poster art covering the walls. Or you can choose a deluxe room with a queen- or king-size bed, private bathroom, and air conditioning, but no matter what room you choose, it's bound to include exquisitely simple design

features. When you are making your reservation, ask if a room with partial water views is available. Offering stylish comfort that's right on point, Ace Hotel is the ultimate lodging for the urban nomad on a mission to experience sleek, twenty-first-century design and affordability in a historic Belltown building. Overall, it's an economical sleep within blocks of Pike Place Market and Seattle's ever-growing network of art galleries, retail stores, and restaurants. *IB*

Hotel Deca

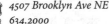
4507 Brooklyn Ave NE
634.2000
www.hoteldeca.com

Smack-dab in the middle of the University District, Hotel Deca is super convenient for travelers who prefer staying in "neighborhood" Seattle and not "big city" Seattle—parents of students at the nearby university, repeat business travelers, and youngsters like me who are just looking to have a good time getting to know the city. The lobby, complete with 1920s-style mural, comfy leather sofas, and Chihuly lighting, is set up with wireless Internet and is almost always abuzz with action, whether it's a group of local cops on their regular coffee break or some prom couples fluffing their bangs and fixing their ties. The rooms are simple but comfortable, with large TVs, city views, and antique bathroom fixtures (that work well!). It's good to get away from the buzz of downtown and still stay in a straightforward hotel. *SB*

Best Western Executive Inn

200 Taylor Ave N
448.9444
www.bestwesternwashington.com/hotels/best-western-executive-inn

The Best Western Executive Inn, located in the heart of Seattle just a few blocks from downtown, is nestled against the Experience Music Project (EMP) and the Space Needle. My view was better than any TV show could ever be: every few minutes I could watch the monorail glide past the hotel and into the tunnel of the EMP. In the filtered monotone light, the EMP looks like a blob of gum, sort of like Willy Wonka meets recycled airplane parts. My double room on the top floor was clean and sparse, but the location, affordability, and service are the reasons to stay here, not the interior decor. I found I slept better here than at some of the other, more luxe hotels around downtown—it was quiet, it was smoke- and chemical-cleaner-free, and my bed was firm, just as I like it. *SB*

Mayflower Park Hotel

405 Olive Wy
800.426.5100
www.mayflowerpark.com

Mayflower Park Hotel is on an especially interesting block of downtown Seattle, and every time I enter the lobby I am impressed with the magnificent flower arrangements. The historic building has been nicely refurbished to reflect the British colonial style of the decor. Comfortable beds, incredible service that outshines that of many other hotels, and a supremely convenient location all make this a worthwhile pick for a beautiful night in Seattle. *SB*

Pan Pacific Seattle Hotel

2125 Terry Ave
264.8111
www.panpacific.com/seattle/overview.html

The Pan Pacific Seattle Hotel is a new hybrid hotel that caters to wealthy locals living on the top floors and travelers who stay in rooms in the bottom two thirds of the peach-colored tower. Across from Vida Spa (see pages 26 and 181), the hotel features its own 24-hour fitness center, a SLUT stop (see page 22), and a Whole Foods Market, so it's easy to stay put in these plush rooms. I enjoyed the oversize bathtub and toilet-side telephone, making use of both on as many occasions as I could during my three nights at the Pan Pacific. It was one of my favorite stays in Seattle, in part because of the comfortable, modern atmosphere, the interesting characters I met while I was staying there, and the exceptional experience I had both in the room and at the spa. *SB*

MUST see & do....

a) 1st & 2d Starbucks
a) Pike Place Market.
c) Space Needle ☼
d) University Village
e) Seatte Public Library
f) Pacific Place.
~~$~~

Downtown
- 43
- 70
- 25
-

- 425 - 786 - 6144   40
- 425 - 256 - 8150   Rodrigo
            3150

Bed-and-Breakfasts

Staying at a B&B in Seattle is like staying in a local's nicely decorated abode. Often owned and operated by longtime residents, these spots vary in price and amenities but are ideal when it comes to value and comfort. When you stay at a B&B, you can assume that your money is going quickly back into the local economy. Plus you don't have to worry about that morning meal!

Shafer Baillie Mansion

907 14th Ave E

322.4654, 800.985.4654

www.sbmansion.com

This Tudor revival home on Capitol Hill is ideally situated just blocks from Volunteer Park (see page 92) and the restaurants and retail shops on Broadway. Shafer Baillie Mansion sits on Seattle's renowned Millionaire's Row and abounds with period furnishings and eclectic antiques, from the ornately carved wood-paneled entry hall to the five individual suites themselves. Owners Ana Lena Melka and Mark Mayhle exemplify supernal hospitality and are dedicated to making the mansion your dream home away from home. The opulent staircase is an excellent place to hold a wedding ceremony, which Ana Lena and Mark take into consideration, offering their space for such an occasion. DL

Pensione Nichols Bed and Breakfast

1923 1st Ave

441.7125

www.pensionenichols.com

Being half English, Dutsi Bap, the official poodle of GrassRoutes, loves the combination of Pacific Northwest heritage and European sense and sensibility at Pensione Nichols Bed and Breakfast. He is also quite fond of the idea that it is a pet-friendly establishment, which partially makes up for the fact that he's not allowed in Pike Place Market. Antique furnishings all the way from Sussex, England, as well as stunning views of the Puget Sound and the awesome Olympic Mountains from a suite balcony should please human guests. DL

Washington State Bed and Breakfast Guild

800.647.2918

www.wbbg.com

Whether you choose to find lodgings in Seattle or anywhere else in the beautiful state of Washington, this volunteer association provides a comprehensive network of resources for the public and its member B&Bs throughout the state. The Washington State Bed and Breakfast Guild has also developed high standards of cleanliness, hospitality, and safety for its members, as well as a strong voice for these locally owned inns. The Guild's recommendations are reliable and in line with its ethic of promoting quality lodgings. DL

Salisbury House

750 16th Ave E

328.8682

www.salisburyhouse.com

Salisbury House, located on a quiet residential street, is a small bed-and-breakfast with five comfortable rooms. There is a glass-enclosed sun room overlooking the private gardens where you can have coffee before going into the dining room for a complimentary meatless breakfast from 8 to 9:30am. On cooler days, you can sit in front of the fireplace and read the local morning paper or the *New York Times*. It is great to make arrangements for breakfast to go for the aimless walking that is such a pleasure of this city. IB

Pumpkin Coffee Cake

The owners of Salisbury House will even share some of their delicious vegetarian recipes with you to cook at home, like the Pumpkin Coffee Cake recipe we snagged.

Serves 8 to 12

Topping

¼ cup brown sugar

¼ cup sugar

½ teaspoon cinnamon

2 tablespoons butter

½ cup chopped pecans

Cake

½ cup unsalted butter, room temperature
1 cup sugar
2 eggs
1 cup sour cream or plain yogurt
½ cup canned pumpkin
1 teaspoon vanilla extract
2 cups flour
1 teaspoon baking soda
1 teaspoon baking powder
1 teaspoon cinnamon
½ teaspoon nutmeg
Dash nutmeg and cloves
½ teaspoon ginger
½ teaspoon salt (omit if using salted butter)

Preheat oven to 325°F. Grease and flour a 9-by-13-inch baking pan.

In a small bowl, combine the sugars and cinnamon for the topping. Cut in the butter with a pastry cutter. Stir in the pecans.

In a large bowl, cream the butter and sugar for the cake. Add the eggs one at a time, beating well. Add the sour cream, pumpkin, and vanilla extract. In a medium bowl, combine the flour and remaining dry ingredients and mix well. Add the dry ingredients to the wet ingredients and mix until just combined. Spread the batter in the prepared pan and sprinkle with the topping. Bake for 40 to 50 minutes, until cake tests done.

Hostels and Camping

There are some convenient bargain-basement lodging options in and around Seattle. If you're looking for camping, expect to stay a little way outside of the city, but if you'd like to stay at a hostel, you'll find a few choices right downtown.

Hostel Seattle

6200 Seaview Ave NW
706.3255
www.hostelseattle.com

With reliable WiFi, complete breakfast included with the bed price, and clean accommodations, this is a good budget lodging choice not too far away from the main drag of the city. Friendly workers can also suggest good local eats and fun activities for daylight or afterhours. *SB*

Green Tortoise Hostel

105½ Pike St
340.1222
www.greentortoise.net

The most convenient budget lodging is Green Tortoise, which has the same name as the infamous bus service that runs up and down the West Coast in hippie fashion. Steps from your shared room are the hubs of downtown and Pike and Pine, and the price for a clean bed in a dorm room of eight hovers around $30 depending on the season. Call ahead to inquire about private rooms if that is your preference—either way, there is a constant influx of foreign travelers and young concertgoers to meet while you're staying here. *SB*

Seattle Tacoma KOA

800.562.1892
www.seattlekoa.com

To me, KOA seems to be a whole culture that's slightly over my head, but I do love that it has campsites closer to downtown areas than most state parks do. The Seattle KOA site is across from the Green River, just under 25 minutes away from the downtown area. KOA hosts mostly RVs, but hookup-free tent sites and those big enough for car camping are also reservable. Regular guided tours planned by the campground take visitors around to the main landmarks of Seattle, but I'd just hitch a ride with them and do my own exploring (that's just me). *SB*

Fay Bainbridge State Park

360.902.8600, 360.344.4431
www.parks.wa.gov/parkpage.asp?selectedpark=Fay+Bainbridge
Check in by 2:30p or call

Bainbridge Island is a beautiful ferry ride away from the center of Seattle commotion, and it's one made daily by many island dwellers. Camping at the 17-acre camping area inside Fay Bainbridge State Park offers the best of both worlds: total Washington nature and small-town wonders within a boat ride to the biggest city in the state. Call ahead to book a site near the 1,500 feet of saltwater shoreline in this park. *SB*

Other Camping Recommendations

Farther afield are **Doe Bay Resort and Retreat** (*www.doebay.com*) and **Moran State Parks** (*www.parks.wa.gov/parkpage.asp?selectedpark=moran*) on gorgeous Orcas Island. At **Lake Easton RV Resort** (*www.lakeeastonresort. com*), you'll find ample tent sites for non-RVers.

Other parks to search online if you're interested in a pre- or post-Seattle camp-a-thon are as follows: Lake Cushman in Hoodsport, Dash Point in Federal Way, Dosewallips in Brinnon, Deception Pass in Norland, Wallace Falls in Gold Bar, and Deception Pass in Oak Harbor. Each of these have campsites for those with tents.

Other Recommended Stays

There are tons of places to rest your head here in the Emerald City, so here are a few others we recommend. There's much more info about these and more at www.grassroutestravel.com/directory.

Greenlake Guest House

7630 E Green Lake Dr N
866.355.8700
www.greenlakeguesthouse.com

The College Inn
4000 University Wy NE
633.4441
www.collegeinnseattle.com

Chambered Nautilus Bed and Breakfast Inn
5005 22nd Ave NE
522.2536, 800.545.8459
www.chamberednautilus.com

Three Tree Point Bed and Breakfast
17026 33rd Ave SW
669.7646, 888.369.7696
www.3treepointbnb.com

Bacon Mansion Bed and Breakfast
959 Broadway E
800.240.1864
www.baconmansion.com

Westin Seattle
1900 5th Ave
728.1000
www.starwoodhotels.com/westin

Calendar

For film festivals, see page 146; for the Seattle Tilth annual calendar of environmental events, see page 76.

January

Seattle Chamber Music Society Winter Festival
Last weekend in January
Benaroya Hall
www.seattlechambermusic.org

National Geographic Live Speaker Series
Last Saturday in January, opening night
Benaroya Hall
http://events.nationalgeographic.com/events

Seattle Boat Show
Last week in January
Qwest Field and Event Center
www.seattleboatshow.com

International District's Lunar New Year Celebration
Late January/early February
International District, S King and 5th Ave S
www.cidbia.org

February
Seattle Improvised Music Festival
Second week in February
Chapel Performance Space
www.seattleimprovisedmusic.com

Northwest Flower and Garden Show
Early February
Convention Center, 7th Ave and Pike St
www.gardenshow.com

Take Part in Art Festival, presented by ArtsFund
Last two weeks in February
Discount and pay-what-you-can tickets to incredible shows at various locations
www.takepartinart.org, click on "festival" link

March
Seattle Rainman Triathlon
First Sunday in March
Start: Evans Pool in Greenlake
www.seatri.org (other runs found here, too)

Northwest Women's Show
First weekend in March
Qwest Field and Event Center
www.nwwomenshow.com

St. Patrick's Day Parade
Second Saturday in March
Start: 4th Ave and Jefferson St
www.irishclub.org/parade.htm

Ballard Parade for Nordic Constitution Day
Third Saturday in March
Start: Adams School at 62nd and 24th aves NW
www.syttendemaiseattle.com

Green Festival
Last weekend in March
Washington State Convention Center
www.greenfestivals.org/seattle

Vegfest
Third weekend in March
Exhibition Hall, Seattle Center
www.vegofwa.org

Wine Rocks
Last Saturday in March
Gibson Guitar Showroom, 159 S Jackson St, Pioneer Square
www.winerocksseattle.com

Moisture Festival
End of March through first week in April
Various locations
www.moisturefestival.com

April

Seattle Cherry Blossom and Japanese Cultural Festival
Third weekend in April
Seattle Center
www.seattlecenter.com/events

Ballard Jazz Festival
Last weekend in April
Various stages throughout the Ballard neighborhood
www.ballardjazzfestival.com

May

Seattle Tilth Edible Plant Sale
First weekend in May
Meridian Park, Wallingford
www.seattletilth.org/events

Asian-Pacific Islander Heritage Month Celebration
First weekend in May
Center House, Seattle Center
www.seattlecenter.com/events

Playwrights Festival
Throughout May
Burien Little Theatre
http://seattleperforms.com

Northwest Folklife Festival
Last weekend in May
Seattle Center
www.nwfolklife.org

Sasquatch! Music Festival
Memorial Day weekend
The Gorge Amphitheatre
http://sasquatchfestival.com

June

Seafair
Throughout the summer
Seattle Center and various other locations
www.seafair.com

Seattle Peace Concerts
Sundays, early June through September
Woodland Park, Gas Works Park, Volunteer Park, and others
www.seapeace.org

Wallingford Garden Tour
First Sunday in June
Various homes in Wallingford
www.wallingford.org

Father's Day Barbecue
Father's Day (second Sunday in June)
Woodland Park Zoo, 550 Phinney Ave

Fremont Fair
Third weekend in June
Various locations in Fremont
http://fremontfair.org

Northwest New Works Festival
Two weekends in June
Behnke Center for Contemporary Performance
www.ontheboards.org

Centrum Port Townsend Writers' Conference
Ten days in mid-June
Fort Worden State Park
www.centrum.org/writing/writers-conference.html

Northwest Mahler Festival
Second two weeks in June
Meany Hall and Shorecrest Center
www.nwmahlerfestival.org

Olympic Music Festival
June through first weekend in September
Festival Grounds, Center Road, Olympia
www.olympicmusicfestival.org

Greenwood Car Show
Last Saturday in June
Greenwood Ave and 72nd St N
www.greenwoodcarshow.com

Torchlight Run
Last Saturday in June
Start: Quest Field
728.0123
www.seafair.com/events/torchrun

Pridefest, Pridefeast, and Parade
Last weekend in June
Downtown Seattle
www.seattlepridefest.org

July

Milk Carton Derby
First Saturday in July
Green Lake
www.seafair.com/events/mcd

Bastille Day
July 14 and the closest weekend to that date
Seattle Center
www.seattle-bastille.org

Wallingford Seafair Kiddies Parade and Street Fair
Second Saturday in July
Wallingford Ave between N 43rd and N 45th sts
www.wallingford.org

International District Festival
Second weekend in July
Hing Hay Park
www.cidbia.org/events

Bite of Seattle
Mid-July
Seattle Center
www.biteofseattle.com

Bainbridge Bluegrass Festival
Last weekend in July
Battle Point Park, Bainbridge Island
http://bainbridgebluegrassfestival.com

Ballard SeafoodFest
Last weekend in July
Throughout the Ballard neighborhood
www.seafoodfest.org

August

Arab Festival
First weekend in August
Seattle Center, Fisher Pavilion
www.arabcenter.net

Summer Chamber Music Festival
Late July through mid-August
Various locations
www.scmf.org, www.seattlechambermusic.org

September

Bumbershoot
Labor Day Weekend
Seattle Center
www.bumbershoot.org

Seattle Tilth Harvest Fair
Second weekend in September
Meridian Park, Wallingford
www.seattletilth.org/events

The Great Wallingford Wurst Festival
Last weekend in September
St. Benedict School, 4811 Wallingford Ave N
www.stbens.net/wurstfest.shtml

Sustainable Ballard Festival
Last weekend in September
Ballard Commons Park
http://sustainableballard.org

October
Wallingford Home Tour
First Saturday in October
Various homes around Wallingford
www.wallingford.org

Earshot Jazz Festival
Mid-October through first week of November
Various locations
www.earshot.org

Elysian Pumpkin Beer Festival
Third Saturday in October
Elysian Brewing Company, Capitol Hill location
www.elysianbrewing.com

November
Pike Place Tree Lighting
Last Saturday in November
Pike Place Market
www.pikeplacemarket.org

December
Winter Solstice Fire Festival
Second weekend in December
Seattle Center
www.seattlecenter.com

Ice Skating Rink

December through January
Fisher Pavilion, Seattle Center
www.seattlecenter.com

New Year's Labyrinth Walk

December 31
St. Mark's Episcopal Cathedral, 1245 10th Ave E
www.saintmarks.org

Urban Eco Resources
Helpful things

Single Spark Calendar

singlespark@riseup.net
Curious about what goes on behind the scenes of Seattle's free spirits? Find left-wing, community-based radical events on this monthly bulletin, which is posted around town and can be e-mailed directly to you at your request. Ask for the latest edition so you know what's on when you're in town. *SB*

Centrum

www.centrum.org
Centrum, tagged "a gathering place for artists," is a major asset to all of the arts movements passing through Western Washington. The ongoing Writers' Exchange program encourages new writers to hone their skills, the jazz and blues courses teach this American form of music in both theory and performance, and the Young Artist Project brings youth into the mix of talents buzzing around Centrum. Look it up if you are a creative type and you find yourself heading toward Seattle or its environs. *SB*

Seattle LGBT Community Center

www.seattlelgbt.org
The Seattle center for the lesbian, gay, bisexual, and transgender community is a wonderful resource. It hosts classes and events, book clubs, and support groups—anything and everything that's a need of the community is a concern of this center. *SB*

Seattle Young People's Project

www.sypp.org

Promoting education justice and community support for youth, the initiatives of the Seattle Young People's Project cover vast topics. The overall aim is to give a voice to youth, to "give a loudspeaker for our opinions and views," as one 16-year-old member wrote on the project's website. *SB*

UnScene Seattle

www.unscene.com

The little green square of info inside the Seattle edition of UnScene is an updated independent business guide that's loads of help for anyone navigating the downtown area. Easy-to-read maps highlighted with local finds are on both sides of the free foldout. You can find this handy guide at centrally located coffeehouses in Seattle. *SB*

PoetsWest

www.poetswest.com

The written word is cherished in many different ways in Seattle—in loud song lyrics; tonal, poetic phrasing; ghostly stories; comedic tales; and phenomenal paragraphs soon to be printed in best-selling paperbacks. The PoetsWest web site is a clear resource of local poets' groups, readings, workshops, and even new books that have come out from native writers. The carefully worded ponderings of Seattleites are at your fingertips here! *SB*

Earshot Jazz Calendar

www.earshot.org/calendar/calendar.asp

This nonprofit organization exists to promote a continuous influx of world-class jazz into Seattle. A surprising number of local talents perform at the shows listed on Earshot's online calendar. *SB*

Seattle Gay News

www.sgn.org

The *Seattle Gay News* has a wealth of newsworthy articles about local topics, many relating to politics and current events surrounding LGBT issues. Pay special attention to the events page at the back of the paper for upcoming fun parties and festivals. You can find the free print edition at coffeehouses around town. *SB*

The Facts

324.0552

The Facts newspaper, headquartered in Seattle's Central District, is a family-run paper known as the voice of the Northwest African American community. Inside are reliable calendar listings and current events pieces. You can find this paper at most library branches and local coffee shops. *SB*

The Stranger

www.thestranger.com

The well-loved *The Stranger* is known by everyone around Seattle. It's the free alternative arts and culture weekly with syndicates like Free Will Astrology and Savage Love, written by locals, and it's definitely worth picking up while you are in town. Necessary, I'd say, as all the new films, concerts, restaurants, and city news are dissected somewhere on these pages. *SB*

SeattlePerforms.com

www.seattleperforms.com

No theater performance, large or small, falls between these guys' fingers. If you are looking for an outing, whether well in advance or at the last minute, this web site will direct you to everything that's going on. *SB*

Allied Arts of Seattle

www.alliedarts-seattle.org

This pivotal organization put up the funds to save and restore Pioneer Square, Pike Place Market, and other structures that are easy to take for granted around Seattle. Find out what urban design concepts are currently on the table by taking part in an Allied Arts of Seattle–hosted event. Without this group, locals would be going into the discussion about Seattle's future without the voice of collaborative sustainable design. *SB*

Seattle Weekly

www.seattleweekly.com

Owned by the same group that runs other weeklies like *SF Weekly* in the Bay Area, this free paper is another contender for local love. You'll find witty columns and the lowdown on city movements and political decisions, plus all the other cultural info you could ask for. Look on busy street corners for your copy as soon as you get into town. *SB*

Seattle Times

http://seattletimes.nwsource.com

This is Seattle's "real" paper. It's no *New York Times* or *LA Times*, but it's worth penciling in a quiet Sunday morning to drink cappuccino and read every page, front and back—my private test for any newspaper. The local section is strewn with almost as much Seattleite lingo as the free weeklies, and the nation/world section takes on international commerce, celebration, and politics with candor and some help from the Associated Press. Restaurant reviews are a highlight, as are the weekly technology pullouts and the free monthly *NWsource Magazine*, an advertiser-biased staycation encyclopedia that comes in handy whether you are a local or new to the city. *SB*

ArtsFund Calendar

www.takepartinart.org

To discover the best music, dance, and theater events in the Puget Sound, look no further than ArtsFund. This calendar lists the free days at the museum, the must-see art films, the newest gallery shows and museum exhibitions, children's entertainment, and live performances. This web resource has had such a strong impact on people's ability to find great inspired outings that the area is now known nationally as a creative hotbed, and not just as the town with the Space Needle. Seattle and the surrounding towns and cities are a rich tapestry of talent, encompassed by the detailed listings on this site. Search to your heart's content, and if you are on a low budget, be sure to check the site at the end of February when all tickets are discounted or pay-what-you-can. This organization bends backward to make it possible for everyone to enjoy "high culture." Read carefully—on any given day there could be 30-some options for your sensory pleasure. *SB*

Community-Supporting Banks

Here are a few of the community-supporting financial institutions around town.

Seattle Bank

281.1500
www.seattlebank.com

A small, local, FDIC-insured bank with a loyal following of companies, small businesses, and families, Seattle Bank a great place to get your very first account, since it is so keyed in to financial education here.

Washington Federal Savings

800.324.9375
www.washingtonfederal.com

Of its 136 state locations, Washington Federal Savings (WashFed) has about 10 in and around Seattle. The ultimate state pride can be conveyed by banking here; this bank works closely with the state government and with nonprofit entities and universities.

Banner Bank

1420 Madison St, 709.8314
2815 2nd Ave, 770.7180
www.bannerbank.com

This locally owned bank based just outside of Seattle has a reputation for loaning to independent businesses and young entrepreneurs with tight business plans.

Frontier Bank

5602 15th Ave NW (with branches all over the city)
783.0300
www.frontierbank.com

Frontier Bank is a reliable neighborhood bank for Seattleites and suburbanites with an understanding of thinking globally and acting locally. Although this bank was tempted into partial ownership of reverse mortgages (which it has since parted with), the better part of its funding and investment is from thriving businesses across the state. Helpful online service and fully insured banking make this a far better choice than the chain financial institutions.

Alternative Energy Resources

Natural Gas

City of Seattle
Charles Street Facility
1030 7th Avenue S
Daily, 24 hours
386.1159

Puget Sound Energy
Georgetown Operating Base
6500 Ursula Place S
Mon–Fri 8a–5p
253.476.6202

1122 75 Street SW (Everett office)
Mon–Fri 8a–5p
253.476.6202

3130 S 38th St (Tacoma office)
Mon–Fri 8a–5p
253.476.6202

Clean Energy Fuels Corporation/Port of Seattle Sea-Tac Airport CNG Facility
19425 28th Avenue South
Daily, 24 hours
800.663.4555

Clean Energy/Pierce Transit Public Access Station
3898 94th St SW (Tacoma)
Daily, 24 hours
800.663.4555

Electric

Seattle Electric Vehicle Association
www.seattleeva.org

Electric Bikes Northwest
4810 17th Ave NW
547.4621
www.electricvehiclesnw.com
Sales: Mon–Fri 11a–6p, Sat 11a–4p
Service and parts: Tues–Fri 2–6p, Sat 12–4p

MC Electric Vehicles
1200 South Dearborn St
328.1750
www.mcelectricvehicles.com
Mon–Fri 8a–5p, Sat 10a–4p

Biodiesel

www.nearbio.com
Send the location of the nearest biodiesel station to your cell phone

Seattle Biodiesel
www.seattlebiodiesel.com

BioLyle's Biodiesel Workshop
4512 38th Ave S
354.6802
www.biolyle.com

Dr. Dan's Alternative Fuelwerks
912 NW 50th St
783.5728
www.fuelwerks.com

Laurelhurst Oil Biodiesel Station
4550 Union Bay Pl NE
523.4500
www.laurelhurstoil.com

Seaport Petroleum and BioFuels
7800 Detroit Ave SW
971.7999
www.seaportpetroleum.com

Grange Supply, Inc
145 NE Gilman Blvd (Issaquah)
425.392.6469
www.grangesupplyinc.com

Fuel Cells

Nu Element, Inc.
2323 N 30th St, Ste 100 (Tacoma)
253.573.1780
www.nuelement.com

Neah Power Systems
22118 20th Ave SE, Ste 142 (Bothell)
425.424.3324
www.neahpower.com

Index